50

D0941624

THE PROBLEM
OF JESUS

THE PROBLEM OF JESUS

A FREE-THINKER'S DIARY

by

JEAN GUITTON

P. J. KENEDY & SONS
NEW YORK

The Problem of Jesus is the author's abridgement of his two volumes, *Le Problème de Jésus et les fondements du témoignage chrétien* and *Le Problème de Jésus: Divinité et Resurrection* (Aubier: Paris, 1953).
The translation was made by
A. GORDON SMITH

First published 1955

To the memory of
JOHN HENRY CARDINAL NEWMAN

CONTENTS

Chapter   Page

     PREFACE   xi

PART ONE: THE CHRISTIAN TESTIMONY

    I   THE CRITICAL APPROACH   3

   II   THE DIFFICULTIES OF THE CRITICAL APPROACH   12

  III   THE MYTHICAL APPROACH   24

  IV   THE DIFFICULTIES OF THE MYTHICAL APPROACH   29

PART TWO: DIVINITY

    I   PROBLEMS OF ORDER AND METHOD   51

Resurrection and Divinity: distinction between the two beliefs, p. 51; Messiahship, Resurrection, Divinity: the historical genesis of the ideas, p. 52; The logical genesis of the ideas: the significance of Arianism, p. 53; Comparison of the two beliefs and their justification, p. 56; For contemporary man the examination of Divinity should precede that of Resurrection, p. 58

   II   SOURCES OF THE BELIEF IN THE DIVINITY OF JESUS   61

Divinity and Testimony: the words of Jesus and the faith of the Christian communities, p. 61; Divinity and the Jewish background, p. 62; Prophecies and Divinity: prospect and retrospect, p. 63; Divinity against the pagan background, p. 65; Conflicting conditions for the criteria of Divinity, p. 66; The spirit of the proposed inquiry, p. 66.

  III   THE ENVELOPMENT OF THE SEEDS   68

A.—*Jesus and the Jewish values of his day.* Jesus and Solomon, p. 68; Jesus and Jonas, p. 68; Jesus, Moses, and Elias, p. 69; Jesus and David, p. 71; Jesus and John the Baptist, p. 71; Jesus and the messengers who preceded him: the Parable of the Vine-Dressers, p. 72; Jesus and the good and wicked angels, p. 72;

B.—*The Relationship of Jesus to Javé*. Jesus calls God his Father, p. 74; Jesus sets himself apart, p. 76; Jesus and the Sabbath, p. 77; Authority to forgive sins, p. 78; Jesus the final judge of conscience, p. 80; The relationship of Jesus to the Spirit, p. 82; Testimony before the powers, p. 83; The relationship of Jesus to the Father, p. 83; Passage relating to the divine 'Ego', p. 84; Other texts, p.85.

IV THE SIGNIFICANCE OF THE ENVELOPMENT   87
A.—*Envelopment and Authenticity*. The chief characteristic of the foregoing 'logia': the difference between virtual and apparent content, p. 87; The accidental aspect of the implicit assertions, p. 91; Virtuality never the outcome of fabulation, p. 92.
B.—*Other aspects of the resistance of facts to fabulation*. The verisimilitude of the historical background, p. 94; No retrospective projection of the risen Christ, p. 95; Some doubtful passages, p. 96.

V THE RESULTS OF REFLECTION ON THE FACTS   100
Emergence in the Jewish mind of belief in Divinity: the double theological problem, p. 100; The element of chance, p. 103; Paulinism: its antecedent improbability and explosive character, p. 104; The doctrine of Paul, p. 107; The Johannine contribution: its improbability: history and theology, p. 109.

PART THREE: RESURRECTION

DIFFICULTIES   120

I THE ORIGINAL EVENT   121
The first historical difficulty: the problem of origin and emergence, p. 121; An inductive reconstruction of the original phenomenon, p. 122; Were the visions objective? p. 124.

II RETURN TO LIFE   126
The first philosophical difficulty, p. 126; Resurrection and return to life, p. 126; Resurrection and sublimation, p. 127; Material body and spiritual body, p. 130; Sublima-

Chapter   Page

tion, p. 132; The problem of the ultra-human, p. 134; The
allegory of the fourth dimension, p. 136; What is a body?
p. 138; Obscurity, p. 140; Summing up, p. 141; Is it possible to have experience of a sublimated body? p. 141.

III THE DEVELOPMENT OF THE TESTIMONY   143
Improbability of the documentation, p. 143.
A.—*The First Phase: General Affirmations.* The primitive
professions of faith, p. 144; the discourses in the Acts, p.
146.
B.—*The Second Phase: Narratives, Circumstances, and Answers.*
Mark's account, p. 147; Matthew's account, p. 147;
Luke's account, p. 148; John's Gospel, p. 151.
C.—*The Third Phase: Harmonizing and Summarizing,* p. 153.

IV THE CHARACTERISTICS OF THE EVIDENCE   155
The contemporary attitude to the documentary evidence:
its subjectivity: absence of primitive verification, p. 155;
Faith and history: opposed standpoints: the character
of the Gospels, p. 156; Historicity and attestation: from
thematic to circumstantial assertion, p. 162; The Resurrection and mental expectations, p. 165.

V APPARITIONS AND MYSTICAL EXPERIENCES   169
The resemblances, p. 169; Some characteristics of mystical experiences: the social background, p. 170; The
impression of reality, p. 171; Spiritual mission and message, p. 171; The apparitions of Christ and perceptions,
p. 172; The strangeness and ambivalence of the experiences, p. 174; The appeal to earlier tradition as a test of
authenticity, p. 176; The presence of a vocation and a
mission, p. 178; Investiture, p. 179.

VI HOW THE APPARITIONS DIFFER FROM MYSTICAL
EXPERIENCES   181
The apparitions to the apostles not mystical visions, p.
181; Insertion in the texture of history, p. 184; The identity of the character of Jesus, p. 185; An objection to correspondence, p. 186; The apostles' doubts, p. 187; The
Jewish idea of objectivity, p. 188; A difficulty: the Damascus apparition, p. 190; The 'metapsychical phenomenon'
explanation, p. 192.

Chapter   Page

VII THE SIGNIFICANCE OF THE EMPTY TOMB   194

Significance of negative experiences, p. 194; A suggested
explanation: the empty tomb as the final stage of faith's
magnification, p. 195; Difficulties in the way of reducing,
p. 198; Discussion of the prophetic argument, p. 201; The
Gospel evidence concerning the empty tomb: its virtual
presence in the earliest preaching, p. 203; Its plausibility
for the genesis of faith, p. 204.

VIII THE NATURE OF THE APPARITIONS   206

The Resurrection-in-itself and the Resurrection-for-us,
p. 207; Perception and presence, p. 210; Presence and
body, p. 211; Message and event, p. 213; Two meanings of
historicity, p. 214; The significance of Emmaus, p. 216.

IX EXPLANATORY DEVELOPMENTS   218

Attestation and explanation, p. 218; The state of mind of
the first Christians, p. 219.
A.—*The First Phase: the pre-theologies of the Resurrection*, p.
220; The ante-Pauline theology, p. 220; *Maran Atha*,
p. 221; The Petrine theology, p. 222.
B.—*The Second Phase: the pre-theology of the Synoptics:
moment and duration*, p.225 ; Mark, p. 225; Matthew, p. 226;
Luke, p. 228;
C.—*The Third Phase: The explicit theologies:* p. 229; The
Pauline view of the Resurrection, p. 230; The Johannine
Gospel, p. 231; Paul's soteriology compared with the
theology of John, p. 234.
D.—*Allied developments in dogma*, p. 236; The descent into
hell, p. 236; Kindred dogmas in Mariology, p. 237.

PREFACE

FOR those engaged in advancing some branch of knowledge, it is no easy matter to give thought simultaneously to the methods they are using and the principles they take for granted. To act, and to reflect on one's actions, are necessarily two distinct operations. Nor is it perhaps desirable, amidst the ardours of research or in the sudden enlightenment of some new discovery, to pause to distinguish how much is due to accepted ways of thinking, a principle taken for granted or some latent belief, and what is really an original truth, a newly discovered fact or a really vitalizing idea. Drawing such a distinction is a proper task for somebody else, whose approach should be one of critical contemplation.

For the last fifty years or so, in mathematics, physics, biology, and history, much attention has been devoted to the methods and assumptions of scientific research; indeed scientific progress is inseparable today from a philosophical criticism of the sciences.

It has not been the case with the science of Christian origins. This has seen a remarkable renewal in the course of the last century, but it has never undergone any process of self-criticism; it has been pursued often enough in a spirit of objectivity, but not in an atmosphere conspicuously serene.

The reason for this is that it is a branch of knowledge incompatible with any 'impartial' conclusions. One of two alternatives is always presupposed. Because of the nature of the object to be known, the problems of historical criticism are inseparably interlocked with those of philosophy.

Yet whichever the chosen standpoint that calls for allegiance, what should be required here above all is logic: the distinguishing, in the act of knowing, between what is contributed by the mind and what is contributed by the fact. This 'logic of religion' is still in its infancy. One may even wonder if it has yet come to birth.

Impressed by the need for it, I have made a start, almost alone, on this unfamiliar path. Adopting the affirmative option, which I believe I can justify, I have tried to find the elements of a logic of Christian origins.

This logic, of which the present work forms a part, presupposes a knowledge of contemporary exegesis under its three modes of approach, the rationalist, the Protestant, and the Catholic. It aims at defining difficulties and possible solutions; then, by comparing them, at finding if one of these solutions fits the integral data of the problem better than the others.

Since it is impossible to study a question like this without starting from some initial hypothesis, it is as well to state this hypothesis at the outset. It is apparent enough that I have undertaken and pursued this inquiry with a predisposition in favour of the Christian solution.

I have, however, always been scrupulous to separate principles of interpretation from facts, difficulties from solutions; and for this reason, I think, my study may also be profitable to those who reject my conclusions.

I would like to see a similar study made from the unbeliever's point of view. By confronting one type of investigation with the other, it ought, theoretically, to be possible to draw the elements of an objective solution.

Works of criticism, important though they are, lose something of their value if they are not preceded by a critical examination of criticism. Without this cleaning-up process the observer is in danger of projecting into his findings what are in fact hypotheses, though he mistakes them for facts.

My appeal throughout is to the intelligence, to that power of joining things together which makes it possible to grasp the harmony and consequences of our thoughts, while keeping them all in view at the same time. For this reason I have made it my aim to shorten rather than expand this book. I think every *synoptic* work ought to be fairly short: the evangelists were of the same opinion.

*   *   *

I know that this study will have two sets of opponents among readers for whom it was not intended.

Among unbelievers there will be those who declare that I am simply trying, as so many apologists have done in the past, to prove the truth of religion. This is to ignore what is original in the book, which sets out in a spirit as rationalist as such a subject permits, allowing private judgement all the freedom that belongs to it. My religious leanings are not disguised, as are so often the anti-religious leanings in writings that profess to be scientific. And I can claim, I think, that I have done all a Christian may to understand positions most opposed to the Faith.

My other opponents will be Catholics who disapprove of my progressive method; these will hold that I concede to the sceptical more that I should. But this is to forget that I am adopting the viewpoint of one who is wholly outside the Faith, a mere seeker, with no explicit light to guide him but that of nature and the facts 'as they are known' (*Rom.* i 20). A serious inquiry is necessarily slow and laborious, to be undertaken by stages.

And there will be some, too, who will regard these questionings as vain. Faith is sufficient, they think, and it is impossible to raise such problems without troubling many consciences. If their hearts counsel thus they should read no further. . .

An unshakeable faith is a treasure indeed. Yet Newman was not in error when, speaking of simple believers with 'little intellectual training', he said they 'have never had the temptation to doubt, and never the opportunity to be certain'.[1]

*   *   *

This book is presented in the form of a free-thinker's journal. This free-thinker is a thoroughly estimable character. He is absolutely honest: too much so, if that were possible. He stands for pure reason, slow-moving, almost too prudent, craving firm supports, refusing to go forward except on firm ground. Though he would check everything for himself and never quit a line of thought till he has pursued it to its deepest lair, he is clearly anything but a sceptic philosophically; he goes his own way, weighing the pros and cons, and especially the cons. If he finds the latter so attractive, this is due to his caution; he mistrusts what is asserted by mere belief, anything that is not the result of meticulous consideration. Each of us should have his enemy at his side and argue with his opposite. Though truth to tell, as will appear in due course, this free-thinker of mine is by no means my opposite. He stands for my own reason in a state of calm, when it restricts its acquired certitudes and maps out for itself a procedure that is ideally logical. He is a very different person from Pascal's *libertin*. He is not enlisted in the cause of evil; rather

---

[1] *Grammar of Assent*, p. 211. And, long before Newman, Pope Gregory the Great observed that he derived less benefit from Mary Magdalen's faith than he did from Thomas's doubting: *Minus enim mihi Maria Magdalena praestitit quae citius credidit quam Thomas qui diu dubitavit* (quoted from the Roman Breviary, 3rd Nocturn at Matins of the Ascension).

he has enlisted and persevered in the cause of good. He is a stranger to anything like inward drama, unless it be that of an intense curiosity. He seeks, not, it is true, 'with groaning', but with confidence, with care and peace of mind. He is ready to submit to what his conscience requires of him. Only he cannot anticipate it, and perhaps his favourite maxim would be that saying of Valéry's: 'If you would destroy some opinion, you must first master it better than the ablest of its defenders.'

PART I

THE CHRISTIAN TESTIMONY

I

THE CRITICAL APPROACH

I WANT to take advantage of this placid week in the high peace of summer to clarify my ideas about Jesus. It is high time I did so. I have now reached middle life; it is impossible that I should come by any entirely fresh knowledge, or that my requirements should grow less exacting. I think I have sounded all the ideas on the subject and made an inventory of the possible solutions. What is more, I think I have attained the sort of unbiased state that is needed for calm inquiry, and my present situation is so secluded that I am in no danger of being moved by emotional considerations.

I have read on the problem all the books which anyone may reasonably be expected to have read, and I know something of the necessary sciences bearing on language and history. Admittedly I am not a specialist; this, I know, is a failing these days, at any rate for purposes of making a career; but it rids me of some of the specialist's limitations and gives me the satisfaction of being able to note where the specialists go astray, whether through forgetting their principles or through ignoring the work of their neighbours. I have also sometimes the advantage of watching their labours from above and seeing how the trenches they are digging diverge or converge, which is something that those doing the actual digging cannot observe. What I lose in knowledge personally acquired, I gain in the understanding of knowledge acquired by others.

I am not a believer, which allows me more freedom in forming hypotheses. Nor am I an unbeliever, for precisely the same reasons, and because what I want—too much, I am sure—is that my mind shall be in complete control of its work. I do not share that learned credulity known today as rationalism, yet I love reason above everything in the world. What lies deepest in me, I believe, is a horror of premature certitudes, of beliefs and unbeliefs too hurriedly adopted. I prefer to have a grain of assured truth rather than a mountain of mingled truths and errors. And what I look for everywhere is the ounce of certitude which is all but incontestable. That is something I can build on. What I want above all is the feeling of security. I am one of those ultra-cautious people; I prefer to go a very long way with my opponent, even to let him have the better of me, rather than by clever debating to gain a facile victory. I have often been reproached for this, and it is as well I should recognize the fact and admit it. In matters like these, however, *prudence* is so rare that what many consider a failing I regard as an advantage.

I am also concerned for order, again possibly too much: I don't want my thoughts to wander haphazard; I want them geared together like the mechanism of a clock. To my mind uncontrolled thinking is too like dreaming. If I could, I would like to see all my thoughts at once, so that I could keep in view their mutual relationships and marshal their arrangement. I want them, at any rate, to hang together securely, as was once the fashion, like links in a chain. It is a happy chance that in my present state of privation I have hardly a book in my possession; so I shall not be tempted to use foreign bodies to fill up gaps in my own mental equipment. My energies will be devoted primarily to reflection.

I can see the task is going to be difficult. I shall not be able to devote to it more than an hour a day. But it is a good thing to break off and let the nights help.

The first question concerns the right attitude of reason to a tale of miracles, like all those contained in the Gospels.

I decline to take up in advance, as so many do, a purely negative position; on the other hand, I want to take the line I regard as the most prudent. To explain these allegations of unprecedented and preternatural phenomena (such as the resurrection of the dead) there are two possible hypotheses. The miracle may have actually happened. Or it may have been related without its having happened.

Apparently, when presented with these two alternatives, I ought to decide in favour of the second. It is the more probable. Every day people think they see strange and marvellous occurrences: they may take to be miraculous things that are not so really (as people once did thunder); they may give credence to rumours impossible to verify, or when under some such influence as enthusiasm or fear they may interpret something unusual or singular as miraculous. And I know, for I have seen it myself, that the most honest witnesses can be deceived by prejudice, by being too hasty, by the effects of mass-hysteria, especially when (as is the case with religion) some very lively emotion is involved. Such genuine errors are common enough and history records them even in sceptical ages, whereas the occurrence of a fact contrary to the laws of nature is to say the least extremely rare. Not that I would deny that any such breach of determinism is possible: that would be a betrayal of my reason, which I want to be thoroughly supple and unbiased. But such an accident is extremely improbable. Believers, belonging to the Roman Church or orthodox Protestantism, have doubtless sound reasons for their faith in miracles, and among them, I know, there are those with scientifically trained minds who may be mistaken but certainly cannot be suspected of dishonesty; but apart from this handful of the educated and enlightened, no one pretends today to have witnessed a miracle properly speaking. I exclude crowds; also women and children; and I leave out of account those backward peoples who have no clear idea of what is meant by law. The implication would seem to be that as means of observation and verification improve, the less chance there is of witnessing a miracle. It may be argued, of course, that God denies signs to a faithless age that seeks to be assured of his non-existence; but it can also be maintained that the number of miracles varies in inverse ratio to the diffusion of scientific methods. Yet what would happen if I actually saw with my own eyes, and were therefore bound to admit, some plainly preternatural phenomenon? I have sometimes asked myself this, and the answer is, I think, that it would be my first duty to deny the fact and call it an *appearance*, as a man would do if he saw a ghost in the gallery of some haunted castle, or—to take a simpler case—who saw a stick bent in water and used his reason to straighten it.

When I examine historically the explanations men have given before the beginnings of science, I observe that whenever they felt they must *explain* strange facts by invisible and supernatural causes, they have always succumbed to magic and superstition: as for instance when they made up fables to explain storms, eclipses, and meteors; or even when, more recently, they attributed maladies of the mind to direct intervention by God or the devil; or again when they see in the origins of great religious movements, such as Buddhism or Mohammedanism, an exceptional and superhuman phenomenon, whereas the history of religions and a critical examination of the original documents make it possible to reduce these exceptions to the common measure and see them as esctatic phenomena produced by mass suggestion. True, it may be very wrong to apply this 'reducing' method to the religion of Moses, of Jesus and Pascal;

for reasons I have examined at length elsewhere, I know that Christianity is an exception to the exceptional and therefore merits some special treatment. Taking account of the posterity of Jesus and the sublime figure of Jesus himself, one would be justified in adopting an exceptional procedure and forgoing the rule of excessive caution. But it may be that *just once* in history the combination of chance and the forces of illusion produced something more, a highly improbable success and an extraordinary effect of grandeur, that this effect once realized had a captivating influence which lasted on, thanks to its intrinsic beauty and its interest for humanity. Once more I want to be as circumspect as possible and adopt, as I prefer doing, the most unfavourable hypothesis; then if I have to discard it later it will be for no exterior reasons but for its own shortcomings. Even if I had a Christian's scruples in the matter, I could still justify my method, for it was St Augustine who said, in connection with the reluctance to believe shown by the apostle Thomas, that Thomas's doubts did better service to future believers than did the firm confidence of the other apostles.

What I propose to do, then, is to seek, in the *mélange* presented to us in the Gospels, on the one hand what is historical, that which is soundly attested and actually happened, and on the other hand what has been added by the imagination of the fabler.

A highly delicate operation, for what is to be the criterion? In a religion like Christianity, which challenges (at any rate in its origins) our sense of the possible, how difficult to distinguish the real from the fictitious! Who is to determine the bounds of the impossible? Who will provide us with a ready and reliable means of deciding, among the mingled incidents of the story, what actually took place and what has been added on?

Even as I ask the question I hear one reply. It is that the religious historian is really in a privileged position compared with the secular historian. His criterion by which to judge what he must accept or reject is so rigid in character that the distinction will be effected automatically and accepted by everyone: it is that provided by the *laws of nature*. Any alleged fact that is contrary to these laws must be discarded.

So I shall try using this rule. It is perfectly simple, perhaps too perfectly simple. There are many, I know, who are not afraid to use it openly, categorical as it is. It is by presupposing it that unbelievers justify their conclusion; so much so that for many of them it has the authority of a dogma. It was laid down in the past by Spinoza, by Voltaire and Renan; today Brunschvicg, Delacroix, and Valéry all defer to it. This is the company I propose to join. I shall adopt, if I can, a mental outlook indistinguishable, it would seem, from the type of reasoning used in science, perhaps any type of reasoning. The rule will allow me to trace the exact line which separates *history* from *faith*, the possible from the impossible. I remember noticing in the past how closely associated these two aspects are in the primitive documents, and how the factual and the marvellous overlap in the apparent unity of the evidence. But an uncritical acceptance of this fact is to solve the problem by recourse to mystery. And I am not one of those who admit the mysterious at the outset: I accept it only when I am bound to, when there is no other solution.

I propose, therefore, to retain as historical, or virtually so, whatever science, philosophy, and human experience represent to me as possible and likely to be true. I do not, you will notice, say it *is* historical. Whether a reported fact is historical is something it is impossible to tell at a glance. All I say is that facts in conformity with human possibilities *may* have happened. If these coincide with historical events that are known for certain, if they imply logical sequence, a connected train of events, and intelligible continuity, I shall call them true, or at any rate plausible. I shall allow them at least the degree of certainty I allow to the secular history of the period.

I shall, on the other hand, describe as illusory—apocryphal, legendary, fabulous, 'fact of faith but not of history'—all that science and reason regard as impossible.

Jesus, say the witnesses, died and rose again. His death is probable: I retain it as historical. His resurrection is improbable: I relegate it to the region of mere belief.

This rule will make it possible to draw a certain and always easy distinction and make a clear separation of the *objective* from the *subjective*. And to these I shall apply very different explanations.

The events I retain as probable and historical will be explained by *objective* causes: by motives drawn from our knowledge of man, his desires and fears, his interests and intrigues, generosities and resentments; or else by the interplay of political causes, by those mass movements to which the individual is merely a party: or even by causes which operate invisibly, at the lowest level in economics, at the highest in those irruptions of the Spirit which occur at the beginnings of great mystical movements. But whether I am considering motives of which the historical actors were themselves aware, or whether I am weighing those secret movements discernible only in the after-effects which make themselves felt at the social level, I shall never take leave of the purely natural; I shall always remain within the bounds of the cosmos.

As for the improbable events, which it is agreed I shall consider as *non-true* and a-historical, I shall seek causes for these also. I shall not regard them as an unexplainable enclave in an otherwise organized universe. But instead of looking for the causes in any conformity with some real object exterior to the mystical subjects witnessing them (which is what these subjects affirm them to be), I shall seek them in what is hidden from these subjects, their own dispositions, or in the latent energies of social groups. This procedure, I know, will arouse indignation, and I shall soon have it pointed out that since only these subjects had anything to do with the 'reality', and were its only observers, I shall be depriving myself of the only immediate source of information. And it is certainly true that a scientist who so proceeded, and repudiated in advance the evidence of the only observer, would be acting quite irrationally and denying himself all he had to go upon. But what justifies my principle is precisely the fact that it is not with the realm of nature that I have to do: the phenomena reported in religious experiences do not belong to that close-knit whole of phenomena which I call the universe. It would therefore be unreasonable to apply here the methods of explanation that are applied to accounts of unusual facts of nature and marvels of the physical world. All the more so because it is possible, as I said just now, to reduce to vanishing point these 'preternatural' phenomena—irrational and miraculous facts—by finding an adequate explanation in psychological or sociological causes, causes which are purely interior and subjective.

And to return to this question of probability, it is surely more probable that these facts belong to the order of dreams or madness, and so get back to cosmic limits and cosmic laws, rather than that they should be highly exceptional realities, a defiance of the regularity and necessity of order. Consequently I shall try, as far as I can, to explain the evidence by subjective conditions and wholly interior mechanisms. If such mechanisms are unknown to the subjects and repudiated by them, this will be no proof of their unreality, because the consciousness of the experiencing subject enlightens and grasps only that which the psychic activity expresses outside itself, not the preparations and undercurrents of this activity. Besides, for these witnesses to recognize the truth of this natural explanation would be to admit that they were deceived; this is more than we can ask of them, for no one can be expected to give the lie to himself. So the objection that the immediate actors contradict the results of this scientific method is a necessary consequence and leaves me quite undisturbed.

I propose, therefore, to explain the visions of these earliest witnesses by *subjective causes*. Various types of explanation are possible here and I am not pretending to enumerate all of them. One is psychological, based on processes of hallucination, analogous to dreaming, where the subject projects some desire or vision that exists only for himself. Another explanation could be provided by social phenomena: people thrown together, especially when they share some common hope or fear, are apt to see their power (or their weakness) multiplied, and so can perceive in common what is not really there, even attributing to this creation of their desire or terror a stronger reality than that of physical objects. I can envisage also a more historical explanation: one which accounts for the birth of beliefs by the needs of a particular religious society, by the creative force of tradition, by the power of language, of speech, and all those narrative devices which *create* the object they describe, and finally by the combination of different beliefs, their juxtaposition and fusion. I could imagine even other types of *causality*. Who knows that we have not in us a myth-making power, similar to the passion-creating power of the *libido*? Or who knows if the impersonal thought of humanity may not proceed, as many have thought, from synthesis to synthesis, and religion be explained logically like a process of thought, miracle being simply a dialectical stage? And possibly these different explanations could be combined in various ways, what is doubtful in one being completed by what is certain in another, and each borrowing the certainty it lacks itself. I cannot say whether there is a single mind capable of embracing all these explanations at once and seeing their agreement, basing them, too, on a sceptical philosophy and developing them with all the reasons, intellectual and emotional, for not believing. But if there is such a mind I see its goal very clearly.

Is it feasible now to proceed to this separation in such a way that a history of Jesus is still possible? Will it not mean stripping that history of all that constitutes its charm and attraction, and that peculiar quality of a life humanly lived which the Gospels will always offer the human heart? This no doubt is the hardest point. But if ever nature combined the gifts of artist and critic and created a religious soul detached from religion, clever enough to harmonize these two modes of explanation and pass from one to the other without a too obvious break, then there would be one capable of writing about Jesus as I would do now. There has been such a man, though I feel there was room for him before he appeared. It is very rarely that a situation occurs without a man capable of bringing it about; either he feels it and adapts himself accordingly, or else it is just destiny. Renan wanted to be an historian and believed he could write a Life of Jesus precisely as one could write a Life of Caesar: namely, seeing in Jesus an interior development and in his history a linking together of incidents and a correspondence between incidents and results, just as in any ordinary human life. At the same time he rejected everything preternatural. The following passage of his seems to me characteristic of the method I have laid down. I quote it, not because I attach any exceptional importance to it; perhaps these days a disciple of Renan's would smile at the 'explanation' he gives; it might even be that Renan himself was being ironical when he offered it; the example, however, illustrates my point. He is writing of the Resurrection, or rather of the apparitions that led to belief in it:

> Anyone of perspicacity could have told already, that Saturday night, that Jesus would return to life. The little Christian community worked a miracle that day; through the intense love it bore him, it raised up Jesus again in its heart. It resolved that Jesus would not die. The love of these passionate souls was truly stronger than death; and as passion is nothing if not communicative, lighting kindred sentiment like a torch and so propagating itself indefinitely, at that hour Jesus, in a sense, had already risen. All that remained was for some trifling material fact to give grounds for belief that his body was no longer here below, and the dogma of the resurrection would be founded for ever.
>
> The cities of the East are mute after sunset, so indoors there would have been very deep silence: every little noise could be interpreted in the sense of universal expectation. And expectation normally creates its object. In those decisive hours, a breath of wind, the creaking of a window, any chance murmur may determine the belief of whole peoples for centuries. The breath of air is felt, sounds are thought to be heard. Some declare they have distinctly heard the word *schalom*, 'happiness' or 'peace'.

I see this as an excellent example of what I call the *critical* approach. Apart from the miracle, all the evidence is preserved. At the same time belief in the miracle is explained by normal and natural causes: temperament, enthusiasm, pent-up passion that can be released by a mere nothing; add to this the characteristics of Eastern towns, the silence that follows dusk—and reason triumphs!

It keeps all that was contained in the texts; on the rare points where it is bound to intervene it conjectures causes that might well have entered into the texture of the story. The apparently broken threads are repaired and the miraculous has insensibly faded away. On the face of it the testimony stands in its entirety. Actually it has dissolved into thin air.

II

THE DIFFICULTIES OF THE CRITICAL
APPROACH

THE conclusion I came to yesterday was that the content of the Gospels must be subjected to rational criticism. I explained the grounds for doing so and accepted them in all their apparent plausibility. I was pleased to discover that these principles, which I had established by myself before consulting the books that expounded them (thus following Leibniz's advice), corresponded well enough with what I found among the critics. Indeed I could congratulate myself on having deduced Renan! If he had not existed I should have had to invent him; and I think I can say that—except, of course, for the charm of his style—I should have invented someone very much like him. But I have no intention of calling a halt to my thinking, which is nothing if not mobile, and I shall not make this a permanent position—strong though it is, or at any rate seems to be—before I have made an inventory of the others. Besides, I want to see what it commits me to, and how far.

I am well aware that once a theory has been formed there are two ways of looking at it. The angles can be smoothed down, the shadows relieved with reflected lights, and the whole touched up like a too candid photograph; alternatively one can stress its geometry and lay bare its structural essentials. It is obvious to me that Renan, a man of fastidious taste, chose the first of these methods and used an anaesthetic to deaden the effects of his critical operations. But my choice is the second, for it is the truth I am looking for.

The whole question, it seems to me, is to decide whether the grounds of the critical approach are sound. Yesterday I had some misgivings about this. I wondered whether perhaps Christianity should enjoy some privileged treatment, or whether one should apply to it the ordinary law that applies to the interpretation of the fabulous. Out of prudence I decided to be as negative as possible. I deliberately broke up the evidence and divided it into two classes: the objective, which I kept; the subjective, which I explained by certain impulses unknown to the subject. I was well aware that my explanation of the mistakenness of the witnesses, prudent though that explanation was, rested upon an anterior denial of the experience. I might have been right in denying it in advance, it may have been incumbent on reason to do so; but it leaves my conscience a little uneasy. Like one who has expressed a daring opinion in public and awaits a murmur of approval from the audience, I should much like to see some kind of corroboration in the historic experience itself.

I spent a long time last night trying to find what I might call experimental confirmation. Obviously I cannot hope to reconstruct the Gospel scene and see if the characters really behaved as I suppose, whether the witnesses were the dupes of the illusion I suggest, whether eastern cities were really silent, whether love begot visions, and enthusiasm all I conjecture it did, but there is, I perceive, a much surer and more decisive method than this. It is to see whether the impossibility I assume *a priori* may not rest upon another sort of impossibility, wholly independent and different in kind, namely an *a posteriori* impossibility. What I mean by this is a proof of the historical unreality of what the Gospel stories relate. As a result of reflection, my reading of modern books by the opposing schools and my meditations upon Renan, I feel I must be more precise about the judgement I formed yesterday and work it out further.

The point is this: the idea of impossibility is not clear in itself and I can see two kinds of historical impossibility. There is *a priori* or philosophical impossibility, which proceeds from a clear perception of what makes sense or else from a logical deduction. For instance, it used to be the fashion for students of rhetoric to compose, in the manner of Lucian or Fénelon, dialogues in the Elysian Fields between Socrates and Descartes. (The subject one might, perhaps should, set them today, would be a dialogue between, say, Valéry and Racine, or between Peter the Great and Stalin.) Obviously there could be no such discussions except in Elysium. The impossibility is palpable. More palpable still would be the violation of first principles: a whole smaller than its part, an effect without a cause. This *a priori* impossibility is so strong that it can reduce sense experience to mere appearance. It is this that persuades us that the sun is what the astronomers tell us it is, not a great white ball comparatively close at hand. And it is this that compels fanatical adversaries of freedom, Spinoza and Taine for example, to deny the facts of experience on the grounds of initial impossibility.

But it is evident to me that there is another sort of impossibility, that which I call *historical impossibility*. This is not the result of reasoning anterior to experience; it rests on *incompatibilities* in the experience itself. These incompatibilities, once they are recognized, make it possible, with all but absolute certainty, to distinguish forgeries and mis-statements, as cross-examination can 'catch out' the guilty. To take a flagrant example: if in some wartime correspondence, dated 1916 and referring to an air-raid, I find mention of 'Flying Fortresses' and 'Liberators', I know at once I have here a forgery (or else an interpolation). Not because it is unthinkable or impossible *a priori* that there should have been planes so named in the 1914 war, but because I know from other sources that these types and names were not in evidence till 1943, and that a confusion is very possible, especially since people constantly tend—through laziness, inaccuracy, or ignorance—to conceive the near past in the image of the present. Here, then, is proof that a document, if it is all in the same strain, is a forgery.

There are certainly occasions when it is hard to say whether the impossibility we are confronted with is of the *a priori* or *a posteriori* type. Our judgements are a combination of the two. This ambiguity is tiresome to the logician. It is hard to say, for instance, whether the famous proposition 'All men are mortal' implies a judgement anterior to experience, or whether it is something verified by an indefinite number of observations. Do we mean that so far everyone we know of has died sooner or later, that we have never heard of anyone being immortal? Or do we mean to convey that there is so deep a relationship between the human essence and mortality that the one term necessarily implies the other, even though the mind may not grasp the implication all at once? Should the proposition 'Miracles don't happen' be interpreted in the first of these senses or the second? Do we mean that miracles *never have* happened, or that they *cannot* happen? I have often encountered such difficulties and I have a feeling I shall often meet with them again. They are a permanent ingredient in human logic. I have a feeling, too, that these two attitudes, of verification and *a priori* affirmation, as it were feed one another and overlap, each borrowing from the other for its own reinforcement. I see this happening clearly over the question of miracles.

In practice, I should remark, and in spite of appearance, *a posteriori* impossibility is the more objective.

In principle it should be otherwise. *A priori* impossibility should by rights be peremptory and make an end of all argument. But it is a tricky thing to define the impossible *a priori*. There is no knowing whether what is contradictory to our logic may not be otherwise in the logic of nature. In the sciences what we call a fact, since it is thrust upon us with brutal force by experience, is often what was once an *a priori* impossibility: gravity, vacuum, attraction, magnetism, the speed of light, quantum theory, the curvature of space, atomic energy. On the other hand, I have now come to recognize that *a posteriori* impossibility is decisive. If the metal in this piece of jewellery is recent, if the mode of reckoning here supposed was unknown in history till a century later, if the monument alluded to did not yet exist or existed no longer, if the expression quoted was no longer in use or not yet, then I am sure of the forgery, and absolutely sure. And the slightest indication of *a posteriori* impossibility is enough to bring down a vast edifice in ruins.

And perhaps one might add, by way of corollary, that when there is no indication of *a posteriori* impossibility and when not only so but the narrative being examined seems to have historical verisimilitude, then it is improper to plead *a priori* impossibility.

So in connection with the impossibilities in the Gospel tradition I shall make it a rule in future to ask the critic this question: 'Do you reject this on grounds of *a posteriori* or *a priori* impossibility?'

I have looked into one of Renan's books, which happens to be in the desolate spot where I am, to see if he appears to have been aware of this distinction. I think he was. Oddly remarkable is the appendix to the thirteenth edition of his *Life of Jesus*: 'Concerning the use to be made of the fourth Gospel in writing the Life of Jesus'. He had used the fourth Gospel for chronological purposes, to explain the movements of Jesus from place to place, a number of circumstances in his Passion and even his apparitions. And he defends himself by appealing to the veracity of John's testimony in a number of cases. He accepted the Johannine episodes, after the method which historians normally use, to the extent to which he found they agreed with Jewish or Roman archaeology, with human nature and general probability. Thus when Jesus, consumed with thirst, asked for drink, and a soldier offered him some of his sour wine on a sponge, 'Very natural', comments Renan, 'and thoroughly sound archaeologically.' The *crurifragium*, he tells us, and the thrust with the lance were 'quite possible'. Elsewhere, too, he talks of the 'high standard' of the topography, of the 'historical justice' of the situations. It is not my business here to make out a list; I merely remark the old sceptic's respect for the historical details in this, the most 'spiritual' of the Gospels. As far as one can see he never pleads *a posteriori* impossibility in the public life of Jesus. I should have been interested to see some. It would have been pleasant to learn that Pilate never existed, that Nazareth and Cana were mythical places, that the pool of Bethesda never had the five porticoes mentioned by John, that Jews were never crucified, or that in the year 33 the government of Palestine was not in the hands of a procurator...

On the other hand I have found him maintaining stoutly *a priori* impossibility. It is reaffirmed in his Introduction to the *Apostles* in terms that leave no room for doubt. 'Besides', he writes, 'how can one pretend to take literally any document that contains impossibilities? The first twelve chapters of the Acts are a tissue of miracles. But it is an invariable rule of criticism to allow no place to the miraculous in any historical narrative.' He adds, it is true: 'This is not the result of any metaphysical system. It is simply a fact of observation.' But in this he is mistaken: an observation, however extensive, can never prove an impossibility.

I am fully aware of the difficulty of deciding how far a judgement is based on the impossibility of what-cannot-be-observed and how much on that of what-has-never-been-observed; just as in morals it is hard to say whether horror at some crime is due to what-ought-not-to-be-done or simply to what-has-never-been-done: anyhow the two combine in what-is-not-done. But I cannot help observing that the non-existence of a judgement of historical impossibility takes something from the value of one of logical impossibility: it emphasizes very strongly its arbitary and purely conventional character. I shall therefore have to examine afresh what I will call the paranormal in Christianity. If this is a unique religion, with an exceptional development, why deny *a priori* that there could have occurred at its origin some releasing force beyond the powers of nature?

For a unique event there should be an equally unique cause. Perhaps it *is* in order here, and only here, to suspend the ordinary rules of prudence, just as it is in order, in the case of specially monstrous or dangerous criminals, to suspend the normal safeguards of Justice. This may be the time to reflect on what I would describe as 'the intelligent reaction to the exceptional fact'. However that may be, the fact remains that in this case, that of a document in which paranormality arises solely from the assumption of impossibility, my conscience is uneasy. The hypothesis of an un-heard-of exception, however strange, would give me the immediate advantage of being able to examine the documents with a calmer historical conscience; for I am faced with the extraordinary paradox that in this particular case (and in this one alone) it is the attitude of the 'sceptical critics' that is dogmatic, in that it lays down a law anterior to the facts on the ground of certain principles; whereas the attitude of scholars who are believers is scientific, because it allows the mind to accept the facts without qualifying them beforehand. The first determines and closes the field of research, the other leaves it open. 'In exegesis', it has been pointed out very justly,[1] 'believers are in an enviable position. They can accept frankly, and in their completest sense, documents which the critics receive with bias and try to subject to a hazardous process of winnowing.'

But the consequences to be deduced from this, as I clearly foresee, are so serious that I cannot resign myself to pursuing them yet: not, at any rate, till I have examined another possible solution.

I had undertaken, in any case, to examine every hypothesis in turn and I cannot break off half way. The theory I have been con-sidering so far regards as of primary importance the ordinary historical element. There is another which proceeds in the opposite direction, holding the 'historical' element to be something derived, secondary, and frankly fabulous. Profounder reflection would doubtless show me that this second way of looking at the subject, though it appears at first sight a reversal of the first, is somehow derived from it. I have a presentiment of this today and I must think it over tomorrow. It is getting late and I am tired.

* * *

I spent the day yesterday defining the logical framework of what I have called the *critical* method.

I tested its strength and its weakness, its value and its drawbacks, and incidentally I learnt much about the working of the human mind. Making such observations, which add to the knowledge I have of myself, gives me greater pleasure, I must confess, than the pursuit of reasoning. But today I want to resume my journey and discover where my reasoning was leading me.

I observed that the criterion of *a priori* impossibility, which ap-peared to be the most objective and is held by many to be as rigid

---

[1] By M. Couchard in *Le mystère de Jésus*, p. 110.

as an axiom, was in fact quite elastic and depended on individual sentiment. Obviously the idea of impossibility varies with the idea one forms of natural possibilities, and though I am no great age I have seen it change considerably with the progress of science. For instance, if healing by suggestion is admitted to be possible, one could not object to Jesus' healing the sick; if the possibility of meta-psychical phenomena is granted, then one must yield where some of the apparitions are concerned. Can one really say *a priori* whether any given fact is possible or impossible?

I also note that the critical approach is much more arbitrary and unstable than it appears at first sight. I felt this yesterday, when I was expounding it as though it were my own and accepting its mode of procedure. Now I must bring it into the light and examine it.

The aim of the critical method is to be a compromise, a *via media* between the complete sceptics and genuine believers. It allows the former their negation; the latter, everything but the miraculous. If I place myself in the shoes of the sceptic, or of the ordinary, impartial, and indifferent reader, I can share his lack of conviction: the critic concedes too much, he is caught between two contradictory demands, neither of which he satisfies adequately.

Take the cardinal events in the life of Jesus. The final chapters of the Gospels recount the death of Jesus and his reappearances. It is on this recital that the faith of the Christian depends: it teaches *simultaneously* that Jesus died and rose from the dead: *mortuus, sepultus, resurrexit*. For the Christian it is all of a piece, written by the same hand, a kind of 'seamless robe'.

I do not know that this belief is well founded; all I say is that it is logical. If the Christian admits the evidence for the *Passion*, he is justified in admitting the evidence for the *Resurrection*. It comes from the same mouth. It is written down in the same apparently narrative style, it is presented by the same group of witnesses.

It is not so with the critical school, which has to adopt two entirely different attitudes, according to whether it is dealing with the Passion or the Resurrection. I have explained why, and it is perfectly clear. From the critical point of view, the Passion is wholly credible; the Resurrection, on basic principles, must be rejected.

But if its *a priori* impossibility compels me to discard the account of the Resurrection, I am compelled at the same time to reject the trustworthiness of the witnesses, their balance, their sanity; or else I must suppose the account of the Resurrection is just symbolical, a later addition, begotten of faith and the workings of the newly born tradition. This being so, and since (as I insist) the tone, the style, the quality of the testimony are identical in the two cases, I hardly see why I should employ two sets of weights and measures, accept the truth of the Passion narrative and reject the account of the Resurrection. The same applies to all the miraculous incidents that abound in the Gospels. It is the same man speaking and telling the story: his accent is always the same; there is no denying his consistent identity. Why believe him when he says *this* and not when he says *that*? The *this* and the *that*, after all, are very closely connected. I know, of course, that it is the habit of liars to mix truth with falsehood, and that the lie is not dangerous for the falsehood it contains but for the particles of truth; it is like calumny, the perfidious nature of which is due to its verisimilitude, or like the machinations of the wicked, which are as harmful as they are only because the good are so complacent. So it might be that errors in the Gospels have been cleverly disguised with partial truths. But it is hard to believe that we are dealing here with subtle forgers, who with a jeweller's skill have set in one piece the counterfeit assertion along with the authentic gems of detail.

The mind's tendency will be to follow the sceptical reasoning to its conclusion, not to stop half way.

In reading Renan it is not his scepticism that surprises us, but the fact that he is not more sceptical than he is: that he repudiates the *substance* and retains the *accidents*; that he dismisses the evidence for what is the kernel of the whole matter, but has such an affection for the empty shell. Why keep so much history? Why such confidence in these documents, when the whole principle behind them is a fable? Why such respect for one whose moral worth is questionable, whose very existence is open to doubt? Would it not be better to proceed otherwise and more logically, without compounding with piety and going on following the common sentiment of the faithful? May there not be another way altogether of conceiving how the religious IDEA is related to the FACT which was thought to support it?

The difficulties I have been putting forward are by no means new. I was able to discover them for myself, for they clearly emerge upon reflection. Enlightened critics of the Hegelian school objected to Renan on the score of his method; it seemed to them that he went too far in his acceptance of the facts given in the Gospels. And from the logical point of view, which is where I now propose to

C

take my stand, I confess I find it hard to justify Renan, who seems to me to have tried to reconcile the irreconcilable. It was going against the grain. He was working against his own principles: denying to the Gospel all supernatural reality, yet conceding it almost everything else. Could a witness so totally mistaken about the essential be so *little* mistaken about the adjuncts of that essential? For my part I see no escaping the tendency to restrict to an ever greater extent the properly *historical* part of the Gospel narratives, while respecting more and more the part which is certainly *religious*. But I have no desire to mingle the two, less still to make the second emerge from the first as a progressive idealization and magnification.

The fact is, I see quite clearly that for the unprejudiced reader what gives the Gospel that air of simplicity and naturalness is just the initial assumption and constant supposition of the supernatural character of its principal Actor. Take it for a moment that Jesus is God, the All-Powerful and All-Good, momentarily manifest on earth: the Mystery of Love, hidden behind the veil, come for a moment to smile upon us—then everything in the Gospel follows quite automatically; nothing surprises us, all is in place, and *naturally* in place. It is just like this that one can imagine *a priori* that human beings would react to a divine visitation. The secret of the Gospel's hold upon minds, age after age (and doubtless as long as hapless humanity continues to inhabit this lonely planet), is simply due to the way the facts presented to us as real, as having actually occurred, correspond as they do to the idea our hearts form of Love's passing among men. It is no paradox to say that this passing once admitted, by a simple act of faith, no story is less extraordinary and more human, none more simple, more like what we see happening all about us every day; not marvellous, but prodigious; more astonishing for its modest telling than for anything sensational.

On the other hand, suppose Jesus not God, but only a man falsely believed to be God; then the Gospel story has extraordinary singularities. It is exceptional indeed—since the purple mantle of the dead gods was put off—to see a man appear so contradictory as this Jesus of the Gospels, presenting on one side extraordinary virtues, on the other malign dissimulation and a sinister power of seduction. The same applies to his disciples and those who believed in him. They too are a mass of contradictions: admirable in their faith, their audacity, and their fortitude, but deceiving themselves so readily, so ready to be deceived; such lovers of truth as to be willing

to die for it, but wholly incapable of recognizing truth, or distinguishing illusion! And so with the whole history of primitive
Christianity, in one of its aspects a glorious story of missionary
devotion, in another an extremely equivocal adventure suggestive
of spiritualistic experiments.

I suggest, therefore, that Renan's critical method makes the life
of Jesus a phenomenon of quite unprecedented strangeness; it re-
places supernatural with natural miracles, with events, that is,
which psychologically and historically are highly improbable to say
the least. Nor do I see any reason for not applying to these 'natural
miracles' the method Renan applies to supernatural miracles, and
divide these also into two classes, relegating one class to the impossible and retaining only the other as historical. I would then
distinguish two Jesuses: the divinely human Jesus, the charming
pretender described by Renan, and the real Jesus, about whom I
could make statements highly displeasing to Renan, but statements
which there would be no sound reason to doubt.

But the Jesus so obtained has nothing extraordinary about him
and cannot be classed as even genius or hero, sage, or saint. For (as
I have realized by now) the character of Jesus fits no normal pattern.
If he was not above all others, he was below them; if he was not
superhuman, he was subhuman; there is no alternative to either
exalting or abasing him.

Progressive idealization, which is the idea that lies behind the
fundamental axiom of the critical method, seems to me now a very
dubious and perhaps useless theory. How can one think that it was
by degrees, by the accumulation of small touches, by an imperceptible increase in admiration, that Jesus, first loved and admired, then
worshipped, passed little by little from the human rank to the divine? Certainly the documents give no hint of such a progression.
Quite the contrary. The Epistles of St Paul, written about the year
55, convey the impression that Christ had always been conceived as
God's equal, the Lord, whose name is to be accounted above all
other names. There is a definite feeling that for the believer Christ
had been God for the beginning; and this is a much more normal
idea, because the distance from the human to the divine is infinite,
not to be bridged by gradual stages. Apart from this, progressive
idealization required that the event must have been marvellous and
exceptional originally; that the man it idealizes and then worships
should have been *already* at the limits of historical possibility. It is

precisely this that I have now come to doubt. The further I go, the more I am disposed to reduce the fact of Jesus to very simple and paltry proportions, and the less I can understand how any process, however slow, could have turned him into a god.

I have ventured to consult some works more modern than Renan's to discover what *these* regard as historical in the Gospels, and I see that the historical portion is steadily dwindling. That was only to be expected. I am satisfied that I have detected the rational mechanism of this development. It is to be found in the reason itself; not, as the authors suppose, in the facts. I should like to transcribe the conclusions they come to about the historical core whence emerged Christianity.

'That man', reads the description in Guignebert's *Jesus*, 'who either could not or would not talk to the people effectively; that prophet who could do no more than stir the casual labourers of Galilee to sympathetic curiosity'. And it is easy to find passages like this in Loisy: 'A person called Jesus, a native of Galilee, affected more than most by the hope that inspired the majority of his countrymen and disturbed so many of them, but also convinced of the need for his people's moral regeneration to prepare them for the judgement of heaven, made bold to announce the coming of God. After a short spell of preaching in Galilee, where he recruited only a handful of adherents, he came up to Jerusalem for the paschal feast in the year 33, only to get himself condemned, by the procurator Pontius Pilate, to death by crucifixion.' There is something in these pontifical pronouncements, which aim at being purely objective, that for a reader of any taste seems to strike a false note. It is, of course, a kind of emotional froth, the external manifestation of something very deep-seated: a resentment against believers, against One in whom the author had himself believed. But I need not dwell on the matter of taste. The same things could perhaps have been said otherwise. All I want to do is to call attention to the difficulty of stopping anywhere on this logical slope, which leads to reducing to insignificance both the history and the person of Jesus.

It is like seeing a flower with brilliant petals on a mean and unworthy stem. To which it may be objected that origins are always unworthy. But what is unworthy is only the appearance the origin presents to the uninstructed mind, incapable of grasping the presence and operation of true causes. The spermatozoon contains life in all its mysterious entirety and infinite possibilities. In the obscure labours of the poet, as he painfully assembles syllables and sounds, stammering a meaningless language, there lies hidden the idea, the inspiration that will turn this dry dust into a poem. The outward appearance is only the vehicle in which the energy of form lies still concealed. And to the making of Religion, that poem of life and truth, the same must apply also. So I admit that Jesus was what these learned scholars tell me he was. But the lower I set the man and the phenomenon, the higher I exalt the IDEA Christians see underlying both. It is this IDEA which is the object of FAITH. And ideas, as I know very well, are born suddenly. Before, there was nothing; and lo! it is there, and its light illumines all. The human symbols are like a mantle of mist, formed on its way and marking its presence; but the idea itself has nothing in common with earth. It clothes itself in history, yet in itself it is outside history.

So I am now led to adopt a wholly different standpoint; I set my foot on new territory, which will give me, perhaps, a better understanding of Jesus Christ. What I take from Jesus I shall restore to Christ.

III

THE MYTHICAL APPROACH

IN the course of my yesterday evening's ruminations I fancied I had discovered an entirely new method, one that would satisfy all my requirements and set my mind in harmony with itself. Since I have been considering this problem of Jesus I have come to see that the sceptic's solution, the principle of which was proclaimed by Voltaire, is no longer tenable. According to this principle, religions had their origin in the populace, which possesses emotions but not ideas. Imagination makes the god. Admiration is increased by martyrdoms and these epidemics propagate faith. If this has ceased to satisfy me (though Voltaire's explanation has the merit of perfect lucidity) it is because I regard religion, like art and philosophy, as a very pure and very sublime form of activity. However grotesque or barbaric its origins, religion lies deep in the roots of our being. So even if we have no belief in the facts which the faithful consider to be the genesis of Christianity, this is no reason why we should abandon the Christian religion. Its content is eternal because it is composed of eternal *ideas*. The *idea* is the miracle, the miracle the idea.

Yesterday I met an admirer of Alain's. 'In the life of Jesus', he remarked to me, 'all is miracle, from birth to resurrection. Jesus himself is the essence of the miraculous; with him, the natural is marvellous.' And this man was no believer.

I am now going to *test* this idea and see how it squares with the facts of history. To be true, it is not enough that a theory should be acceptable and attractive, for it to have its own internal logic; it must also agree with the facts. Here is the test, I surmise, of every Christian ideology. If Christianity is comparable to an IDEA, it is not the idea of a single mind, translated *afterwards* into symbols, which is what happens in the mind of a poet, and perhaps in all nature, which was first of all a Thought. It is one found and expressed by a community of believers. A difficulty occurs here, for we know little about the conditions of group invention. But it is at any rate an idea strictly related to history, since it would appear to have actually emerged from history. Up till now I had regarded the starting-point of Christianity as a fact, however diminished that fact in comparison with what we are told in the Gospels. But now that I have come to realize how difficult it is to get faith in Christ out of the fact of Jesus, seeing how vast a gulf the mind has to bridge and the little time (we are to suppose) there was to bridge it, I prefer to imagine the opposite process.

Might it not have been that the *Idea of Jesus-God* came first? Was not this belief the logical foundation of all the rest, and the facts a mere symbol, a clothing of this belief? For if a marvellous fact is awkward to explain, this is not the case with the *idea of the marvellous*: this could have come to birth without the fact. Or rather, is not the miraculous fact itself an Idea?

Take the miraculous feeding of the five thousand, an example that has the merit of simplicity. Here are people reclining on the grass in groups. They *discover* they are refreshed, though it is impossible to count more than five loaves to feed them. The thing can be accepted just as it is related, so emphatically, in the Gospel. We may say, if we like, that these multitudes were refreshed with the provisions they had brought with them, or by a happy surprise, or by a generous gift from people who could afford it. The admiration which these poor people had for Jesus, and a kind of confusion between their physical hunger and the hunger of soul which Jesus assuaged with his words, would have caused them to believe they had been miraculously fed. But this is still rather involved. Surely it would be simpler to adopt at the outset that sublime conception of faith, so profoundly expressed in the 'Gospel of the Secrets', that of John, namely, that Jesus is the true Bread of Life. This, after all, is the primary idea. What of the celebration by the disciples, every 'Lord's Day', of the liturgy of the Bread, broken and truly multiplied by the fraction? This would have made them witnesses of an evident but spiritual miracle, and coursing through memory it could have been transformed, I thought, into a pure Idea, the Idea of Christ the Bread, which would have become one with the idea of the all-powerfulness of God, the idea of God's goodness and of the divinity of his Servant. Moreover it corresponded to analogous stories in the Old Testament: those of the manna and the quails, of Elias's miracle for the widow of Sarephta, of that of Eliseus, who during a famine fed a hundred men with twenty loaves. Ideas such as these, once drawn together, descended (so to speak) into the reality of history, there to seek a point of connection; thus the Idea became incarnate in the fact it created. Hence the miracle of the multiplication of the loaves.

The fact is related to the idea, as is the infinitely small to the infinitely great, as accident to substance, body to soul. What has to be accomplished here is a reversal of values, a process to which we have been made so accustomed by idealist philosophy that it has become a kind of intellectual habit. It is not the case of there being a spiritual element in things; rather that there are things dwelling in the spirit, as beings imaged and represented. It is not the idea which proceeds from the fact, but the fact from the idea, like its radiation and effective symbol. This emergence, of course, of the fact from the idea may have been occasioned by some real but accidental fact. It may be that Jesus really existed; that he really blessed, broke, and distributed bread; really fed, with some un-expected sustenance, that multitude assembled in the wilderness. It may be that the memory of this acted as a swifter, more acceptable, and more probable *factification*. But the process is essentially *ideo-fugal*, not *ideopetal*—to use expressions favoured in other connections.

And does not this *ideopetal* process, which makes the Idea more important than the fact, accord very well with religious thought? Which counts more, for the believer, in the story of the multiplication of the loaves: the fact that some people were fed by the side of a lake, or that Jesus is God, master of things material; that Christ by his word can feed the soul, that he is himself the life-giving Bread, multiplied by a miracle in the sacramental species which is renewed whenever the Last Supper is celebrated? There will be no hesitation in recognizing the second as the principal element, and this is fully understood by the author of the Johannine Gospel. In saying that the *Idea* gave rise to the *Fact*, and not vice versa, I am in the true path of faith, following its trail, its daily influx. Not that this would be a reason for my preferring this hypothesis to any other; I have no wish to treat the believer's standpoint with any special favour. But it is always rather awkward to explain some reality of a higher order in a way that the principal actor or author would repudiate. It is very improbable that some experience of your own could be explained by a stranger, who never had it, more truly than you can explain it yourself. You were there; he was not. It is doubtful if all his knowledge can make up for this. One should distrust the explanation of some passage in a poem which the poet, if consulted, would disavow. I am well aware, of course, that my mythical theory would scandalize believers, because their faith seems to them to rest on well-established facts; but they would be scandalized less, I think, than they would be by the hypothesis of critical rationalism. The latter undermines both the *grounds* and the *objects* of faith, whereas the mythical hypothesis disturbs nothing but the grounds; it respects the objects, conceding them still a very deep significance. Not only this, but by prescinding from the sphere of events, true or false, and of testimonies, whether sincere, insincere or doubtful (the battleground of partisans and opponents), I might very well secure some advantage. It is always a good plan to try to by-pass an issue, and see if there is not some other language, some other set of concepts, in which to express the same ideas; but they must be new words and new concepts, not debased by custom and the heat of controversy.

Leaving miraculous stories for what is most essential in Christianity, I am willing to admit that the idea of God-made-man—or rather of God-himself-made-one-of-us, with all our human nature, including even suffering, weariness, and temptation—is of all the ideas conceived by man the most beautiful and most true. God being conceived as the most perfect of beings and man as the most perfect of his works, the relationship between Creator and creature would still be imperfect, and as it were *exterior*, unless God became man by a second and unutterably wonderful creation. The humanity of divinity and the divinity of humanity require, so to speak, that God should become man for love of us, and also, if I dare say so, for love of himself, since to abase oneself is really to love oneself.

So here I return (though reversing it) to Pascal's argument from 'figures'. He proved the truth of Jesus by the resemblance he bore to the figures that symbolized him; and if Jesus is historical one cannot but recognize, along with Pascal and his Church, that the accomplishment in real history of types so diverse and circumstances so various can be explained only in one way: by a miracle of divination on the part of the prophets, an adaptation of the *before* to the *after* which requires for its cause none other but the God of Jesus. But if God is not historical, nor yet his Gospels, then there is a more natural explanation of the resemblance of Jesus to the figures of Jesus. It is no strange adaptation of reality to its predictions, but the composing of a fictitious reality to agree with the predictions. If there is so strong a likeness between the *after* and the *before*, it is the *after* that is copying the *before*. If the Emmanuel was so much like what he was expected to be, it is because the expectation begot the Emmanuel. If Jesus was born of a virgin, it was because Isaias would have him miraculously conceived; because the Idea was congenial to faith, which copied Isaias in the account of the infancy. The whole life of Jesus, his words, his miracles, his Passion and Resurrection, were all of them outlined beforehand in the Scriptures. And the Gospels were composed in accordance with the already existing portrait.

These are the considerations to which I have now been led. I realize that they are very different from the common idea, indeed that they verge upon the paradoxical. They would be logically sound if Jesus had never existed! But apparently he did exist. I have reached these conclusions, not because I find them intellectually fascinating, but simply owing to the difficulties of the opposite position. What I shall have to do later is to strike the balance and see how I stand. Thought must be left to pursue its course to the end.

IV

THE DIFFICULTIES OF THE MYTHICAL
APPROACH

WHEN I was last pondering the subject, I made an endeavour to grasp the merits of the mythical approach: it seemed in some respects sound, with a loftiness of conception and a certain plausibility. Yet there is no denying that it has awkward elements, and these I propose to examine very carefully. I have now completed my circuit; there is no other position I can fall back upon; so my case might well seem desperate if it were not that I have a cool head and am ready for anything that may result.

The mythical theory may have difficulties, but it has at least the merit of coherence. Like Spinoza's philosophy, it relies less on proofs than on internal logic. Its negations will not appear extravagant or brutal except to those who have shirked the mental effort to make them. In Strauss, as in Couchard, though in different degrees and with more restraint in the former, there are to be found specimens of the philosopher's temperament. The value of their systems lies in their criticism of contemporary rationalists. As I said before, it was only to be expected that polemics would sooner or later follow the same type of argument. I foresee a new Loisy in the twenty-first century who will take up positions similar to those of his original, and a new Couchard to attack him and in turn provoke yet another Loisy. It was thus that Paulus had produced Vater and de Wette, Krug and Gabier and Strauss; and Strauss had given rise to Renan, who returned to a solution similar to that of Paulus. One could, in fact, draw up a genealogy, in which every father begot his contrary, only to rediscover himself in his grandson: *Paulus autem genuit Strauss; Strauss autem genuit Renan; Renan autem genuit Loisy; Loisy autem genuit Couchard. Et post magnam tribulationem.* . . There is no doubt a renewal for criticism in the discovery of fresh documents, in novel points of view and ingenious comparisons, but there is only a definite number of possible points of view; the arguments are limited; and it is strange to observe how modes of thinking alternate, how they reproduce and resemble one another.

I will dwell for a moment on the fundamental thesis, that which carries the mythical contention to its limits and concludes that Jesus never existed. This, I feel instinctively, is historically not tenable. No one likes better than I to understand precisely how things happen, but this is something I am unable to understand; none is more eager than I to accept the boldest theories, but this one I cannot accept.

Take this belief that arises suddenly, these 'apparitions' with no antecedent history: how hard it is to think that the life of Jesus could have had its origin in Scripture alone—in this and a few apocalyptic visions! It is no explanation to offer a theory that fits *grosso modo* the appearances of the physical world. An explanation must make the theory seem probable to all who know the limits of human credulity and something about human psychology. I know that at the birth of religions the power of sentiment, together with the lack of irrefutable evidence, may explain the occurrence of unaccountable events; at the same time, *homo religiosus* is not a person who can be made to believe anything.

Take the missionary life of Paul, which is so well known to us. It cannot be explained except by a belief in a *terrestrial* crucifixion, in a *terrestrial* life of Jesus and in a real society founded by Jesus, one in which Paul himself is incorporated. But was I perhaps wrong to attack so easy a prey and so give the impression that all the mythical school is so easy to dispose of? What we have to discover is precisely how much the fabulating faculty can do, and in so far as it can make up facts, to decide the limits of the mind's creative power. I note, too, that fabling, or at any rate a certain restrained fabling (which remains to be defined), may be necessary for the actual perception of an historical fact. When the mechanism of perception is analysed it will be noticed that what is involved is an activity of the mind, the projection of a possible scheme or form of structure which goes beyond sense-data, transforming these into a mental object which it thus admits into our interior life. Why should it not be the same for the perception of what we call an historical fact? Why should not this require anticipations, narrative schemes, symbols, and reconstructions of such sorts and types as would be (as it were) projected by the witness upon the factual datum, thus allowing him to grasp it and make it a fact? So I would not quarrel with the statement that just as a thing is perceived thanks to a true hallucination, so a fact is known by means of veridical fabulation. All I would ask is a definition of the basic difference between the true hallucination which is necessary and healthy, and the false hallucination which is pathological; between veridical hallucination which is indispensable to the telling of the story (and perhaps to historical understanding), and the lying hallucination that creates myths and legends. There ought to exist some complex criteria by which we can judge if the hallucination is *true*, the fabulation veridical. It is these criteria I want to discover.

I will venture to offer a few.

In the myth, it seems to me, the whole framework is romanticized. The myth-maker, whether he is consciously so or not, is disdainful of the history of his invention, of its geography and sociology. Or else, if he gives it an apparently historical background, this is a projection into the past of the various circumstances, rites, and institutions among which the myth-maker himself lives and thinks. How could it be otherwise? All he can invent is what he has seen.

A second characteristic of the mythical narrative appears to be the continual exaltation of the principal character, who is raised above historical conditions by all the prodigies reported of him. He is a typological personage, schematic and one-sided, not so much a person as an example, a desire, a thought clothed in flesh, and therefore a symbol. Finally there is the conventional and accessory character of the minor personages, who are there simply to exalt the exceptional being, and all they have to do is to resemble and reproduce him.

The whole question is obviously whether the Gospels belong to the mythical (and allegorical) type or to the narrative (and evidential). Is there enough variety in the features, and are these features numerous and objective enough to allow us to say that the Gospel writings, as we actually find them, were drawn up probably by people who were contemporary with the events, and were undoubtedly themselves involved in the events they describe? And can we conclude that the fable hypothesis is lacking in verisimilitude and highly improbable? With his own rigorous logic David Strauss himself maintained the importance of this criterion when he wrote (in 1835): 'The Gospel story would be unassailable if it were established that it was written by ocular witnesses, or at least by people very near to the events they describe.' Because, he added: 'Though mistakes, and consequently false information, might have been introduced by even ocular witnesses, yet the possibility of unpremeditated errors (and premeditated deceit is easily recognized) can be confined within much more narrow limits than it can when the narrator is separated from the events by a longer interval and is reduced to relying on the information supplied by others.' Strauss does his best, of course, to minimize all the reasons for supposing that the writers of the Gospel were contemporaries, and his most specious argument is to compare them with the editors of the Mosaic books, and to represent the conditions in which the New Testament was written as similar to those in which the Pentateuch was assembled.

Before applying this principle I want to gauge its force as nearly as I can by a method I always like employing.

Bergson, I remember, relates in one of his books how he was present at a discussion on telepathic intuitions, the apparent knowledge some people have of what is happening miles away. The debate was being conducted on an intelligent level and turned on the truth of these intuitions and the conditions required for believing them. Someone had said that what was needed was the statistics of the true and false cases. At this Bergson pointed out that a single divination, provided it were circumstantial and verified in every particular, had a right to be considered as true. In this he was appealing to a principle which is one with reason itself: that disorder is incapable of producing order, chance of producing intelligence. Consider now this fabling faculty. If an individual or a group, by some process or other, invents an incident that has not been witnessed, it is no more possible for the invention to be always correct than it is at roulette for the number chosen by the player to turn up every time—unless, of course, the table is rigged. When I use my imagination to invent a scene which I never witnessed, I may well hit by accident on a detail that happens to be correct. I may well imagine the death of a friend in Australia. But if I also imagine that he was injured in the neck, that this occurred at midday, that contrary to his usual custom he was wearing a striped waistcoat and had six shillings and five pence in his right-hand pocket: then, if this combination of independent details turns out to be verified by the facts, it will have to be recognized that my mental operation was not that of invention but—whatever its mechanism—a kind of vision at a distance. The fabling faculty is strictly limited. What is more, it is possible to define its limits. The probability of fabling diminishes in inverse ratio to the number of contingent details that come to be verified, by either historical research or psychological probability.

Now it is certain that the places mentioned in the Gospels are real. Those who live in Palestine can recognize the sites, the distances between them, the differences of landscape, the descriptions of the Holy City, its monuments, its surroundings, its peculiarities. The incidental references, presupposed rather than stated (for the *vis testimonii* is not concerned with these details), relate to such htings as the pools of Siloe and Bethsaida, Cedron and its valley, the Mount of Olives, the Temple and its portico, the Lithostrotus, Gethsemani, and Golgotha. All this, we know, is perfectly correct; more so, sometimes, than one would think.

If we hold that the fabling faculty produced such exactitude in the background, an accident was to occur to make this even more improbable. In the year 70 a catastrophe destroyed Jerusalem: Palestine was sacked by the Roman legions, Jerusalem razed to the ground, its Temple destroyed and its sacred observances terminated for ever; the Abomination of Desolation was to reign there ever afterwards; all that had existed before remained only a memory. A new order took the place of the old, one that bore no resemblance to it.

Now when a writer of fiction imagines the past he cannot but project into it what he perceives in his present surroundings. Flaubert, it is true, when he wrote *Salammbô*, took minute care to avoid anachronisms and all false notes, and such was his imagination that he could breathe life into all the dry dust he had collected. But Flaubert was an aesthete, living in a scholarly age, toiling hard in his study; very different from this is the imagination of the myth-maker in a society aflame with religious fervour, inventing, as best he can, the scene in which the legend of his hero must be enacted. There is little likelihood of his reconstructing it accurately, especially since accuracy would serve no purpose and be wholly unappreciated by his religious public. Indeed, the truer the local colour, the greater the risk of marring the edification it was intended to effect; the absence of familiar surroundings and contemporary customs would give an impression of unreality. The necessity of imagining the details of ancient history as conforming to those of the present is fully realized today, and the faithful brought up to expect as much would be greatly shocked if in a stained glass window Jesus were to be depicted in his oriental truth and Nazarene colouring.

However, I am prepared to admit that in a number of details the fabling process could have hit upon the truth by accident. We may also suppose that some memories of the old days had been transmitted orally. But they would have been confused, vague, and insignificant memories, and I see great difficulties in supposing that fabulation could ever reconstruct that Judaic-Roman world which came to an end in the year 70, with all the peculiarities so hard to explain *afterwards*. There had been such an entanglement of jurisdictions and parties, of institutions and interests. Politically, to take that aspect alone, there had been astonishing complications: Judaea, governed first by Archelaus, the son of Herod, but later administered by a Roman procurator, dependent upon the imperial legate in Syria; Galilee, on the other hand, owning allegiance to Herod Antipas the Tetrarch, who was a vassal of Rome. Judaea itself was an 'occupied' country, and we know well enough from bitter experience what clashes and equivocal situations are brought about by foreign occupation and the superimposing of authorities. All this is extremely hard to *re-imagine*, even for people who have lived through it. Now in the Gospels, when they are describing, for instance, the trial of Jesus, we discover the exact picture (even when it is given incidentally by authors whose main concern was certainly not historical accuracy); it is the picture, I repeat, of the ambiguous relationships which then existed between the Jewish authorities and the political power of Rome. This Jewish microcosm, so peculiar in structure, made up of so many chance elements, this unstable world that was to founder in the catastrophe of A.D. 70, is here completely reconstructed, the various schools of thought, the different parties, confront one another with perfect verisimilitude: the Herodians and the Pharisees, the Sadducees, John's former followers, and the disciples of Jesus. It is hard to think that all this was re-invented (especially as the narrative would have nothing to gain from such an effort after local colour, as laborious to undertake as it was superfluous to the end in view), and so reinvented as to be entirely satisfying to a scholar of the twentieth century.

So the myth hypothesis, which accepts such fabulation, can hardly be said to meet the requirements of history. Strauss himself felt this. I am thinking here of the Gospels of the public life. He had other things to say of the Gospels of the Infancy, which have not the same character of historicity. But I am leaving these on one side, because they do not affect my fundamental argument.

I said just now that one of the two rules followed by fabling is the *heroicizing* of the principal character and his peers. This can be observed in any legendary cycle, whether it be that of Charlemagne or Napoleon.

I can see there are deep-lying reasons for idealizing the person of Jesus.

There is no denying that the earliest Christian communities, as they are presented to us in either religious or secular history, had feelings for Jesus that amounted to worship. When Pliny, as proconsul of Asia Minor, encountered these early Christian societies, what struck him was the fact that these fanatics worshipped 'Chrestus' as if he were a god. Reading the least contested of the Epistles of St Paul, one has the impression, here too, of divine worship. It was in the celestial sphere that Christians set Jesus. In the letters of Paul to the Ephesians and the Philippians, Christ is a being pre-existent and post-existent, transcending the bounds of history. The Christians of these earliest times believed he had overcome death, that he was beyond the human state, risen up, in glory, the supreme Judge, the means of attaining immortality, the Redeemer. Even if they had thought of providing a history for this extraordinary being, what likelihood was there that they would have steeped him in the ordinary conditions of human ignorance and human limitations? A Gospel so constructed would at least have been full of prodigies and heavenly manifestations, of demiurgic achievements revealing the power of the Creator. Imagination might have multiplied such prodigies indefinitely: there was no fear of shocking the faithful, for faith is always accommodating and far from fastidious where probability is concerned. Admit that Jesus is God and you can safely make him do anything.

Again, since these communities had a hierarchical organization and rites, the Gospel they had thus fabricated ought to contain discourses on the institution of these rites and on the priesthood, laying down beforehand the rules that were to govern the Churches now in being. This is what the Jews had done in the case of Moses, making him foresee and preordain every single detail of the Temple liturgy.

But I can see nothing corresponding to this in the earliest Gospels, particularly in Mark's, the most primitive of them all. And this is what worries me. Here the person of Jesus is not exalted above the human state; indeed an ingenuous reading of the Gospels

D

of Mark, Matthew, and Luke might convey the impression that it was not a God made man they were describing but merely an exceptional prophet.

It has become a commonplace to note how the Gospel conjures up for us a closely observed countryside, with oriental features but with all the permanent characteristics that belong to every country-side: all over the world we find partings and returnings, fishing and harvesting, funerals and weddings; fathers, mothers, husbands and wives, children, friends and enemies; exaltation, despair, and anxiety; moments of calm and sudden storms; peaceful provinciality, political revolutions, the age-long contrasts between village and city, alternating seasons, and the monotony of fresh beginnings.

A Protestant friend has just shown me a passage by that incisive writer Karl Barth who expresses what I mean much more vigorously than I can:

It is not a moral or Christian world, not an imaginary world that is here described to us, but quite simply and artlessly the ordinary world as it goes its way without a care for anything else, not interested in great events but concentrating wholly upon little facts, humble human relationships. Here is a typical ne'er-do-well, welcomed back by his father—after all, he is his father!—with quite incomprehensible kindness; here is a judge who feared neither God nor man, and a shrew who got the better of him; a king who embarks on an unwise war and beats a retreat while he still has time; a speculator who sinks the whole of his fortune in order to acquire a valuable jewel; a sly old rascal (a typical war profiteer) who contrives very cleverly to get possession of treasure he has discovered by accident; a sharper who deals with money as if the rights of property were non-existent; children quarrelling in the street; a peasant sleeping comfortably while his fields do his work for him; a man who falls among thieves—such things do happen!—and has to wait some time for the compassion of a Samaritan, though the world is full of very pious people; a whimsical host, who in spite of refusals on all hands insists on filling his house with guests; a woman living alone, who loses a penny and is as much perturbed as if she had lost everything; a good man and a sinner side by side in church and both behaving quite consistently. How commonplace it all is, how free from illusions; from the point of view of eschatology, how completely pointless! But only because this is human life, something real, entirely surpassing the eschatological. No artistic style, no literary form; but a deep understanding of everyday happenings, in all their integrity, in all their rational necessity and perfection.[1]

But apart from these facts of common observation, which from all I know of romantic invention (as I have studied it in myself as well as in others) make it so difficult to accept the myth hypothesis, there are others that are stranger still, because they are not so easily noticeable; they are not on the surface of what we see but hidden in the byways.

What do I find when I open this Gospel of Mark's? Why, that the brethren of Jesus came to restrain him physically because they thought he was mad (iii 21); that he could perform no miracle in Nazareth (vi 5); that in the middle of working a miracle he had to stop and begin again (viii 22); that he would not allow people to call him 'good master' because only God is good (x 18); that he admitted he was ignorant about the day of judgement (viii 32); that he felt weakness in his agony, forsaken on the cross (xv 34). As for the apostles, they are represented as inattentive, bewildered, incredulous, stupid, and cowardly. It almost looks like a deliberate intention to discredit them. Jesus himself reveals his identity with what might seem excessive caution and reserve. His divinity is as it were in shadow, and one can well understand how Arius, reading these earth-bound Gospels, saw no reason to believe in the divinity of Jesus. His humanity, on the other hand, is evident in almost every line we read: he is at his ease with people, speaks their language, converses with women; he is tempted, he weeps, he is grieved, he trembles, implores, he actually dies, and without anything in this to distinguish him from others, just as though his power had come to a sudden end.

I am equally astonished at the strangeness of his nature and at the way these descriptions conform to it; for they conform not only with his surroundings, as I have said, and with the time in which he lived, but also with human verisimilitude. It is not in books that I find this last criterion, but in my own intimate experience. If those who have suffered can recognize themselves so easily here, if this narrative contains the vocabulary and (as it were) the whole encyclopedia of our afflictions, it is doubtless because it rests on a foundation of truth, and truth actually lived. The imagination of the fabler is very little good at evoking these mysteries of weakness and sorrow. I have no wish to let sympathy obscure my judgement,

[1] K. Barth, *Parole de Dieu et parole humaine*, pp. 71-2.

but it seems to me unreasonable, through an excess of intellectualism, to deprive oneself of something that also belongs to the intelligence, namely the *humus* in which it strikes root. Our intelligence rests on a kind of sense of the possible: it is experience focused on a single point. And for the accomplishment of this, pain also has its place. I know, for I have often observed it, that suffering—at any rate if it is accepted—develops the ability to grasp shades of meaning that are imperceptible to those in health; it develops a keener power of analysis, a sounder sense of the possible and of the impossible; it develops, above all, a distaste for shams, for all that verges on insincerity.

Lastly, it is striking that these first Gospels never lay down rules about the beliefs, rites, and institutions of the Church. If they had really been the work of priestly fabulation it would have been so easy to invent discourses by Christ about the Church and the episcopate, the eucharistic assembling of the faithful, the baptismal initiation, the Trinity, and the Holy Spirit. I am talking now of the first three Gospels, not of the Johannine which doubtless reflects rather more the contemporary life of the Christian communities. But this is just the point: why do the first Gospels differ in character from the Gospel of St John, and why do they (seemingly) do a disservice to the cause on behalf of which they were written? For a simple and impartial reading of the Gospel might serve to refute the dogma of the Church: it contains hardly anything of what appears in the professions of faith, in the liturgies of the Churches. And this was the reason why in the sixteenth century the diffusion of these documents in the vernacular was a menace to the faith of the masses in the Roman Church. 'Why!' the more simple-minded might exclaim, 'here are the very words of Jesus; there is no further question what I have to do. . .'

So everything points to the fact that the drawing up of the Gospels was entirely uninfluenced by the beliefs of their compilers, though, given the violence, the novelty, and the fervour of those beliefs, one might have expected *a priori* that such an influence would have been inevitable. The generation that was presented with those theological works, the Epistles to the Romans, to the Ephesians, to the Hebrews (in which the Christ-Jesus is exalted above the angels to the very throne of God), was the same generation that saw the composing of these prosaic writings in which Jesus appears so human and so lowly, so humiliated, so restrained in all he says, so unprodigal of prodigies; in which he is spoken of in flat and matter-of-fact terms, the impassiveness of which, as can be seen in all the accounts of the Passion, only increases with the gravity of the events described. I find this contrast most striking. I can hardly realize that St Paul and St Mark were contemporaries, still less that Mark's Gospel was written *after* Paul's Epistles, which chronology nevertheless compels me to admit. There must be some explanation of the *contemporaneity* of these two contrasting types.

It might perhaps be said that the memories of the human Jesus were so vivid in men's minds that *history* was too much for theology; that it was impossible to impose on Christian people a description of Jesus so different from that given by quite recent witnesses. But in that case how are we to account for the fact that these communities, which accepted the extremely human portrait of the Prophet Jesus, accepted also, and *simultaneously*, the image of the Christ-God —unless the former image already contained the germ of the latter? This is one of my difficulties. I must make a note of it.

It may be there are other, strictly technical reasons, for suspecting the myth hypothesis; but I have been making it my rule to accept nothing I am unable to understand by myself and to put down in clear terms.

If I reject the myth theory, it is because it seems to me to be utterly incredible that imagination could reconstruct any portrait so complex as that of the Christ we see in the Gospels. So this compels me to consider once more the hypothesis that the witnesses were telling the truth. What I am bound to recognize, at the least, is that the Gospel contains much more truth than one might think.

To return once more to the person of Jesus. In the mental landscape we are considering he is right in the centre of the picture and must be watched very keenly at every turn in our path: we may, if we are lucky, perceive some new feature, or (what is more likely) see an already familiar feature in fresh surroundings and a new light.

What I notice first of all is how humanly life-like he is. He is not built up, like a character of tragedy, by a juxtaposition of themes. Nor can his personality be reduced to one dominant faculty: it is made up of blending contrasts, dissonances in harmony; there is strength and gentleness; an accessibility very rare in the great; incessant toil, yet giving an impression of leisure; serenity and fervour; uncompromising doctrines, yet refinements in the application of them to cases; absolute justice, yet an indulgence for frailty; the idea of the unapproachable, with an insistence on trifling duties; haste to complete his course, deliberation in its accomplishment; courage, without the running of unnecessary risks; community life and poverty; a delicate respect for womanhood and for solitude; a calm transparency in acts and words, which makes Abraham by comparison seem over-wrought, Moses fanatical, and Elias hot-headed—and always some mystery that both repels and attracts; in conversation a Socratic familiarity, but majesty, too, in the solemn declarations concerning himself; a sense of his privileges, of his equality with God, yet a love for the lowest place and for all that is basest.

He is a true Nazarene, a townsman, a worker in wood, a doctor, a prophet and an apostle, a slave and a king, vanquisher and victim; yet somehow none of these aspects, however short the interval between their appearances, ever seems to make the rest unintelligible: hence an impression of his having amassed a whole number of lives, performed how many incompatible missions and conflicting duties! Yet all this variety takes nothing from his simplicity; all these differences are complementary, like the contrasting aspects of sky and earth in the landscape I see before me as I write.

It is, indeed, not historically impossible that this portrait has been made up of a chance collection of mosaics; but the more I reflect on their unity, so evident to the mind, the more improbable I regard it that we have here either something purely fabulous, put together at hazard, or a sophisticated work of juxtaposition. It is the sort of harmonious disorder, divergence corrected by a deep internal unity, which I see in concrete objects, in history, and in nature, in my own history, my own secret and individual existence.

The work I seem to see here is one composed without forethought, with occasional touches, unexpected contributions, and very little order. Here are threads stitched together, expressing very little of the collector's personality, who seems to have effaced himself completely in his sources. Yet from these sparse fragments there emerges the figure of a human person. It is what happens in the making of a posthumous memoir: the letters which the subject has written at different times, anecdotes, and gossip are all collected haphazard. The result will look patchy, it will be full of gaps and sometimes contradictory, yet the effect of these glimpses will be to make the subject come to life.

I have been carried along by the current of my thought. I wanted to go forward, relying, as I thought I must, on this stream, and now here it is returning to its source! I feel I am moving in a circle. So it is evidently time for one of those 'general reviews' which Descartes recommends. This should help to correct the judgements I have been forming on the way and allow me to see how they are linked together. For it is, I think, in their mutual relationship that their value, if any, lies.

What hampers the examination of the problem of Jesus (and of course all problems) is that the difficulties tend to come so thick and fast that one is bound to meet them with partial answers. There is a risk of succumbing to that kind of giddiness brought about by concentrating on the *part*, of tiring oneself out with worrying over details when attention should be entirely directed to the *whole*, with a constant returning to first principles. I am always coming across this in books dealing with these particular questions. The fascination of little things leads to ignoring the big ones. This is where quality suffers. The acuteness of the exegete is not unaccompanied by a tendency to humour very ordinary weaknesses. I noticed it myself when I was working at this subject which is so intellectually attractive. On the field of battle there is such an exciting smell of powder; controversy has its mischievous side as well as its charm! And the pleasure of guess-work has much more spice than the pleasure derived from certitude. The reason, no doubt, is that when you demonstrate a truth it is so convincing that every reader thinks he could have discovered as much for himself; you are made to feel just a tiresome intermediary! Geometry can get on without Euclid. The more perfect your reasoning, the less kudos you gain by it. Euclid is buried in the oblivion of the obvious. But if, on the other hand, we offer conjectures, and these border on the improbable, they reveal the highest degree of imaginative power: they are suggestive, like a work of art, and like a work of art they will bear the author's signature. At the same time the very uncertainty of the theory is a stimulus to defend it: to the pleasure of invention there is added the pleasure of doing battle. At the height of the combat, while repelling inept assaults, you can go on chanting the refrain: 'It was I who made this guess; no one ever thought of it before, not in this particular way, with the finer points I have enriched it with, the hall-mark of my own mind!'

For my part, the method I have adopted saves me from adding yet another guess to the rest: all I am attempting to do is to define and criticize possible hypotheses according to the unchanging types to which they all conform.

I have examined the documents in the possession of the early Christian communities, documents that give an explanation of their faith while depicting the portrait of a person called Jesus. This personage was simple enough. The narrative that presented him was simple. The faith that accepted the testimony about him was simple. It was the very simplicity of the fact, the simplicity of its assertion and the simplicity of the faith in it, that looked like leading me, if I accepted it all at the outset, to metaphysical beliefs I felt I could never hold, beliefs which, to say the least, appeared to me pointless. I therefore decided to put aside these beliefs and explain the phenomenon presented by these documents by means of certain procedures long approved by the sciences, excluding, at the outset, the possibility of any paranatural element. If my method was unsound it had at least the merit of honesty: it made no secret of its initial principles. Methods are free and they should be judged by their fruits. I took into account the danger of judging experience by the light of an axiom accepted *before* the experience; but it was a fair risk and I was willing to take it.

So the hypothesis I considered first was that which allowed me to retain as historical most of the statements made in these apostolic memoirs, while rejecting the marvellous element and explaining it by causes that were purely subjective. But since this meant rejecting the very essence of the testimony, I saw no plausible reason for retaining the historical element. I found it, moreover, difficult to understand how subjective causes, which ultimately boiled down to plain hallucination, could in so short a time have produced Christianity. It appeared fantastic to me to make the Christian religion rest on a spiritist adventure, on romantic idealization, or the fever of some collective excitement.

In consequence I turned to the opposite theory and toyed for a time with the philosophical notion that what came first was the religious element, based on a profound faith, and that fabulation had metamorphosed the legend, or even created it. But here I was flung once more against the exigences of history, for I recognized that the human mind could never have reconstructed a story so circumstantial, or such a highly complex human portrait.

I join the myth-theorists in saying to the critics: 'It is very hard to think that our poor Nazarene could possibly, in the Jewish monotheistic *milieu*, have been turned so quickly into a God.'

But I join the critics in saying to the myth-theorists: 'It is hard—even harder—to suppose that imagination, either alone or with borrowings, could have created a legend of Jesus so historical in form and so perfect in its verisimilitude.'

The critical school of thought is unable to explain how Jesus, if he had always been held to be a man, could have become so quickly a God.

The myth school make it quite unintelligible that Jesus should be described as so human.

What the first is up against is the sudden divinization (or virtual divinity) of Jesus. The second has to face the fact (even more incontestable) of his humanity, of his truth to human nature, and the fact that his historical environment is so completely verified. The first will not be disturbing to anyone with an artistic sense of history, including its less obvious aspects, but it cannot satisfy one who has a sense of its depths, a *religious* sense of history. The second is apparently satisfactory to this divine or theological side of human thought, but it scandalizes the historian, and the conclusions it is driven to in the end are absurd.

So it looks to me like an interminable process of rebounding from one hypothesis to the other.

Is there no way of reconciling the two? Might one not perhaps allow that the myth, instead of being poised in the void and *creating* a history, discovered this history already in existence, and that the myth of Christ the Redeemer, whatever its origin (a transposition, perhaps, of the Greek mysteries?) came to fertilize the extraordinary facts we are given about Jesus? Could we suppose the myth to have been purified by history, history to have been exalted by myth? I know that Loisy once supported this idea, and I quite understand why he had to. This ex-cleric, with a mind so penetrating and religious as his, could not explain Christianity, as Renan did, by a process of increasing idealization. A mind with any feeling for historical realities could not possibly accept the myth-making explanation. But at the point of intersection of these two theories (provided they were perfected and a mutual adjustment effected by a judicious clearing of ambiguities) might not the true solution emerge? One would need to discover first a society in which the myth-type of thought about Jesus could have come to birth. It would also be necessary to safeguard the historicity of the story of Jesus in all its major features. Loisy set about this. Paul, so he thought, came under the influence of the pagan mysteries. But what these mysteries lacked was a sound doctrine of divinity; their salvation myths had no connection with history. But the religion of Jesus, thanks to Judaism, had a doctrine about God, and thanks to the Gospel it possessed a history. Loisy later revised this theory, which (as he soon discovered) bristled with difficulties. How imagine Paul, that implacable Jew, so tolerant of the mysteries of paganism? How should the earliest followers of Jesus adopt a belief in redemption and divinity if such a belief were not there already? That was why Loisy had to postpone to nearly the end of the century belief in the divinity of Jesus and in his heavenly pre-existence.

But I am quite unconvinced by this attempt to make the myth hypothesis more probable by diluting it slightly in time.

I am willing to admit that Paul of Tarsus may have felt the influence of the pagan mysteries. I see various elements conjoined: the presence of Paul where the mysteries were celebrated, the fervour of Paul's own temperament. But what I also see is the improbability of these elements being related and combined in a Jewish environment and in the person of Paul, and then getting accepted by the Christian communities.

Besides, for a hypothesis to be accepted as true, it needs to be something more than logically possible. To such non-impossibility there must be added also psychological probability and some positive indications of the possible and the probable becoming facts of history.

The same applies to the criteria of interpolation. Except possibly in mathematics, there are elements of opposition, elements of diversity in all our thoughts and speech. It is always possible, by a mental operation, to divide an intellectual construction into two parts, of different tone and even opposite aspect, decide that they cannot be the work of one pen, and that one of them, regarded as more perfect or otherwise, was added by a skilful editor. But if such a suggestion is to be taken seriously we need some objective signs of interpolation, a notable difference in style or allusions. Without these objective signs, the theory of an interpolation will always be vitiated by the mentality of the exegete.

I fully realize that this sort of critico-mythical theory may be more congenial intellectually in that it retains the advantages of both opposed theories, each of which it appears to correct with the other.

But the thing I find it hard to believe is the *gradual* birth of a belief which is asserted in the very earliest documents and found given at the outset with Christianity itself: I mean the worship of Jesus. On this point, the type of thought we may associate with M. Couchard will always prevail over the other. And what I think is more difficult still is to understand how these mystical and already gnostic bodies (whether Paulinist about the year 50, Judaic-Hellenist of the year 100 or thereabouts, or Marcionite round about A.D. 200) could have invented or accepted any such documents as the synoptic Gospels, where Jesus is presented as a human and not as a celestial being, as flesh and not simply *pneuma*. Here again criticisms of the Couchard type will always carry the day.

I have the impression, moreover, that it would be possible to show that the divine character of Jesus never needed to be super-added to the primitive faith, that it can be found included in the earliest accounts, those of the Gospels and the Acts. But this would call for a more elaborate study which I am not concerned, nor competent, to undertake at present.

I have now reached a point rather difficult to pass. I do not wish to exaggerate anything. I have no time at all for those who allow their thinking to be affected by sentiment, by the train of their desires or fears. I can hardly forgive Pascal for corrupting his thought with his famous 'wager'. But I cannot forgo the use of my eyes and I want to take all into exact account.

I have found these reflections of mine an enormous strain on mind and will. I had to guide my thinking and hold it back from going too fast; this proved to require a great expenditure of energy; it was the exertion used to battle against oneself, perhaps the hardest exertion of all.

I wanted to find a way in accordance with reason. The two modified and middle ways I clearly perceived and defined before examining them, and now they have each been examined in turn. They present serious difficulties; each returns you to the other; and if you put them together they decline to be reconciled.

So all that remains is the two extremes, which I refused to conceive possible, or at any rate had no wish to examine too soon. There is nothing for it but to accept nothing or accept all.

Here, *to accept nothing* means precisely this: I cannot think to deny both the *ordinary* and the *extraordinary*, because however extreme my negation, even if it meant denying the existence of Jesus and of the early Christian communities (who can say, after all, that all this Christian prehistory was not fabricated by some tenth century monk, by a sixteenth century chronicler, or even by a contemporary scholar or sect?)—yes, even if I pushed my denials, as the Devil counselled Descartes, to the very bounds of the possible and the absurd, the fact would still remain that these documents exist, that we can read and handle them; also that they have a meaning, and Jesus therefore at least a literary existence. There is a minimum that must be accepted, and this is it. So complete rejection means saying: 'I decline to go further, I propose to be content with Jesus as a phenomenon; I shall add it to other historical phenomena, presented to me by the printed page and begetting in me thoughts no less delightful than those which the physical universe does. These explanations offered me are just other thoughts superimposed on the first: an elucidation, you think, but to my mind they are simply a new set of phantoms, which threaten to destroy the whole dream with a disturbing idea of *reality*, the most treacherous of nightmares and one I would gladly forgo.'

But this position is not really tenable. It is, I know, the position of the majority, for whom the religion of Jesus has no meaning at all, or else seems wholly artificial and unreal. This impression is due to their extreme ignorance of the subject. It cannot be mine—unfortunately! I would certainly enjoy more calm if I knew nothing about it.

That being the case, it would seem the only thing to do is to accept the Whole, to admit that the supernatural and the natural elements are as substantially linked together as the evidence asserts. For the evidence is not that 'Jesus made the multitude sit down on the green grass by the sea' and that 'he saw the loaves multiplied;' the testimony bears on the fact that Jesus MULTIPLIED the loaves for the multitude sitting on the grass. The testimony is not that Jesus died and was buried and *afterwards* appeared; the fact which it insists upon is that this Jesus who died and was buried was the *very same* as he who overcame death. What the evidence asserts is the intimate connection between the historical and meta-historical.

I tried to deny this connection, to assume it was illusory. But I have now examined the different types of hypothesis that *undo* this connection, only to discover that they are by no means clear in themselves and present very weighty difficulties (or so it seems to me), all the more so for being handicapped by an initial denial. All would be now simpler if I could accept the remaining hypothesis, namely the possibility of this effective connection and therefore the truth of the evidence.

I have now reached this point: I no longer refuse to read the Gospels in a receptive frame of mind; I admit the possibility of their truth. This is not to say I shall read them like a believer; but at least I shall examine them without prejudice. Such a position may look simple and easy, but it has been a long struggle to reach it. The stakes were such that I had to proceed with the utmost wariness; and I have, I believe, honoured reason with my doubts.

Certainly my present position is not that of a believer who accepts the whole. I no longer deny that the evidence *could* be true; I no longer whittle down or pare away mentally what the documents assure me actually happened. But this does not mean that I shall cease to be critical, accepting *en bloc* the historicity of every part of the Gospel tradition, nor yet that I shall forgo my private judgement and take refuge, like one making harbour in a storm, in the safe waters of faith. To illustrate what I mean: I cannot accept as historical, in the sense in which I understand history and evidence, the account of the Temptation, for there was, as far as I can see, no one there to witness it. And I am not in the believer's position, who admits, by reason of the dogmas which bind him, facts that cannot, in the normal way, be established as historical.

Nor do I pretend that one does not meet with occasional examples of exaggeration, of stylization in these documents, or even of historical error. This would call for a minute examination of every detail, a task I cannot possibly undertake. But this does not affect the essential point, which is the reality of the connection between history and the supernatural element incarnate in history, in other words the *general* truth of the evidence.

Here is the point to which I return after this long detour. No, it is not impossible that this is true testimony, that these facts, in all essentials, did actually take place on our planet two thousand years ago. I can say no less—and no more. This means more work in store for me. Now, I can see, I shall have to tackle the problem from another slant and make a study, perhaps, of what *adherence* really means and how it is transmitted. May the Spirit save me from ineptitude here and allow me to penetrate the very heart of the spiritual so as to see how the testimony actually came to birth, alike in the individual consciousness and in society. A wholly different undertaking, this: one that I feel sure will prove more attractive and not call for those interior struggles that are so exhausting.

PART II
DIVINITY

I

PROBLEMS OF ORDER AND METHOD

RESURRECTION AND DIVINITY:
DISTINCTION BETWEEN THE TWO BELIEFS

I HAVE become convinced that there are two problems I now have to resolve: whether Jesus rose from the dead and whether he was God. A decision on these two open questions is included, as I see it, in one indivisible act of faith.

The Church's earliest documents lead one to think that in the earliest times there was one necessary and sufficient condition for being baptized, namely adherence to 'Jesus-the-Son-of-God'. This implied acceptance of the *fact* of his 'resurrection according to the Scriptures' and of the *dogma* of his mysterious unity with the Father. Even today, if a Christian had only a limited time to expound his faith (like the deacon Philip to the eunuch of Queen Candace) and so had to ignore inessentials, what he would be bound to mention would be the resurrection and divinity of Jesus.

But I suspect that these two notions are distinct, both in origin and importance. Which of them, then, should I examine first?

I put this question to a Catholic friend: to which of these beliefs, I asked him, was he more committed? He was, I could see, somewhat taken aback and seemed hardly to understand what I meant. The two things went together, he told me. According to him, if Jesus worked miracles it was because he was God, since God alone can perform miracles; the resurrection, he continued when I pressed him further, is the proof of his divinity. At this I observed that, according to Scripture, Elias in the Old Testament and St Peter in the New both performed great miracles, yet no one believed either of these was God. 'You can't', I told him, 'be more exacting than the Holy Ghost.' He agreed, then, that the miraculous by itself is no proof of divinity, that the latter must be known by revelation and had in fact been taught both by the Church and by Jesus when speaking of himself.

I perceived that my friend, like most believers, was unaccustomed to make distinctions among the beliefs he accepted. He held them all to be equally necessary, since they proceeded from the same source, which was the Church speaking in the name of God. He declined to recognize a hierarchy among these different teachings. I admired this point of view and would have liked to share it. It is faith regarded as the possessor of truth. For faith refers to the source of all truths: it mounts from the sun's ray to what interests it more, the sun itself. From the point of view of the owner of a field, the flowers in it are all of one and the same origin; they are all his inheritance. But I am unable to share the believer's viewpoint. I am still floundering in that outer region where my rule is to measure the importance of each question by the difficulty I have in answering it.

MESSIAHSHIP, RESURRECTION, DIVINITY: THE HISTORICAL GENESIS OF THE IDEAS

To return to the question of the relative importance of the two dogmas.

To disentangle the problem better, I propose to use a distinction I have found helpful elsewhere: it is to consider separately, first the order in which ideas unfold historically, and then the order in which they would have to appear if their history were ignored and one concentrated solely on their logical importance. For chronological order, as I have already observed, is something totally different from logical order.

Having read most of the books devoted to the subject, I believe the major questions raised are those of the messiahship of Jesus, his resurrection and his divinity.

If I consider the genetic process I notice a continuous transforming of one of these aspects into the next. I might almost say we have three phases of a dialectic: the *Messiah* is continued in the *Risen Christ* and completed in the *God*. But there is much more to it than this.

When we look to see how these beliefs could have engendered one another in a Jewish atmosphere, what is noticeable is that the Messiah question so enveloped both the others that the Jewish mind was incapable of seeing Jesus as risen from the dead, or even as God, without relating this perception (or conception) to some particular feature of the Messiah. Yet in the mental expectation of the Jews there was no place, at any rate consciously, for the unique resurrection of the Messiah, nor yet for his divinity; least of all for a

Messiah who was God, yet also, in history, a man like others. Official Jewish thought imagined a resurrection, but it was a general resurrection, for all at once, and it marked the final consummation of time. Also, in one of its prophetic traditions, Jewish thought accepted a quasi-divine Messiah, 'riding on the clouds of heaven, that was yet a son of man'; but this was an eschatological being, closing the cycle of history, not subject (seemingly) to the conditions of history. When seeking to understand the fact of Jesus, the Jewish mind set him in the messianic category, and it can hardly be denied that Jesus represented himself to his contemporaries as belonging to this category and fulfilling its expectations. In the messianic thought before his day there were possible links with resurrection and divinity. There is no thinking anything new without also having recourse to previous thinking, even though this may involve profound modifications: thus the questions that were to concern resurrection and divinity emerged, for the Jews, from questions concerning messiahship. It is this that makes the Gospels so hard to understand.

For the modern mind these problems of messiahship have lost their interest; the expectation of the Messiah corresponds to nothing in our mental background. It was different with the Jews. When Peter sought to proclaim the Resurrection and justify it in the eyes of the Jews of Jerusalem, he must needs refer to their ideas of the Messiah; the Resurrection, he explained, had now conferred on Jesus the character of divinity which the Messiah was to possess: it was this that made him 'the Lord'. The idea of the divinity of Jesus was similarly based on that of sonship, an idea that belonged properly to messianic thought, since the Messiah, in a special way, was 'the Son of God'.

THE LOGICAL GENESIS OF THE IDEAS: THE SIGNIFICANCE OF ARIANISM

But suppose we consider the development from another point of view: not that of historical links and transitions, but that of the nontemporal logic of faith. Then all appears in a different light: messiahship does not imply resurrection, nor resurrection divinity.

Jesus could have been the expected Messiah without performing all the miracles recorded in the Gospels, and without overcoming death. He might have been, in the guarded words of Bergson, only the 'chief of mystics'. He could have been the founder and head of a

Christian Church without thereby being necessarily divine. The proof of this is that nowhere, except at Corinth, was the Resurrection contested by *Christians* during these earliest centuries, whereas the divinity of Jesus soon met with opposition, at any rate in the way it was expressed, as we can see from the historical origins of Arianism.

The existence of a Church with God for its author, guarantor and perfecter, does not depend, fundamentally, on the divinity of its founder. Let us suppose that Jesus was only an incomparable envoy of God, the instrument God used for founding his Church. Then, the Church once founded, the instrument would have disappeared, to belong henceforth, like all heroes and saints, to history alone, even though he was the sublime model of those heroes and saints. This is far from inconceivable. Christ, in such a setting, might have been thought of as still living and interceding for the Church, which is precisely the role faith attributes to the Virgin. Jesus could have been the founder, the original member of this hypothetical Church, but he would not have been *worshipped* by that Church.

This is not the Christianity we see held by Christians, even at the very beginning. But it is, at least, a plausible Christianity; one might even say it is a Christianity more in accordance with the age-long expectations of the Jews, with their presentiments of what the Messiah would be.

Arius, I think, was a man of no great stature intellectually. I see him as typical of those popular spokesmen who in every age have known how to echo its subconscious urgings and have possessed that peculiar genius for agitation. What is really surprising is that Arius had so much popular support and so many episcopal allies; also surprising are the subtle revivals of Arian doctrines after the Council of Nicæa, at which Arius himself had been solemnly condemned. This makes me think that in the eyes of the faithful there was something in his teaching that had a traditional air.

The first principle of Arianism was the postulate that has been so fruitful in philosophy and science, and is almost indistinguishable from reason itself, namely economy or sufficiency, not explaining an effect by a superfluous cause. I should be pursuing, quite obviously, a dangerous course if I were to explain lightning as the effect of divine power, instead of seeing it as an electrical discharge. Similarly, for the founding of the Church, as for justifying the Christian faith and liturgical worship, was it necessary, asked the Arians, that Jesus should have been God? Was it unavoidable to have recourse to a fact so incomprehensible, to accept such a handicap, for such it was, in converting the pagan world of Alexandria or Constantinople? The divinity of Christ meant admitting the existence of plurality in divine Being, since Jesus-God and God-the-Father must necessarily co-exist, yet without destroying the necessary unity of the first principle. What a mystery! What was perhaps even more incomprehensible was the necessity of allowing a descent of the divine into the elements of this physical world of accepting an historical subject in whom humanity was actually penetrated with divinity. Arius would have effected an economy here, not violating Scripture or primitive tradition, but interpreting both in a restrictive sense. And may he not have felt that by diminishing the difficulties which the Faith presented to the unbelief of the time he was bringing it a positive access of power? He was removing a major obstacle to the intelligence of his contemporaries, whether they were Jews or pagans; he was diminishing the interval that separated the Faith from the loftier forms of paganism, the loyaller forms of Judaism and the most religious type of philosophy. Arius might be likened to a Christian of the present day who in the hope of getting Marxists to accept a Catholic Gospel would consider dropping some particular dogma as inopportune, perhaps too pessimistic, or too inadaptable.

It had the merit of simplicity, this idea of Arius's: if Jesus was not God, but only the most perfect and exalted of creatures—and much more than that: the most cosmic, the most spatio-temporal, the most co-extensive-with-the-universe—then how many difficulties are smoothed away! What a future for the Faith in this world of ours! Arius had on his side not only the Old Testament tradition concerning the Messiah, but also the apparent teaching of the synoptic Gospels, which do not appear to speak of divinity, certain texts of St Paul and even some of St John, which seem to make Christ the first of creatures, or at any rate a subordinate reality.[1]

---

[1] This tendency to make Christ a supercreature, which continues during the next century in the Nestorian tendency to separate the humanity of the Nazarene from the divinity of the Word, was to have important and disturbing consequences; it had an influential section of the episcopate on its side and on two occasions it nearly triumphed. Newman, in his famous *Essay on the Development of Christian Doctrine* (p. 320) gives the year 493 as the date when the Catholic tradition was in greatest danger, the whole of the East being dominated by the opponents of the Council of Chalcedon and all the West by those of the Council of Nicæa: the Faith in its integrity was held only by the Pope, by a few great bishops, and by the rank and file of the laity (*fidelium sensus*). See *The Arians of the Fourth Century*, pp. 445 and 467, and my *Philosophie de Newman*, p. 175.

COMPARISON OF THE TWO BELIEFS
AND THEIR JUSTIFICATION

The attempt I have been making to understand the contingency
of certain statements of faith was not wholly foreign to medieval
thought. Thus St Thomas shows how the virginal conception was
not a necessary condition of the incarnation of the Word: God
could have entered this world by means of ordinary marriage. Or
again, according to the Common Doctor, God could have created
the cosmos *ab aeterno*.

Christians, like all other human beings, are accustomed to think
everything must have been what it is. This inevitably weakens their
faculty for wonder.

What I would like to do now is to compare these two questions so
as to see what can be done to help throw some human light on
each of them.

From the point of view of proof, I see them as very different.

The Resurrection, at any rate at first glance, sets a problem
analogous to those of experience. It is so presented in the creed,
where it seems to depend on a verification identical with that of the
death and burial: *mortuus, sepultus, resurrexit*. The knowledge that
Jesus rose from the dead implies an investigation similar to that
conducted by a judge, an historian, or a coroner. It is a question of
deciding whether Jesus, his real death established, was recognized by
witnesses as having recovered possession of his body from the tomb.

But how are we to know whether Jesus *truly* rose from the dead.
The word *truly*, which we find in the earliest documents, proves that
the question arose at the very outset. And we can see in the Gospels
how the believers tried to dispel their own doubts or convince sincere opponents. Their method was to ascertain that the witnesses
were not prejudiced in favour of what they had seen; that they were,
in fact, expecting something different; that they had very great
difficulty in convincing themselves of a happening that seemed at
first, though wholly within range of their personal experience, impossible, unreal, and fictitious; that their sanity and impartiality
must needs be admitted; that the testimonies were numerous and of
different kinds, in agreement and from the very outset progressive.
From the beginning, in short, it was the method used by the modern
historian for weighing evidence and distinguishing the true from the
false. It is the method, too, of the psychologist and psychiatrist to

establish whether a subject is healthy or morbid, if he is the victim of hallucination or normally perceptive.

It is quite otherwise in the case of divinity. No miracle, however great, can be held to prove it. Power, of course, and especially *ease* in the use of power, suggests, in the Gospel narratives, a super-human being; even more, it suggests a person acting as God would act. But these conditions are not enough to decide whether he who works these prodigies is God. Least of all was it sufficient in Jewish eyes. God, they believed, could communicate his power to men; even 'the spirit of evil' could produce prodigies with his permission. They did not think of arguing from the fact of a miracle, done in God's name by his presence or his power, to the identity of God with the worker of the miracle. Peter was true to this tradition when after the Resurrection he came to describe Jesus as 'a man duly accredited to you from God', and as one whom God 'raised up again, releasing him from the pangs of death'.

This way of looking at it is correct. That God can suspend the laws he has ordained, and that this is a direct effect of his power, is understandable. That a man can be the instrument of this effect of power, that he obtains this by prayer, this too is well enough. Nor is it inconceivable that a man can have this divine power (as it were) delegated to him. But between this and the idea that a man *is* God, as the Christian faith asserts, the gap is *infinite*. What could possibly induce the human mind to accept a belief so incredible *a priori*?

Nothing but the actual testimony of the person in question. The divinity of a human being cannot be proved by any fact, however extraordinary; it must lie in an attestation by that human being concerning his person, his intimate self, his 'secret'. Miracles, it is true, sublime deeds and good works, perfect and holy behaviour, the sublimating of human nature—all these may amount to so many signs, inducing belief in his word when he claims a quality not verifiable in itself. But in the last resort, when it comes to knowing what a person is in the hidden depths of his being—WHO he is—he alone can be witness. His word is his word. This is testimony at its purest: testimony on the part of him who asserts, faith on the part one willing to believe but unable to prove. An act of truth in the one, an act of faith in the other.

It is thus I have reached the idea that the problem of knowing whether Jesus is God is very different from all the rest; it has no connection with wonder-working. It rests on inner testimony alone, and this can be had from none but the very person of this Jesus. This, I think, is what the Gospel of St John makes clear: one can see there the consciousness which Jesus had of his divinity and the method he chose to get that divinity recognized. The consciousness was direct, the method indirect. Jesus had accomplished great works; he had therefore a right to be believed, on his own word, when he said he was one with the Father.

The difference I observe between these two problems, of divinity and resurrection, provides a light to guide and order my inquiry. I can see now that I must not follow the course I had originally proposed. This was to begin by studying the possibility, plausibility, and probability of the Resurrection, because I regarded the Resurrection as the cardinal sign of divinity, and therefore that which I should criticize first. Now I think it better to begin by examining the divinity of Jesus Christ.

FOR CONTEMPORARY MAN THE EXAMINATION OF DIVINITY SHOULD PRECEDE THAT OF RESURRECTION

One initial reason is that the *greater* has the advantage over the *less*: a man who was convinced that Christ was God would have little difficulty in accepting his resurrection, or *a fortiori* the fact that he was the Messiah expected by Israel.

There is a second and deeper reason. A word is not a miracle. Each of us can say what he likes. A *reported* speech may not be that which was actually *uttered*. Nothing is easier for a writer than to put words never spoken into the mouth of some historical character. This, incidentally, is why I shall have to examine very carefully to see if the criteria which I mentioned just now permit me to decide whether what Jesus said of himself was not the invention of faith. But suppose for a moment that I have reason enough to admit the authenticity of these words. Then I am entitled to say that I am in touch with Jesus (though not so emotionally, of course, and without the personal presence) quite as much as the first witnesses; much more so, at any rate, than when these witnesses tell me of miracles.

I would even suggest that in one sense my very remote historical situation, which allows me to take a synthetic view, gives me advantages over those immediate witnesses. Direct contact can have an obscuring effect: there is such a thing as superabundance, the disadvantage of surprise, the impossibility of stepping back and taking a wider view. Each witness individually might have heard no more than a single saying of Jesus in one particular situation. But I know them all, in their right order, in their agreement and development.

Between the present age and that of the Origins, time has spun a very long interval. And even if this long interval were reduced, and I were living (say) at the end of the first century, my knowledge of Jesus would still have been necessarily through the medium of witnesses. Where I now stand in the flux of time, twenty centuries away, I can and must ask the following questions: Did these first witnesses actually experience what they say? Was it their intention to be historical witnesses, in the sense we give to the expression now and to the attitude implied? Were they not influenced by their previous religious beliefs, by the beliefs of the communities they belonged to, or again by contact with neighbouring cults? And even granting the reality of the initial fact, I am still entitled to ask: Were the sick who were healed so very sick after all? Was he truly dead, this dead man raised to life?

When we are confronted with a statement about a happening, the note of certitude we get from actual witnesses can never be provided by an inquiry undertaken after a long lapse of time, above all after the death of the original witnesses whom we should so much have liked to interrogate personally.

But it is different when we have to do, not with a *fact*, but a *word*.

There are means of deciding, I suppose, whether a saying attributed to an historical character could really have been uttered by him, or whether it is a projection of the hearer's or narrator's thought. Without anticipating results I have not yet reached, I can indicate even now some signs that show whether a saying is authentic: the number and diversity of the circumstances in which it is reported, the difference between the saying and what was expected of the person who said it, the resemblance it bears to other sayings of undoubted authenticity. At all events, if such criteria existed, I think in my present state of mind I would accept more readily the idea of a word or *saying* of the Lord's being authentic than I would the idea of a miraculous deed or *act*. Many believers will attribute this to my scientific prejudices. They are at liberty to do so.

In any case miracles, which are simply manifestations of power, cannot really imply doctrine. They are no help to grasping intimate reality. On the other hand 'a saying of Jesus' gives me access to the mystery of a person.

For all these reasons I prefer to tackle first the question of divinity.

If I were to succeed, an obstacle would be removed and the Resurrection would appear less improbable. I would suspect it was not just an event among others and that it would allow me to approach the mystery of God. Afterwards, and only then, I propose to return to particular miracles. And I am inclined to think that this procedure, which is more in accordance with the requirements of modern thought, may well have been that of the Jews who were first converted to Christianity, of Peter, for instance, and Peter's associates.

II

SOURCES OF THE BELIEF IN THE DIVINITY OF JESUS

DIVINITY AND TESTIMONY:
THE WORDS OF JESUS AND THE FAITH OF
THE CHRISTIAN COMMUNITIES

SO far I have been proceeding in the logical field, where I have
felt fairly at home. Now I meet with a difficulty. I have brushed
against it already, but now I must confront it face to face. Granting
we have a document in which statements are made by Jesus about
his divinity, and these, as I have said, are the only conceivable
'proofs' of it; granting even that I have serious reasons for judging
these passages authentic and in circulation among the Christian
communities somewhere about the year 60 of our era: *what is the
probability that they reproduce the actual words of Jesus, and not the faith of
these primitive communities?* I must admit I see here certain difficulties
in the believer's position and I am surprised that he seems so little
aware of them.

If it is true that a *declaration* made by a rational and moral human
being is the sole means of access to his intimate self, it is equally
true that the counterfeiting of such a declaration is astonishingly
easy. Apart from the fact that the person himself may easily be in
error and that his claim to outstanding qualities may be made out
of pride, ostentation, or mere delusion, it is very easy for any forger
who wants to create a religious legend to put into his hero's mouth
an affirmation of superhumanity or divinity. All he has to do is to
make Christ say 'I am God', or use an expression like 'God and I
are one', and the whole thing is done. Here the drawback to the
proof lies in the facility of counterfeiting it.

I would add, too, that though no miracle is involved in saying 'I
am God' (for these simple words imply no derangement of the cosmic order), the probability that they were uttered by Jesus during
his life on earth appears to me far more improbable than the invention of a miracle. And the reason is that to invent his assertion of

divinity does not call for any effort of the imagination, whereas to invent a miracle means imagining time and place and circumstances, and this involves knowing quite a number of historical and geographical facts.

DIVINITY AND THE JEWISH BACKGROUND

I am going to look at the matter now from the point of view of Jesus himself.

Suppose for a moment that he is the God faith proclaims him to be: what I want to discover is how he could impart the certainty of it without having recourse to miraculous revelation, considering the historical context in which he appeared and the particular mentality of his contemporaries.

To do so he would have to communicate a unique confidence in his truthfulness and at the same time a presentiment of his superhumanity. This implies extraordinary deeds, or at any rate a superhuman mode of human existence. After this, the least hint of the secret of his being, however unexpected or incomprehensible, might well receive consideration.

For this to be possible the gap would have to be bridged between the content of the affirmation and what his disciples expected; the essence of the affirmation would have to be held possible. Now what we have to decide is whether, in the eyes of Jews, that affirmation of the divinity of a prophet, or even the Messiah, could have any sort of plausibility. If the mental habits of the Jews tended in a wholly different direction, could he, *even if he had wished*, have proclaimed his divinity without working a miracle on their understanding?

Now if there was one certitude in Israel it was that of the *divine unity*. This was a truth deep-rooted and racial, coursing in their blood. The religion of Islam is simply the revolt of this Semite blood against attempts to insert plurality into simple Being. Between Mohammed and Allah lies a gulf there is no bridging. It is against the scandal of such a bridging made by Christians that the muezzins make their protest five times a day. The one sanctuary at Jerusalem was to the Jews of old the very symbol of this fierce monotheism. And it should be noted that a belief so absolute as this, protected by clear symbols, institutions, and castes, could allow plenty of latitude in other directions. One can see this in Catholics. Their belief in the exclusive divinity of Christ warrants exalting the Virgin without danger of idolatry. In the same way, however sublime the Messiah in Jewish speculation, the postulate of God's unity set the Messiah at an infinite distance from Javé.

Moreover this God of Israel was not to be represented. The task of the prophets had been to sweep away the material symbols (like that of the calf) under which he had formerly been worshipped. Images were forbidden by the Decalogue. The sacred name itself, amounting as it did to a rudimentary image, was never pronounced in the later ages of Judaism.

Considerations such as these enable us to gauge the Jewish system of taboos, impossibilities, and repulsions.

PROPHECIES AND DIVINITY: PROSPECT AND RETROSPECT

What I have just said, which is very clear to my mind, runs counter to an opinion often expressed by the Fathers: namely that in the Scriptures the Messiah had been already proclaimed the Son of God, begotten from all eternity.

Nothing suggests that in time to come this argument in its traditional form will ever have the importance it had for the Fathers, or even in the time of Pascal. It is probable, at any rate, that it will have to be thought out again in the light of more recent knowledge.

Considered as a proof, the argument, like most prophetic arguments, is ambiguous. *Not because it fails to prove enough, but because it actually proves too much.* Suppose Scripture had spoken with complete precision of a mysterious Being, possessing all the characteristics of a human being, yet fundamentally identical with God. Suppose it were a classic of the Jewish schools, this announcement of a Messiah-God. Suppose Jesus had appeared in a society that expected the coming of a transcendent Being equal to God. Even so it would always be possible to suppose Jesus was deliberately playing this God-role, thrust upon him by the fact of this very expectation, or allotted to him by popular opinion or the writers of the Gospels. A too perfect resemblance between the reality and the expected image invites the hypothesis that the reality was actually modelled upon the image. The ancient apologists, of course, were largely influenced by the Jewish mentality, for which an event attained full historic reality only if it had already been predicted; it was this that led them to exaggerate both the precision and the amplitude of the prophetic texts.

On the other hand, for a proper understanding of the prophetic argument it is necessary to distinguish between its *prospective* and its *retrospective* aspects. Without this distinction all is obscure; with it, everything is perfectly plain.

Every event has a retrospective action on its origins and antecedents. Some ingenious examples were given by Bergson. No one, he pointed out, before the Romantic age, every talked about the romanticism of Racine; it was in the restrospective glare of Victor Hugo that Racine was seen as a figure or type. There were some of the seeds of romanticism in Racine, but before they could be observed the potentiality had to become actual. Similarly, after the event, many commentators, re-reading the *Old* Scriptures in the light of the *New* Fact, could see plenty of types and images and announcements, where the original readers, without supernatural enlightenment, could see—though the germs were there—nothing at all. Luke, in the incident of the disciples on the road to Emmaus, throws a very clear light on the way this retrospective knowledge comes about.[1]

Thus the use of the first person plural by Elohim was interpreted as proclaiming the Trinity. The famous *Maleak Javé*, arresting the arm of Abraham as he was about to sacrifice Isaac or speaking to Moses from the burning bush, was regarded by the Ante-Nicene Fathers as a personal appearance of the Logos. The Resurrection itself was to be found in the eighth verse of Psalm 7: 'Thou wilt come back to thy throne.'

We know, too, how Judaic thought in Palestine, during the period before Jesus, tended to stress the external influence of divinity, God's word, his glorious presence, his name, and avoided mention of his mysterious and immanent aspect; the use of such expressions avoided the necessity of pronouncing the Holy Name. It was enough to think of it through the medium of certain attributes. This hardly made for belief in a doctrine of God's duality. Afterwards, it is true, the divine attributes—his word, his dwelling, his glory—came to be referred to Christ, as can be seen in the Johannine prologue:

> The Word was made flesh,
> And came to dwell among us,
> And we had sight of his glory.

[1] As I shall show presently, the Passion and the Resurrection acquired in their minds historical consistency only when Jesus showed them how they were announced in the Law, the Psalms, and the Prophets. Or again, the scene of the Transfiguration, considered as historical in Peter's Second Epistle, has less weight for him, as a proof of Christ's glory, than the word of the prophets (2 *Peter* i 16–21).

But not without transforming the original sense. A new and unsuspected fact had intervened, which reinterpreted a text detached from its context and from the mentality which begot it.

Suppose even that the learned speculations of the philosophers about the Word (such as that of the Jew Philo) had been familiar to the people and that the Palestinians among whom Jesus appeared had had some expectation of an intermediary: there would have been a considerable difference even so between the ideas of *intermediary* and *mediator*. The intermediary is something belonging to a system of philosophy, the dichotomous, hierarchizing system of the Platonist. Thanks to this 'intermediary' the distance is halved: it is possible for God to abase himself to man's level, it is given to man to mount towards God. This is no historical person, wholly divine, grafted on time, with a true function of mediating by oblation.

Before Jesus there are no signs of any development by Jewish thought of the germs already present in Scripture or any flowering of an anticipated theology of the Incarnation, as there had flowered before the Christian era that anticipated theology of messiahship or even the theology of the Suffering Servant, the substructure of the Gospel. It is true that in its final and 'Sapiential' phase Jewish thought had defined a plurality of principles in the divine Being, though it is hard to decide to what extent, in the *Book of Wisdom*, the sacred writer regarded the *Logos* and the *Pneuma* as really distinct from that Wisdom itself. But if Jewish theology could provide as it were a *priming* for the idea of divine plurality, even though it regarded the idea itself as unthinkable, it blocked every avenue to the understanding of an historical *incarnation*. Latterly, too, when Judaism had come into such close contact with Hellenic paganism, so rich in 'incarnate' and human gods, it was more than ever incumbent on Jewish thinkers responsible for their faith to emphasize the transcendent aspect of God and the eschatological character of messiahship.

DIVINITY AGAINST THE PAGAN BACKGROUND

One may easily surmise the symmetrical, though inverse, difficulty involved when preaching the Gospel to pagans. To the Jews, as we have seen, an historical person asserting his divinity would have been *incomprehensible*. He would have been understood *only too well* in Gentile circles.

The gods had been in the habit of appearing in human form.

There would have been nothing shocking in the idea that Jesus was simply another god the more. The emperors, after their death, were officially promoted to divine rank: it was what was known as 'apotheosis'. The divinity of Jesus, unacceptable to the Jews, was all too acceptable, in a sense, to the Gentiles. The first heresy was that of the Docetists, who regarded Jesus as a pure apparition of God just like other divine apparitions.

CONTRADICTORY CONDITIONS FOR THE CRITERIA OF DIVINITY

I have long sought a way of escaping from the difficulties which I see exist, so far unsuccessfully. What adds to my embarrassment is that the two conditions my mind requires are in fact contradictory.

Firstly, to be sure that Jesus really claimed divinity I must find texts to this effect which are at least very unlikely to have been concocted afterwards. The chief criterion of the 'improbability of fabrication' must be sought, I think, in the conflicting of such texts with the inventive tendencies of early Christianity or with the mentality of the Jews at that time. The more a statement conflicts with the mentality of those who report it, the less likelihood there is that they did not produce it but had it imposed on them.

Secondly, the passages containing such an assertion of divinity must always be such as could have been uttered to a Jewish audience. There must be a probability that Jews, hearing such statements from the lips of Jesus, could at least have tolerated them. In the absence of these conditions I would hesitate to say that any such accounts or statements were historical.

I find myself torn between these two contrary requirements. The texts must conflict with the mentality of their hearers before they can be regarded as authentic; also, for them to be historically probable, they must in another aspect respect this mentality.

THE SPIRIT OF THE PROPOSED INQUIRY

This preliminary investigation has been rather heavy going. What I propose to do now is to forget my own ideas and draw up a list of passages in the earliest Gospels which contain statements by Jesus concerning himself.

Observing a cautious rule which I intend to apply always, I shall distinguish in every case (as far as it is intellectually possible) be tween the FACT and the INTERPRETATION. Every interpretation contains in part a personal judgement. I know it is a vain hope always to make this difference between the *fact* and the *idea* one forms of the fact, because (as it will be urged) the mere act of choosing one fact from many already presupposes an idea. However, my thinking is not angelic but human: I shall do my best. The utmost I can hope is that an opponent of my ideas will not find so very much to reproach me with.

Also, in the following chapters, I want to concentrate entirely on the mental significance of certain texts. I shall simply classify them in a particular order, draw the reader's attention to them and try to determine their character.

In any case, I think, the *real* importance of a text is not the same as its *logical* importance. The more it has the air of teaching something, the more suspect it looks. On the other hand, the more incidental, the more significant. That is why I shall leave aside a number of texts which according to traditional apologetics I should have used first. But if the content of those I retain is *equivalent* to that of those I leave alone, the omission is of no importance. Very possibly it may even be to my advantage.

I shall first have to examine the passages where Jesus compares himself to certain Old Testament characters whom the Jews conceived as endowed with outstanding powers, either in this world or the next.

I shall not be concerned as to whether these characters ever really existed or with what they actually were in history; it will be enough to determine what they stood for in the mind of a Jew contemporary with Jesus.

III

THE ENVELOPMENT OF THE SEEDS

A. Jesus and the Jewish Values of His Day

JESUS AND SOLOMON

IN the popular mind, Solomon was unquestionably the King of
kings, powerful among the powerful, wise among the wise. He
appealed to the mass of men by his spendour. All that was highest,
in the political order and in the domain of knowledge, was his. And
Jerusalem was his city: as heaven was the throne of God, so Jerusalem was the city of the Great King (*Matt.* v 34–5).

Now Jesus, incidentally, claims to be greater than Solomon: *A
greater than Solomon is here* (*Matt.* xii 42; *Luke* vi 31).

JESUS AND JONAS

What idea did Jonas convey to the minds of people in the time of
Jesus? At the very least he was a legendary prophet with a fixed
place in popular memory. In the unconscious mental workings of
the Jews, the 'sea monsters', like the original 'deep' (*Gen.* i 2), or the
'Leviathan' of the *Book of Job* (xl 20) stood for primeval opposition,
the depths of the abyss. As for Nineve, it was the symbol of paganism
in all its insolent might. But Jonas had been quite at home inside
the monster, so much so that he even found leisure to sing. And what
is more extraordinary still, Jonas had done for the most pagan of
pagan cities—that Nineve so vast that it took three days to cross it
(*Jonas* iii 3)—what no prophet had ever succeeded in doing for the
holiest of cities, Jerusalem.

Both physically and morally, Jesus sets himself far above Jonas.
What does he say, *incidentally* again, when he comes to talk about
Jonas? The Gospel attributes to him a saying which is enigmatical
but very significant, namely that the sign he will give will be similar
in kind to the sign of Jonas, but more startling:

'Jonas was three days and three nights in the belly of the sea-
beast, and the Son of Man will be three days and three nights in the

heart of the earth. . . And behold, a greater than Jonas is here (*Matt.* xii 40; *Luke* xi 32).

Because it contains an announcement of the Resurrection, this passage has been held suspect. It is true that a prophecy in circumstantial terms, occurring in an historical work written after the event, cannot be retained at the outset of a critical inquiry, because it is far less probably authentic than invented. I accept this rule. But just now I am not considering this synoptic text as a prophecy of the Resurrection, but simply as a *saying* of Jesus in which he manifestly sets himself above Jonas, just in the same way as he had set himself above Solomon.[1] Even if one reduces the content of this passage to the minimum, there is proof enough here of the impression made by Jesus on the popular mind, in which the concept of Jesus was evidently richer than that of Jonas.

JESUS, MOSES, AND ELIAS
(*Mark* ix 2–10; *Matt.* xvii 1–13; *Luke* ix 28–36)

The Transfiguration is a scene recorded in the earliest preaching. It is found in the three Synoptics. Again I am not concerned with its historical content, only with its significance.

There is no shadow of doubt that (whether or not it has any foundation in fact) this account is based on the theophany in *Exodus*: Peter, James, and John taking the place of Aaron, Nadal, and Abihu (*Exod.* xxiv 9–18). But here it is not the *giving of the Law* but the *seeing of the Messiah*. The whole new Revelation is therefore concentrated in the person of Jesus alone.

The religious significance of the passage is very important; but what I have to consider here, pursuing the method I have chosen, is a kind of summary of the impressions made by Jesus on the Jewish mind. This held Moses to be the personification of the highest authority, legislative and prophetic, as it held Elias, after Moses, the personification of the highest prophetic authority. Elias had been raised up to heaven (2 *Kings* ii 11). It was foretold that he would return before the coming of the day of Javé (*Mal.* iv 5). His being taken up to heaven made him equal to an angel in the eyes of the Jews and his aid was invoked at the hour of death. When Jesus uttered his final cry, calling upon his Father *Eli, Eli,* the crowd

---

[1] And as this statement about himself is quite in the manner of Jesus and as there is no technical sign of interpolation, I am inclined to regard the passage as in all essentials anterior to the events it predicts.

believed he was calling upon Elias (*Mark* xv 35). Elias was to return at the time of the Messiah when all things would be transformed. He was conceived as a kind of pre-Messiah, so it is easy to understand how the Jews believed that they witnessed his reappearance in the person of John the Baptist.

Moses and Elias were associated in the vision of the Transfiguration as the Law and the Prophets were associated. They are represented as the two precursors of the Messiah. This had never been the rabbinical tradition concerning the Messiah. But what is remarkable is that in the presence of Jesus these two precursors vanished into a cloud, while Jesus remained alone.

Clearly a vision of this sort cannot be classified under *history*. It is analogous to an interior revelation. Its presence in the synoptic tradition shows that it belonged to the primitive evangelical *catechesis*. It is a well established fact that in the popular mind Elias was closely connected with the Messiah. It is also undeniable that in the popular mind Jesus was thought of as infinitely superior to Elias— the order of infinity being represented by the act of *worship*.

One might even observe that the primitive evangelical fact is against the equalizing of Christ and Elias. The crowd that was present at the death of Jesus instinctively felt he was calling upon Elias, whereas the Gospel insists that he was not. Nor was Elias the angel of the Agony, who came, according to Luke, to comfort him. Jesus himself was never thought to be Elias returned, nor did the messianic expectation set the Messiah above Elias. Quite the contrary: those who believed that the Messiah would first lead a life of wretchedness looked to Elias to deliver him. Yet in spite of this, the general and ancient acceptance of the Christophany of the Transfiguration shows that Jesus, so far from being Elias, was held to be much more, and in such a relationship to Elias, as he was to Moses, that neither remained very long in his presence.

For many critics, I know, this incident is really an appearance of the risen Christ transposed into the life of Jesus, in spite of the fact that the accounts of such appearances were of a different sort, as we shall presently see, from that of the Transfiguration. But if it is decided beforehand that all expressions of the Messiah's glory are antedated, the consequences are worth just what the assumption is worth. To insist that there were never any prophecies of the Resurrection is to start from a personal opinion about the possible and the impossible. This means facing clearly all the critical problems this choice presents. But the hypothesis that the Transfiguration has been misplaced does not, I suggest, affect my conclusion. Whether the scene should be before or after the death of Jesus, it shows that the mind of the people set Jesus above the *Law* and the *Prophets*.[1]

JESUS AND DAVID
(*Mark* xii 35–7; *Luke* xx 41–4; *Matt.* xxii 41–6)

It matters little whether this psalm is really David's or not, or whether it originally had the meaning this passage attributes to it. What is certain is that Jesus gave it a meaning that implied to his hearers the non-inferiority of the Lord-Messiah to the Lord-God. To the Jewish understanding, *Sit on my right hand* meant *Be my equal*.

Speaking to Jews, who he knew made so much of scriptural proofs, and appealing to David's authority which they regarded as beyond dispute, he demonstrated very skilfully that they were bound to admit his equality with the Father. There is no similar proof for either Solomon or Jonas.

JESUS AND JOHN THE BAPTIST
(*Luke* vii 18–23; *Matt.* xi 2–6)

I am not interested to know here whether John the Baptist was really what the Gospel tells us he was; all I want to know is the idea people had of him at the time.

His influence was great. He seemed the reincarnation of the most popular of the old prophets; for Jesus, too, he was Elias returned (*Matt.* xvii 11). People took him to be 'he who was to come'. Jesus placed himself under his aegis by going to him to be baptized.

Now what is the teaching of Jesus about John the Baptist?

'What was it you expected to see when you went out into the wilderness? Was it a reed trembling in the wind? No, not that; what was it you went out to see? Was it a man clad in silk? You must look in kings' palaces for men that go clad in silk. What was it, then, that you went out to see? A prophet? Yes, and something more, I tell you, than a prophet. This is the man of whom it was

---

[1] In connection with the relationship between Jesus and Elias it may be noticed that the prophecy of Malachias (iii 1): 'See where I am sending an angel of mine, to make the way ready for my coming!' is repeated word for word in Mark, though the latter erroneously attributes it to Isaias (*Mark* i 2). It is John the Baptist who is assimilated to the 'Messenger'. But in that case the parallelism implies that Jesus is assimilated to the 'I', who is divine.

written: "Behold, I am sending before thee that angel of mine, who is to prepare thy way for thy coming." Believe me, God has raised up no greater son of woman than John the Baptist; and yet to be least in the kingdom of heaven is to be greater than he' (*Matt.* xi 7-11).

Jesus claims not only to be greater than the 'no greater', but to be able to confer this excellence on 'the least' of those who follow him.

JESUS AND THE MESSENGERS WHO PRECEDED HIM: THE PARABLE OF THE VINE-DRESSERS

According to the parable of the vine-dressers, given in the three Synoptics (*Mark* xii 1-12; *Matt.* xxi 33-46; *Luke* xx 9-19), a man possessed a vineyard that was in perfect condition. He let it out. Then, when the season came, he sent one of his servants to claim from the vine-dressers the revenue of his vineyard. This servant they maltreated and sent away empty-handed. They did the same to all the other servants who were sent successively and in ever greater numbers; some of them they even killed. At last the owner sent his only son, thinking that they would respect him at least. The son was violently assaulted and put to death by the vine-dressers.

This, beyond doubt, is the vine described by *Isaias* (v 1-7). It is the house of Israel. Javé is its master. Since it bears no fruit, he will have it destroyed. The Father's servants are the prophets of old (cf. 2 *Kings* xvii 13; *Jer.* vii 25; *Dan.* ix 10); Javé sent them to Israel, more and more of them. The only son put to death by the vine-dressers is Christ put to death by the Jews; he is above the 'servants' (in those days only slaves); he is of the same blood as the Father.

JESUS AND THE GOOD AND WICKED ANGELS

The Hebrews believed in the existence of celestial creatures who formed a court about the supreme Being. They were a kind of 'heavenly army', in number past counting. Their occupation was to worship God, to behold him, also to act when required as his messengers. They were, of all beings, the closest to God and the most holy.

As for that day and that hour you speak of, they are known to nobody, not even to the angels in heaven, nor even to the Son; only the Father knows them (*Mark* xiii 32).

There are marks, in this passage, of quite peculiar antiquity and authenticity. It shows ignorance on the part of the Son; and the higher in the divine sphere the Son was exalted, the more shocking this must have seemed to the writers of the Gospels. If they left in the words 'nor even to the Son', it must have been because their source was too unquestionable to reject. Now in this passage, which has no doubt preserved the actual words used, Jesus sets himself above the angels (though on the same level of ignorance) and immediately next the Father.

That Jesus conceived himself as at the head of the angels is what appears incidentally in many other passages. Without insisting on the point, rather seeming to take it as a matter of course, he talks of *sending* his angels, as if he had the same power of *sending* them as that which the Gospel acknowledges in the Father.

The Son of Man will give charge to his angels, and they will gather up all that gives offence in his kingdom, all those who do wickedly in it (*Matt.* xiii 41).

The Son of Man will come hereafter in his Father's glory with his angels about him, and he will recompense everyone, then, according to his works (*Matt.* xvi 27).

Then the sign of the Son of Man will be seen in heaven; then it is that all the tribes of the land will mourn, and they will see the Son of Man coming upon the clouds of heaven, with great power and glory; and he will send out his angels with a loud blast of the trumpet (*Matt.* xxiv 30–1).

When the Son of Man comes in his glory, and all the angels with him (*Matt.* xxv 31).

Dost thou doubt that if I call upon my Father, even now, he will send more than twelve legions of angels to my side? (*Matt.* xxvi 53).

Jesus knows that the angels are subject to him. It may be, as the last passage expressly says, that the power he claims over them is not direct; he holds this power from the Father. But he can obtain it in an instant.

We know that wicked angels, or *devils*, played a considerable part in the imagination of the contemporaries of Jesus. Their power was greater, it was thought, than that of the angels themselves. Jewish demonology evidently derived in many respects from the mentality of the East. These devils' sphere of influence was that governed by the 'powers' which pagan religions took to be divine; for the Jews, the 'gods' of those accursed rites were 'demons', the word used thereafter to describe those beings, created to inhabit heaven, whom their malice had rooted for ever in evil (*Luke* viii 29). They lived in the desert, in waterless places (*Luke* xi 24), and in tombs (*Mark* v 2); they congregated together (*Luke* xi 26); they were especially dangerous at mid-day (Psalm xc 5–6) and in the dark (*Luke* xxii 53). They were the cause of physical and mental diseases and everything else unexplainable and evil.

Now the Gospel shows Jesus as having authority over these devils and as being able even to confer on his disciples the power to subdue them.

The seventy-two disciples came back full of rejoicing: 'Lord,' they said, 'even the devils are made subject to us through thy name.' He said: 'I watched, while Satan was cast down like a lightning flash from heaven. Behold, I have given you the right to trample on snakes and scorpions, and all the power of the enemy, and take no hurt from it' (*Luke* x 17–19).

To these passages there should be added others, impossible to establish as historical since they relate to the intimacy of Jesus in his own inaccessible solitude; but all such texts show *at least* the idea that gathered round Jesus concerning his power over the angels and the service they rendered him. Thus:

And in the desert he spent forty days and forty nights, tempted by the devil; there he lodged with the beasts, and there the angels ministered to him (*Mark* i 13; and in *Luke* xxii 43, the angel that encouraged him in his agony).

In this connection there should also be remembered the initial temptation of Jesus, as recounted by Matthew and Luke, which is at least a sign of that power over the 'prince of this world' that the earliest tradition attributed to Jesus.

B. The Relationship of Jesus to Javé

In this second section I review the texts in which Jesus speaks explicitly of his relationship to Javé and to the attributes with which God was invested by the Jewish mind.

JESUS CALLS GOD HIS FATHER

We know that Jesus calls God '*my Father*', '*my heavenly Father*', '*my Father who is in heaven*'. And God calls Jesus *the Son*.

In Mark's Gospel we find the first germ of this title (*Mark* xiii 32;

xv 39, and allegorically xii 6), and we see it developed by Matthew and Luke. The passages are numerous and no one has ever disputed the fact that Jesus described himself as the beloved Son of the heavenly Father. Any discussion of the manifestation of the Spirit at the baptism in the Jordan and the voice saying *This is my beloved Son* would serve no purpose; even if it were held that the incident is not historical but merely a symbol, it evidently contains no more than is asserted in another form elsewhere.

Jesus introduced men to the idea that God was their Father. He taught them as much as soon as he instructed them how to pray. His own prayer, it would seem, consisted in repeating *Father! Father! My Father!* and meditating on the consequences of this simple and yet most wonderful relationship. And when he came to die, this was his last word. All this has been recalled so often that one would hesitate to say it again if in a matter so profound there could be any real repetition. It is fair to say that in this present age of distress the Gospel contains the only antidote, which is the feeling of an allpowerful affection, enveloping everything in man and expressed in the relationship of fatherhood—if it be understood that included in the divine fatherhood is all the tenderness we commonly associate with motherhood.

But just now what I am seeking in these passages is to see how far we are justified in thinking that he who spoke of a Father he had in heaven can also be regarded as God himself. At first sight the claim to be the Son would seem to suggest dependence and inequality.

To speak of having a Father, of being a Son, especially when adding that men are also the sons of this Father, so far from being a claim to equality with God is rather an admission of dependence and subordination. A Father comes before his Son. Moreover in the Jewish mind the expression 'son of God' implied in itself no idea of divinity. The Messiah was conceived as 'son of the blessed', without this involving any belief that he was God; as the chosen people, the Israelites were all called 'children of God'. The centurion who witnessed the death of Jesus, occurring so much sooner than was expected, said: 'No doubt but this was the Son of God', which implies no belief in what we call divinity. All Luke makes him say is: 'This was indeed a just man'.

But we get a different impression when we examine some of the things Jesus said. Here, as in so many other fields, it is not the most obvious that is always the most significant.

Matthew vi 8–9

'You are not to be like the heathen; your heavenly Father knows well what your needs are before you ask him. This, then, is to be your prayer: Our Father, who art in heaven. . .' The expression 'your Father' is repeated in verses 14 and 32 (and in the parallel passages, *Mark* xi 25–6 and *Luke* xii 30 respectively).

Matthew x 29, 32–3

'Are not sparrows sold two for a penny? And yet it is impossible for one of them to fall to the ground without *your* heavenly *Father's* will. . . And now, who ever acknowledges me before men, I too will acknowledge him before *my Father* who is in heaven; and whoever disowns me before men, before *my Father* in heaven I too will disown him.'

Matthew xii 49–50

'Then he stretched out his hand towards his disciples, and said: "Here are my mother and my brethren! If anyone does the will of *my Father* who is in heaven, he is my brother, and sister, and my mother." ' (See also, for the same expression, xv 16; xvi 17–27; xviii 19, 55; xix 23).

Matthew xxv 34

'Come, you that have received a blessing from *my Father*, take possession of the kingdom that has been prepared for you since the foundation of the world.'

Matthew xxvi 29

'I shall not drink of this fruit of the vine again, until I drink it with you, new wine, in the kingdom of *my Father*.'

JESUS SETS HIMSELF APART

In what Jesus had to say of himself, what is often remarked as an improbable feature is the way he sets himself utterly apart.

For instance he never places himself on the same level with his apostles when it comes to defining his relationship to the Father. He says '*my Father*' when he wishes to signify his own sonship. To the apostles and disciples he says '*your Father*', when he would teach them that God, who is his own Father, is also theirs. One would therefore have expected the equation to be complete, and since the fatherhood is apparently common to all one would have expected that, when speaking to his apostles of God, Jesus would have used the words 'Our Father'. But the Jesus of the Gospels, who teaches his disciples to say 'Our Father', never descends to join them in praying to the Father together.

There are cases where this difference of expression is so marked that it might well give the impression of a subtle distinction. At the Last Supper, Jesus does not say: 'I shall not drink of this fruit of the vine again, until we drink it together in the kingdom of the Father (or our Father).' What he says is: 'I shall not drink of this fruit of the vine again, until I drink it *with you*, new wine, in the kingdom of *my* Father.' It is true that in Mark's Gospel Jesus says simply: 'I shall not drink of this fruit of the vine again until I drink it, new wine, in the kingdom of God.' Possibly Matthew made the addition to clarify the meaning, but if so it must have been the meaning originally understood.

Moreover Matthew's Gospel makes the same fine distinctions in the scene of the Last Judgement: 'Come, you that have received a blessing from *my* Father, take possession of the kingdom that has been prepared for *you* since the foundation of the world' (xxv 34). So does Luke, when he makes Jesus say: 'Behold, I am sending down upon *you* the gift which was promised by *my* Father' (xxiv 49).

JESUS AND THE SABBATH

The sabbath had been observed by God himself after his week's creative labour, or rather joy. In its origin it was doubly divine: by the authority it derived from Sinai and by the divine example of the seventh day.

Now this holy day is treated by Jesus with complete freedom. He gives his disciples permission to pluck the ears of corn; more than this, on the sabbath day he does his own re-creative work, the performing of miracles.

Certainly in the first of these instances he refers to the example of David and the Temple priests; he establishes the principle, so often forgotten by men, that a rule should be applied not merely in its *letter* but in its *spirit*. It was a principle not unknown to the Jews. The rabbis were aware that the positive law is of no effect when it conflicts with man's good, the purpose for which God established it: it is impossible for God to be in opposition to himself. It had been decided, too, in the time of the Machabees, that if the enemy

attacks you, you must fight even on the sabbath (1 *Mach.* i 39–42).
The preservation of life dispensed from the sabbath.[1] Yet Aqiba
had observed that even God had held himself bound by it, in not
sending manna on the sabbath day.

Therefore the point to be observed here is not so much that Jesus
restored the law to its true spirit—the good sense of the rabbis
tended sometimes to do this—as his motives for doing so. David,
he pointed out, had dispensed from the sabbath. He placed himself
on the same level as David. He went even further. What David
did accidentally, in response to personal need, Jesus (we are told)
did by his own personal authority, that which he possessed as 'Son
of Man'.

*The sabbath was made for man, not man for the sabbath. So that the Son
of Man has even the sabbath at his disposal* (*Mark* ii 27–8; *Luke* vi 5).

One might say, as did Loisy, that the 'so that' is not quite self-
explanatory and that verse 28 has the appearance of being added.
It is true that for a Greek mind, so swift to observe consequence, the
connection between these two verses is weak. But even if the second
were a subsequent addition, it would only help to explain the profound idea implied by the *praxis* of Jesus and the implicit conclusion
drawn by the witnesses of what he did.

At any rate, for present purposes it is enough to note that the
impression made on the Jewish mind would be that Jesus claimed
to have special authority to reduce the law to its initial meaning;
and, even more, to break the law so as to *reveal* its meaning.

The healing of the man with the withered hand, performed on the
sabbath day, shows the double dominion of Jesus: over nature by
the miracle, over the law by the day on which the miracle was
performed. This seemed so impious to the Pharisees and Herodians
that they held it to be legal grounds for putting him to death. It
was certainly something that the Jewish mind was unable to
assimilate.

AUTHORITY TO FORGIVE SINS

'Son, thy sins are forgiven thee,' said Jesus to the man with palsy.
There were scribes present who reasoned with themselves thus:
'Why does he speak so? He is speaking blasphemy. Who can forgive
sins but God, and God only?' Jesus at once knew their secret
thoughts. 'Why,' he asked, 'do you reason thus in your minds?
Which command is more lightly given, to say to the palsied man,

[1] See the rabbinical texts in Lagrange, *Mark*, pp. 54–5.

"Thy sins are forgiven," or to say "Rise up, take thy bed with thee, and walk"? And now, to convince you that the Son of Man has authority to forgive sins while he is on earth. . .' (*Mark* ii 6–10; *Matt.* ix 1–8; *Luke* v 17–26).

The passage in itself is clear enough, but it has to be explained according to Jewish ideas. The account in Mark seems to be written by a witness who actually saw and heard. It is here that Jesus first reveals himself as a physician of souls; it is to show his power over souls that he condescends, as it were, to manifest his power over the body. The visible miracle is simply a sign of an invisible act in a different order. But it amounted to claiming a power which the Jews regarded as divine. It was because he claimed to be forgiving sin that those who were present accused him of 'speaking blasphemy'.

Strictly, there is no proof here of any identifying of the power of Jesus with that of Javé. Jesus did not say: 'I forgive thee thy sins,' but '*Thy sins are forgiven thee*,' which means at least that he guarantees the forgiveness of sins by the Father, not that he procures such forgiveness by himself. Moreover in all the texts he seems to make a distinction between the forgiveness of sins *in heaven* and their forgiveness *on earth*. In heaven it is God who forgives sins. On earth he delegates this power to the 'Son of Man', here so named for the first time.

The Jews were also aware that speaking in God's name one man can tell another that his sins are forgiven. It is what Nathan told David (2 *Sam.* xii 13). Such a *declaration* can always be made by one who sees as God sees, which a prophet presumably does. This is something different from a *judgement* of absolution. Such a judgement, in Jewish eyes, belongs to him alone whom the fault has offended. Now, as they saw it, the fault offended God (*Psalm* l 6), and the judgement that absolved it belonged only to God (see *Henoch* lxi 8; lxii 3). The prophet's art of penetrating secret thoughts was communicable (*Jer.* xvii 10; 1 *Sam.* xvi 7; 2 *Kings* viii 10–14); the famous passage about the gifts of the Spirit in *Isaias* xi shows that these gifts were conceived as communicated to the Messiah.

We have therefore here an ambivalent passage. It can be maintained that all it does is to represent Jesus as having the powers of the Messiah, including that of the forgiveness of sins 'on earth'. Moreover the Johannine Gospel shows that a Messiah who was endowed with 'all judgement' was yet, to the Jewish way of thinking, not God. This is still the vision of Daniel and his prophecy of the 'Son of Man' who has been given *all* powers.

But we may still surely ask whether this total delegation of powers conceived by the Jewish mind as proper to God, does not already imply the impossibility of the recipient's being merely human. The synoptic passages I have examined have all this doubtful character: taken by themselves, in their minimum content, they can be interpreted as not transcending the messianic horizon. But in the manner of their expression, in the strength of their assertion, in the 'going to extremes' that such texts involve, we are carried well beyond the minimum content. Hesitating as I do between these two interpretations (the one purely messianic, the other hypermessianic and virtually deifying), I feel I have no right to draw the line between them. The texts must be seen as a whole and all the passages in harmony. As I reflect on these primary data, the impression I get is that they contain much more than appears at first sight and that the scribes had reason to talk of 'blasphemy'.

JESUS THE FINAL JUDGE OF CONSCIENCE

The Son of Man will come in his Father's glory, with his angels about him, and he will recompense everyone, then, according to his works; he will sit down upon the throne of his glory to judge all nations (*Matt.* xvi 27; xxv 31 *et seq.*). It is then, before his Father, that he will be ashamed of those who have been ashamed of him before men (*Mark* viii 38; *Luke* ix 26), that he will disown those who had disowned him (*Matt.* x 33; *Luke* xii 9) and will acknowledge those who before men had acknowledged him (*Matt.* x 32; *Luke* xii 8).

To grasp all that these texts convey it is necessary once more to remember the Jewish idea of the Messiah as judge.

Without admitting the divinity of the Messiah, the Jews regarded as one of his functions the sanctioning of men's conduct. It was for him to judge the living, and sometimes the dead. Such a judgement was strictly a restoration of the people, rather than a judgement of persons as we have since understood it. It completed the terrestrial work of the Messiah, which was the triumph of the sons of Abraham, the victory of the circumcised over the uncircumcised, the latter's fate (apart from a few just men like Job) being to be cast into gehenna.

Here we have still the same viewpoint, but the *spirit* is different. The judgement in question is certainly a judgement of the nations, solemnly decreed in the presence of all conscious beings. As in the popular apocalypses, the Messiah makes his appearance 'booted and armed', a warrior chief surrounded with his bodyguard. Yet in spite of these resemblances it is something quite different from a political restoration of Israel, or even their spiritual restoration. No privilege counts, no social advantage; neither does membership of the chosen people nor even services to God's cause, if these have been rendered from interested motives. On the other hand the friends of God, even if unknown to the world, are to be found among strangers, unbelievers and enemies, whereas some who have proved unfaithful servants will find themselves cast out. Therefore the judgement of Jesus reaches 'the very division between joints and marrow' (namely to thought itself) and with no possible appeal. He has no regard for the decrees of any anterior racial predestination but only for the moral life of the individual; this he scrutinizes in the light of charity, this being the very plenitude of justice. Jesus behaves as if he were Judge-in-himself. What is more, he judges according to the strictest moral law but also according to men's attitude to his message, in fact their attitude—the attitude of each— to his own person, considered as anyone who is poor, anyone who is a prisoner. . . He identifies himself with the moral law. Man's adherence to Jesus, his impulse of love for *him*, is the necessary condition of his eternal salvation.

Consider, now, what this claim implied for the Jewish mind. In order to pass such a sentence, which would determine the destiny of each human being, it was necessary to have access to that which was secret. Such knowledge, according to the Jews (*Psalm* vii 10; *Wis.* i 6; *Jer.* xi 20) was peculiar to Javé, the direct source of all that concerned the moral law. God, as I have said, might reveal the state of an individual conscience to a supreme judge of men, who would be a man like others. But it was an established tradition for the Jews of that day that judgement was reserved to God; the Messiah never appears as judge except in the parables of Henoch, and even there his judgement is not a universal judgement. The day of judgement is 'the Lord's Day' *par excellence*; and as the coming of the Son of Man coincides with the day of the Lord, so the Son's act of judgement coincides with God's. This identifying of time and manner and function makes it hard to distinguish the Messiah's role from the Father's.

To do justice to both aspects of what we are given, of what I would call the 'structure', one would have to say something like this:

everything suggests that Christ is not only acting as supreme judge but identifying himself with the Person offended by sin: *you did it to me . . . you refused it to me. . .*

According to the Jews the power to judge could be delegated. There could be delegated, too, the power to offer oneself as a victim in place of the guilty (this is just the sense of the second Isaias). But the capacity to be affronted by sin in the same measure as God, as if sin against God were also sin against yourself, implies the impossibility of any delegation, and this is not far from identification. Once it is recognized, one may readily admit that it is in another relationship, namely inasmuch as he is a man, that Christ receives this power of judging. So that if in the *inductive* order we argue from the Messiah-judge to the Messiah deified, when we reach this conclusion we can argue *deductively* from the Messiah-God to the Messiah-judge. This was bound to happen on further reflection. We see it in St John, where the deduction has become explicit. The fourth Gospel (*John* v 27) certainly says that the Father has given to the Son the power to execute judgement because he is man, but no one denies that this man, in St John, is also the Son, who is to be honoured like the Father and who is, with him, a single principle of existence.

THE RELATIONSHIP OF JESUS TO THE SPIRIT

Consider now the texts where Jesus speaks of the Spirit *incidentally*. *Believe me, there is pardon for all the other sins of mankind and the blasphemies they utter; but if a man blasphemes against the Holy Spirit, there is no pardon for him in all eternity; he is guilty of a sin which is eternal. This was because they were saying: 'He has an unclean spirit'* (*Mark* iii 28–30; *Matt.* xii 32).

'Believe me' (*Amen*) is a solemn formula which appears for the first time here in Mark. Jesus distinguishes two kinds of blasphemies. Some are pardonable, even though they attack God (such were Job's blasphemies). Others are not pardonable: they are the blasphemies of which the scribes had just been guilty, those called by Jesus 'blasphemies against the Holy Spirit'.

Here the Holy Spirit, designated by the article (*To pneuma to hagion*) seems to have a distinct reality within God himself. The text, it should be noted, makes a distinction between blasphemy against the Son of Man, a sin in some sort human, temporal, and forgivable, and blasphemy against the Holy Spirit (the Spirit of God), a sin as it were divine, non-temporal, unforgivable. One would expect Jesus to say that sin against himself is pardonable, since what he claims to be is the Son of Man. But no. Mark's circumstantial account (which is seemingly the source of the parallel passages) is quite precise. What is unpardonable, a sin not to be remitted, an *eternal* sin, is simply to have said of Jesus: 'He has an unclean spirit.'

What conclusion can one draw from this, other than that Jesus sets himself not in the human but in the divine category? He asserts that the principle of his action is in strict relationship to that mysterious value, named by him not merely 'Holy Spirit' but '*The* Holy Spirit'. So we have here in this ancient text (which it is hard to think is a later addition) the very principle of the distinction, since become traditional, between the *humanity* and the *divinity* of Christ. And I prefer to consider its origin in its earliest form, however crude, before it was affected by later reflection.

TESTIMONY BEFORE THE POWERS

When they take you and hand you over thus, do not consider anxiously beforehand what you are to say; use what words are given you when the time comes; it is not you that speak, it is the Holy Spirit (Mark xiii 11; Luke xii 11–12).

We are here at the solemn moment when the apostles are to be dragged before courts of justice for their faith in Jesus. Then the Holy Spirit, whom Matthew calls 'the Spirit of your Father', will give testimony in the apostles' place. Here again Jesus acts in an order apart, since human testimony about his nature is provided by the presence of the Spirit of God.

These two last passages (to which might be added the baptism of Jesus in the Jordan) were not to become clear until later, when thought concerning the Father's Spirit had been fully developed. But in their primitive form they show clearly how Jesus in his ordinary preaching sets himself naturally in the sphere of the divine.

THE RELATIONSHIP OF JESUS TO THE FATHER

Father, who art Lord of heaven and earth, I give thee praise that thou hast hidden all this from the wise and the prudent, and revealed it to little children. Be it so, Father, since this finds favour in thy sight. My Father has entrusted everything into my hands; none knows the Son truly except the Father, and

G

none knows the Father truly except the Son, and those to whom it is the Son's good pleasure to reveal him (Matt. xi 25–7; *Luke* x 21–2).

It seems strange to find this passage in the Synoptic Gospels. Yet an examination of the style and a study of the different versions provide no objective proof of interpolation. Perhaps the word *know* should not have the meaning a Greek mind would give it. *To know* may mean simply *to be in full familiarity and intimacy with.* But in this case also Jesus sets himself apart from all other beings. He claims to be on relations of reciprocal friendship with his Father, a relationship that no one else can enter. He claims to be the Father's only Son; and, though his Son, his equal in respect of knowledge and friendship. Much more than this, he claims that *everything* has been remitted to him by the Father, and in this *everything* there must clearly be included that which makes him the Son.

This passage takes us outside time. We have to think of the world as vanished out of sight, with two beings only who still remain, deeply interpenetrating in a secret none other may ever penetrate. Only the Son knows the Father; and, what seems even more mysterious, the Son himself is a mystery known only to God.

PASSAGES RELATING TO THE DIVINE 'EGO'

What I am referring to here is all those Gospel texts in which Jesus says, 'But I tell you', which one might almost translate with an emphatic 'My *self* tells you that'. Such texts, recognizable in translation sometimes by the formula 'But I', might seem not more than the stressing required by an antithesis or the desire to call attention to a particular point. But a study of oriental usages shows that this emphatic and sacred 'I' was always employed, in the Jewish and Hellenistic world, in the proclamations of defied kings. Examples will be found in technical monographs.[1]

THE 'EXOUSIA' GIVEN TO THE MESSIAH

The Messiah possesses what he calls 'authority' (*exousia*) which is 'given' to him 'in heaven and on earth', an authority which, as we see in John's Gospel, extends to his own life and death (x 18). This had already been made plain in the synoptic accounts of the

[1] E.g. Kittel, *Theol. Wort.*, ii, p. 1935; Bultmann, *Die Geschichte der Syn. Tred.*, pp. 141 *et seq.*; Schmitt, *Revue d'hist. et de phil. relig.*, 1938, pp. 34–6.

Passion, where we see Jesus dying, as it seemed, quite suddenly, to the astonishment of those accustomed to witnessing executions.

According to Jewish ideas this *exousia* properly belongs to God. It was thought of as an absolute juridical power that admitted of no resistance. It is true that it could be communicated to others: we see Jesus conferring it upon the apostles; Satan himself possesses it (*Acts* xxvi 18; *Col.* i 13; *Eph.* ii 2, and especially vi 12). But the Gospel represents Jesus as disposing of this *exousia* in the same measure as does Javé. Here too it would seem that Jesus and his Origin are one, even though their relationships are different. If the precise nature of this difference is to be defined in the light of these data alone, one would have to say that in Jesus the *exousia* is conceived as *given*, not *giving*; as imparted, not imparting; as something he received, not proper to himself. Here we have the first Christian conception of the relationship between Father and Son as it was later set forth in the Johannine Gospel.

OTHER TEXTS

There are other passages it would have been possible to make much of: they are those which a Christian tends to quote first because they appear most explicit: that, for example, which is generally called 'the Confession of Peter at Caesarea Philippi', where Peter acknowledges that Jesus is the Christ, 'the Son of the living God' (*Matt.* xvi 16); even more, Jesus's own confession before Caiphas, when to the question: 'Art thou the Christ, the Son of the blessed God?' he answered: 'I am' (*Mark* xiv 61).

All I would observe of these texts is that they can be considered *at different stages in the progress of thought*, and it depends on the stage one is at, what light is thrown upon them.

The reason I have not used them is my rule of excessive caution. It is this that has led me to place in brackets—honestly suspending judgement on them—passages that look at first sight too significant or too obviously decisive. But at the stage I have now reached they stand out in a new light. As far as I can see, they contain no assertion more substantial than those in the texts I have examined. Such being the case, why should I reject them? At least I can say that what I recognize as the virtual content of other and indirect passages is here more explicit and sometimes more solemn. In the light of probability it is credible enough that Jesus insinuated 'in divers ways' the secret of his being, and that he revealed it clearly to privileged disciples or in more momentous circumstances.

I propose to reason in the same way about the baptism of Jesus, when a voice was heard saying: '*This is my beloved Son.*' It is not, strictly, an historical fact, because none would seem to have heard it but Jesus himself. Did such sonship imply for the Jews a recognition of divinity?

IV

THE SIGNIFICANCE OF THE ENVELOPMENT

A. Envelopment and Authenticity

THE CHIEF CHARACTERISTIC OF THE FOREGOING 'LOGIA':
THE DIFFERENCE BETWEEN THEIR VIRTUAL AND
APPARENT CONTENT

THE texts I examined in the last chapter—ignoring the commentaries both of believers and unbelievers, because these as a rule obscure their meaning by reading into them either *too much* or *too little*—reveal a characteristic I always find striking, the difference between their apparent content and their virtual, in this case *real*, content.

At first sight they seem to be without significance: one could imagine the same absence of surprise in an Israelite who heard them for the first time. There would be no immediate recognition of any other meaning but that permitted by the official doctrine concerning the Messiah: there is nothing we have found in these texts, in which Jesus speaks of himself as the Messiah, that could not, on first inspection, be applied to the Messiah as the Jews expected him to be.

It is otherwise if one tries, as I have done, to establish the virtual content of these passages. A number of them, perhaps all, go beyond what was commonly admitted of the Messiah. There is more meaning in them than was implied in the Jewish conception of messiahship, because their rendering of the words of Jesus make him calmly claim and presuppose some kind of equality with Javé.

In the concrete language used by the Jews we find no words so exact in meaning as those that were to appear in the Christian confessions of faith: words like *equality, unity, divinity, consubstantiality, divine generation, monogenesis*. So close to physical sensation, the Aramaic tongue, in which the earliest tradition concerning Jesus was expressed, had not at its command the terms which are so useful for excluding philosophical errors, but have the corresponding disadvantage of bearing the marks of human fabrication, besides con-

veying nothing to the popular mind apart from the prestige of the
incomprehensible. If Jesus had used such learned terms—inconceivable in the order of human probabilities—he would have been
talking to no purpose over the heads of his hearers.

Changes of wording, imagery, and even concepts are to be observed in the earliest days of the Church, which turned almost immediately from the Jewish world to the Greco-Roman. It was this
that involved a change of front. This initial accident, which made it
necessary for the primitive faith to be expressed in two registers,
caused it to stand out, as it were, in greater relief, which is always
the way with thoughts that receive two different expressions. The
Jews used such terms as 'Messiah', 'Servant of Javé', 'Son of Man'.
Christians preferred others, like 'Lord', 'Saviour', 'Son of God'.
A theology of glory, it has been said, replaced that of the Cross.
There is no need to go so far to explain these new usages. The first
set of expressions seemed to contain a little less substance of belief
than the second; especially in the ears of a pagan, who could have
no idea of all 'Son of Man' conveyed to the Jews in the way of
spiritual exaltation, with all its reminiscences of the prophecy of
Daniel, where the 'Son of Man' comes forth from heaven. St Paul,
anticipating a lack of response in the minds of Christian converts
from paganism, never used the expression 'Son of Man'.

The other class of words is borrowed from the Greek (*Kurios, soter,
theou huios*), one might even say from the language of imperial
paganism. There the Messiah's abasement would inevitably be less
acceptable, for neither gods nor emperors were ever thought of as
suffering or humiliated. This transposition alone would be bound
to make for a theology of glory rather than of suffering.

The language of primitive terms, transported from its native soil,
calls for historical explanation. It leaves on the modern reader (as
it no doubt did on any reader in antiquity who had had a Greek
education) an impression of vagueness and—in what concerns
divinity—a certain unworthiness. Ideas like 'lordship over the
sabbath', 'power to send the Spirit', 'sonship of man', 'coming in
clouds', are all in themselves imprecise; none of them can be understood properly apart from exegesis. I get just the same impression
when I study (say) the prerogatives of the kings of France and come
across expressions like 'bed of justice' or 'right of remonstrance'. If
I had not some learned work to refer to, which would explain these
terms of the old regime, I could never discover their meaning for
myself.

So in examining the Gospel texts I have set them once more in their proper context, which is that of the Jewish mentality. As I have said, what appears to emerge from these *logia* is the assertion by Jesus of a certain relationship, unique in kind, between his own person and Divinity itself. I can be even more specific: it is a relationship implying that Jesus possesses certain attributes regarded by the Jews of his day as impossible to be delegated, even though their consciousness of this was by no means clear.

To explain this adequately calls for a high degree of exactitude.

It is evident enough that many of the powers Jesus exercised were not regarded by the Jews as peculiar to the divine Being. Jewish thought admitted that God could entrust many of his powers to men. This is what is meant by their idea of a prophet. He was one who had received a share of divinity, a delegation of power, a light on time (past and future), sometimes, as was the case with Moses, an absolute authority. The Messiah was thought of as a prophet in the sovereign order, closing and completing all history. His should have been therefore the maximum of all powers that could possibly be delegated. It was for him, for example, to exercise 'God's justice', being himself endowed with authority to judge.

But it is not a question of whether metaphysically God can or cannot delegate this or that of his attributes. I am placing myself in a particular historical context. I ask myself, knowing the mentality of the Jews, to what extent the divine attributes claimed by Jesus in the *logia* (too numerous, too incidental, and too diverse for them to be all suspect) could have made him appear a 'blasphemer.' In other words, what we have to decide is whether in the eyes of enlightened Jews there was not involved in these claims—so various, so insistent, even if guardedly expressed—something even more unthinkable than intolerable, namely *autodeification*.

An objection can be raised here and I see the force of it. It can always be said that each of these texts, taken by itself, can be interpreted strictly as not beyond the reach of messianic thought. It can even be maintained that this collection of texts does not logically require, when they are all put together, the idea that the Messiah was God. A mere accumulation of assertions of a particular order cannot justify an assertion of a higher order: ten bad proofs do not make one good one. But in the informal logic of real life assertions separately insufficient strengthen one another when they converge. It is quite unthinkable, in my opinion, that the hearers of these *logia* could have retained very long the idea of a purely human being. Each of the assertions is within the messianic scope. None, strictly interpreted, can be said to go beyond it. But when they are all taken together, the manner in which most of them were made compels the conclusion that there was here, for the Jews, something more than a claim to messiahship.

Here, for the first time in the course of this inquiry, I find myself facing the *paradox of the seed*. The seed must have the double characteristic of being without newness, yet at the same time new, *mental and spiritual*. Now the texts I have quoted reveal this double characteristic of seed.

It is perfectly true that the claims of Jesus are all included in the titles of the Messiah, but when each is given its maximum content they go beyond messiahship. From this point of view the ambivalence of the texts is not accidental: it is the equipotential ambivalence of seed, the first aspect of all development.

In a passage I have not mentioned, Matthew's account of the confession of Peter at Caesarea (xvi 13–20), Jesus asks: 'Who do men say that I am?' 'Some say John the Baptist,' they told him, 'others Elias, others again, Jeremy or one of the prophets.' 'And what of you?' Jesus asks. Then Peter answered: 'Thou art the Christ, the Son of the living God.' Compare this with the accounts in *Mark* and *Luke*, and these, you will see, do not go so far. Mark makes Peter say: 'Thou art the Christ' (viii 29); Luke: 'Thou art that Christ whom God has anointed' (ix 20). Mark and Luke no doubt are giving the historical truth of fact, repeating what was actually said. But Matthew's account is historically true in a deeper sense, because he tells us what those who were listening understood by the words. Moreover the expression he uses does not itself imply divinity as such, any more than the confession before Pilate or the words of Peter about the Temple tribute. But there is no escaping the conclusion that if divinity is not implied to the mind of someone limited to a momentary intuition, it is to anyone who has time to reflect, if he has also at his disposal the age-old knowledge accumulated in Israel during the course of ten whole centuries of prophecy. This is the potentiality of seed cast into the earth, it holds life; though with no outward manifestation—except to him who anticipates because he knows already that life is immanent in this grain of dust.

I dare not venture too far, but it seems to me that from these various considerations there emerges a highly probable hypothesis.

I would put it like this: *The assertions of Jesus concerning his mission and his person both in content and form went beyond what could be accepted by messianic expectation, whether popular, official, or deviationist. Everything seems to suggest that Jesus, aware of his identity with God and exercising divine power that was not merely delegated, had so instructed his disciples as to make this claim progressively easier to accept.*

THE ACCIDENTAL ASPECT OF THE IMPLICIT ASSERTIONS

There is another feature that should be carefully noted here. It is the accidental character of most of these texts: they occur in the course of developments where generally the trend of thought leads anywhere but in that direction. They are often incidental.

In the evangelical tradition we have certain very definite doctrinal themes: the difference, for instance, between the old and the new Law, as set forth in the Sermon on the Mount; the theme of the divine fatherhood; the theme of pharisaism. In all these cases Jesus is giving a lesson, and like every teacher he emphasizes, insists, and repeats. When necessary he illustrates with image and parable. He makes use of certain expressions to add solemnity to his statements, such as '*Believe me* when I tell you this' (*Amen, amen, dico vobis*). But in many of the passages I have quoted the *accent* is often on something quite other than the being of Christ. Thus it is accidentally that he speaks of *his* angels; without any necessity, I mean, as far as the development of the argument is concerned. It is as if Napoleon, shall we say, in explaining the strategy of a campaign, happened to make mention of Berthier or his guard. In just the same way the passages in these *logia* where Jesus hints at his own Sonship are not the subject of a solemn lesson, nor even of a lesson sufficiently explicit to convey that he is revealing to his hearers a truth of the highest importance. Their attention at the time is focused elsewhere. Even in the parable of the vine-dressers it is not unlikely that the impression retained was the superiority of the Messiah to the previous envoys, not the assertion of divine sonship. In the account (which seems so early in date) of the absolution of the man with palsy, what was left in the minds of its first hearers and first readers? Doubtless the wholly unique character of this prophet, possibly the power Jesus exercised over sin; but none could then, even in an equivalent sense, have admitted that which we now call divinity. It is even questionable if those present understood that the 'Son of Man' forgave sins. In the incidents that followed there is never a sign of the

Jews coming to Jesus to be healed of their sins or confess them to him, which they did of their own accord when they flocked to John the Baptist.

Casual words and gestures are invaluable for reading the depths of a person's mind, so are indirect thoughts and oblique considerations. When we are bent on some purpose we are always in danger of being carried away, and so tend either to overstate or dissimulate. That is why the apparently insignificant may well be the most significant. And that is why we want to know what Jesus, as it were, allowed to escape, even more than what he expressly declared. The *logia* which concern his relationship with the Father and the Spirit are of greater value, for a naturally critical mind, than the confession at Caesarea Philippi or the Transfiguration, the hymn of triumph or the solemn testimony before Caiphas. Fabulation, the essence of which is to clothe an idea in historical appearance, invariably produces narratives that are highly coloured with a meaning too obvious for anyone to miss.[1]

VIRTUALITY NEVER THE OUTCOME OF FABULATION

Since Strauss, the intellectual objection has come from the school we have described as *mythical*: it consists in stressing the religious basis of a passage in order to reject its historicity. It is because the Gospels have a religious significance that they appear to many to be products of faith.

If this principle in its fullest sense is taken for granted as an initial postulate, there is no arguing with it. But it has no real force. It amounts to saying that every affirmation of faith must be rejected intellectually *a priori*, simply because it has a religious value. But I should like to think that with Strauss, Loisy, or Bultmann the principle is not as absolute as all this. All they mean to say is: 'When a Gospel narrative proclaims a belief, there is no reason to think it was not the belief that produced the narrative.' Here we have a principle of prudence, not a certitude. It does not close the investigation: it is an invitation to continue it. Now the principles I have put forward may throw some light on it. Fabulation, being an objectifying of the mental content, can project no more than the fabulating mind imagines or conceives. If, for instance, it would

---

[1] This is also to be seen in St Paul. The texts in which Christ is most exalted, and especially in *Philippians* ii 5–11, are thrown out in passing, almost absent-mindedly. This implies an unconscious conviction so profound as not even to need affirmation.

present a Christ who is the object of religious belief, it would make him appear 'celestial' or 'glorious'; it would not disguise him with traits that are hidden or ambiguous, opposed or contradictory to the very aims it sets itself. The visible and the visionary are necessary elements in the process of fabulation.

To speak philosophically, I would say that *fabulation cannot imagine virtuality*. What it desires to see, it does not project in the form of seeds, which are necessarily minute, obscure, and disguised. Whether it be in mental background or actual documents—in a 'Tradition' or a 'Scripture'—what it presents as facts are without virtuality: they are all explicit, complete, schematic. There is no approximation. The realities it conceives are the expressive realities it finds to hand in rites and legends, in esctatic phenomena and the dogmatic formulas of primitive creeds.

Fabulation tends to exceed the actual content of a belief, never to restrict, obscure, or 'envelop' it. It is hard to think it would bury it like a seed, especially if one bears in mind that such seeds would disconcert the myth-making communities. Fabulation is never found diminishing faith to the extent of making it a kind of micro-faith, still less a faith 'enveloped', like seed, in a tegument.

I do not know whether orthodoxy would permit the recognition of traces of fabulation in an inspired narrative; it is not for me to say, and the question no doubt depends on the idea of 'literary *genre*'. Is there an historical technique which sometimes involves an imaginary transposition without affecting the essential truth of the testimony? At any rate, in my liberal approach to the subject, I cannot disguise the fact that the Gospels at first sight, when considered simply as historical works apart from any idea of inspiration, present scenes that certainly bear traces of fabulation. Not that this is sufficient proof that they are unhistorical. A man may witness a real scene which is so unlike anything he has experienced before that he believes, as he tells you, 'he has dreamed it'. Improbability, especially in matters religious, is no conclusive proof of unreality. But at any rate we can say that there are certain scenes in the Gospel that are not historical, as we now understand 'history', namely an account of objective and public events, witnessed and reported. One such account is that of the temptations of Christ.

One might conceivably classify passages in the Gospel according to the extent to which they are incompatible with fabulation. If such a critical procedure were attempted I can see that the 'enveloped' statements I have so far mentioned would prove most refractory to the fable-making theory. It is clear that when the sources of the synoptic Gospels were compiled the Christian communities 'were worshipping Christ as a god'; they were accepting the teaching of St Paul, whose principal Epistles cover the period A.D. 50 to 60. Those to whom he was writing bestowed divine honours on Christ.

Therefore, if they had fabulated the Gospel texts, everything would have induced them to represent Christ as claiming divinity. But the source-documents of the Synoptics show the opposite to any such claims to divinity. If I set out to tell the story of a God on earth, I would not begin by embarrassing myself with useless difficulties. I would not show him in his human aspects, in states of weakness or ignorance, nor would I depict his chief collaborators as stupid or unbelieving. I would not disguise my proof with narratives that *prima facie* have no importance and sometimes even look like an express refutation of it. It would be so easy, in composing a Gospel, to make Jesus say whatever the Spirit, at the time I was writing, inspired me that he could and must have said, that he could not *help* having said. Such a reconstruction of the past, according to the rule of 'appropriateness', is habitual with religious writers. In times gone by, believers, when mingling past and present, were wholly unconscious of betraying any trust. To present such fabulated Gospels, in complete conformity with the articles of faith, would surely have been held both laudable and expedient, a work of pastoral merit and availing to salvation.

So I return to the same point: if in spite of all the urge to fabulation, in spite of the loftiest motives drawn from the interests of the Faith and the holiest hagiographical custom, those who described the memories men had of Jesus did not remodel the Lord in accordance with their faith and the interests of their *kerugma*, there must have been some obstinate reality to prevent it, some given facts impossible to ignore.

B. Other Aspects of the Resistance of Facts to Fabulation

THE VERISIMILITUDE OF THE HISTORICAL BACKGROUND

I have already observed how these texts conform to the mental background of any moderately well educated Palestinian at the time of Jesus. But if fabling produced them it would have been very hard put to it to compose them in the form they have. To imagine an able novelist, such as Flaubert or Walter Scott, poring over archaeological remains or the narratives written by bygone travellers, would be to transpose into the past our own very modern pursuits. The *Chansons de geste*, it may be urged, as explained by Joseph Bédier, had originated in the need felt by pilgrims to the shrine of St James at Compostela for detailed information about their route; the author of the *Odyssey*, according to Victor Bérard, had his eyes on the course set by a sea-going Phoenician; in just the same way the Gospel could have been composed in order to explain by historical fiction what were otherwise unintelligible practices or rites. But both the *Odyssey* and the *Chansons de geste* contain that kind of marvellous element which is not to be found in the Synoptics; moreover those who heard those ancient epics never associated them with any faith that led to practical results. The art of historical fiction, learned and scholarly, which would have been required by a writer of the second century if he were to reconstruct a state of affairs that had long passed away, is more than improbable in a highly fervent religious community, concentrating entirely on belief in its Christ-God and with no interest at all in earthly details or the very Jewish colouring of its origins.

As for popular fabulation, of the legendary and hagiographical sort, it proceeds on very schematic lines and its productions are extremely poor and crude. They never attain even a degree of probability.[1]

NO RETROSPECTIVE PROJECTION OF THE RISEN CHRIST

There is another criterion of authenticity, one that rests on a study of the way the human mind works, particularly when remembering: it is the almost inevitable transposition that must have occurred in the story of Jesus after the Resurrection appearances. Why did this not occur on a large scale?

It is possible that the writer, persuaded that Jesus was God, may have added unconsciously and in all good faith some trait that emphasized the transcendence of his model. But just because this instinct was so powerful (and in a sense legitimate) we are astonished that it was not more operative. There is no deciding which are the cases where some such trait may have been added; we can, on the other hand, note numerous occasions when the author must have

[1] See Delahaye, *Les Légends hagiographiques*, pp. 7, 18, 35, 74, 105, 129, 241–59.

been tempted to magnify the strength of his statements and yet did not do so. What could have checked him, if it was not respect for an already established tradition, for facts he judged historic and therefore reproduced, however much he may have been shocked by what must have seemed the too human character of the yet unglorified Jesus?

The Gospels must have been composed long after the Resurrection by believers fully persuaded of their Master's divine and heavenly character. Convinced as they were, when they came to recall the earlier phase, when Jesus actually lived amongst them, it must have seemed to them as it were embryonic, a preparatory stage, so unworthy as to be barely acceptable. When they projected the image of the risen Christ upon their memory of the Nazarene, the disciples must surely have been tempted to embellish. Some must have thought they had carelessly overlooked the divine life which was already present in Jesus, that they needed a beam of light to retrace, so to speak, the line of the past. Some might have thought it their duty to transfer, to the period *before*, what appeared only *afterwards*, but even then was *already* real. It might even be that the *before* and the *afterwards* had come to be confused in their minds.

There is, in fact, one scene in the Gospel which might appear to be carried back to the *before* when it really belongs to the *afterwards*, I mean the Transfiguration. But why should not Jesus, this once, have half drawn the veil? However that may be, what is noteworthy in the Synoptics is this effort to preserve the story of Jesus in its historical *chiaroscuro*, to keep it human, in spite of the clarity of the light that now flooded their belief. The writing of the Gospels was an act of resistance, all through, to the belief of their authors, involving as it did a diminution which would have been most improbable in a work of legend.

SOME DOUBTFUL PASSAGES

My method of examining the implicit may make it possible, I think, to get over a number of difficulties.

Consider first the still delicate question raised by criticism, that of interpolation. A critic like Loisy is continually concerned with it; he believed he was able to detect the work of the 'maximizer', who to a passage originally containing very little doctrine would have added, in the form of glosses eventually incorporated in the text, verses that indicated the development of faith. There is no denying that if we set the three first Gospels side by side we find that a writer adds to a primitive fact, or sometimes subtracts from it, either to allay scandal, to avoid an undesirable interpretation, or to make the Saviour's words benefit from experience acquired in the course of the Church's earliest vicissitudes. There are, in a sense, traces, in the drawing up of the Gospel, of an initial pruning, correlation and elucidation. There is nothing surprising in this. It is a difficult task, never likely to be completed, to detect with certainty, on particular points, the precise nature of this earliest editorial work.

But what we need to discover is whether it affects the substance of the Gospel tradition, whether it adds any element, essentially new, which would not have had a place in the original teaching of Jesus, or in the immediate inferences that could have been drawn from that teaching. In the opinion of the critical school, it does; therefore everything on principle is presumed to be added and interpolated which magnifies the Messiah and make him equal to God. The proof, which in any similar case would be considered essential, would obviously be the discovery (not impossible today) of a text older than the Gospels and not containing the interpolations. In the absence of such a proof we have to be content with guess-work; and very personal guess-work at that, since the guesser cannot impose it on other exegetes, even those of his own school.

In this detailed work, with all its display of subtlety, what strikes one chiefly is the flimsiness of the conclusions reached, especially when contrasted with the author's cocksureness. People will be astonished one day at the superficiality of the *method of synopsis* when applied to the Gospels justly called *synoptic*. It is a surface-synopsis, concerned with the details of construction, not a synopsis in depth, penetrating to those vital elements which in the present case (as doubtless in all living nature) are also those that are most real.

I will give an example of this synopsis of the virtual, which (if I were not reluctant to coin new words) might perhaps be called a *loganalysis*.

In connection with the incident of the man with palsy, found in the oldest Gospel tradition, Loisy pointed out that Christ's forgiveness of sins belongs more naturally to the cycle of Christian ideas than to the teaching of Jesus; hence the probability of an editorial addition, one that would turn an extraordinary cure into a theological proof. Now let us examine this theory from the standpoint we have now adopted.

To maintain the probability of theological touching-up, one would have to prove the existence of a general touching-up in *all* the passages judged *equally* suspect in the earliest version. In the case of the forgiveness of the man with palsy, to be justified in supposing an interpolation I should have to find something similar in other passages of which the content is implicitly equivalent. Then I might well be able to identify the work of a theological editor, correcting a source which he judged too colourless by adding the little difference which exalts the Messiah to the level of God.[1]

From the point of view of a synopsis in depth, the fact that the assertions are so numerous entirely alters the probability of interpolation. It is quite impossible (as no one denies) that in *all* the texts that I have examined there has been either interpolation or a re-editing of the kind that affects what I have called the 'implicit fact'. Some might think they were the work of second century fabulation, but if so they would have to have been fabulated *en bloc*. Of course it simplifies the problem to provide a *fabulator*, for then there is no need to bother about finding an *interpolator*. It is like the procedure of the believer who rejects *a priori* all interpolation but makes no objection to an inaccurate editor.

It is because all these passages—as Jews and Judaic Christians would have recognized at the back of their minds—admit equivalently an implicit divinity, that I am not for rejecting any of them on the ground that divinity is asserted too deliberately. I do not say that some particular passage may not reveal a *development*, or that its appearance in this form should not be post-dated. But what I do say is, that from the critic's point of view the operation then loses much of its interest. If the content of the account of the Judgement is equivalent to that of the incident of the man with palsy, and if the account of the Judgement is admittedly authentic, why be so suspicious of the man with palsy, an episode which taken by itself is not improbable and shows no stylistic trace of re-touching? Since what I am considering is *all the equivalences taken together*, I can afford to abandon any one of these passages; in this or that case I

---

[1] For instance, in the *Matthew logion* concerning the 'general judgement', it would be required to prove: either that it is absent in the primitive source, or (what is impossible here without rendering the text meaningless) that the idea of the Messiah' judgement of mankind has been superadded. Loisy himself remarks that 'the idea of judgement carried out in the manner of a grand assize, presided over by the heavenly Father and the Son of God, [is] not foreign to the Gospel tradition' (*Mark* viii 38 *Matt.* x 32-3; *Luke* ix 26).

have no prejudices at all against Loisy's reasoning. But my concern for the *synoptic*, which means I have no need for *all* the texts, counsels me not to reject any one of them for the *sole* reason that it asserts too much. What I keep my eye on is their collective aspect and what Pascal would have called their 'harmony'. This harmony would be unaffected if a single violin stopped playing.

For instance, it has long been customary to regard as an interpolation the passage in *Luke* and *Matthew* where Jesus confesses to the Father that he is the Son, simply on the grounds, as I have said, that the assertion is not in the tone of the primitive tradition. An argument of this sort has some validity in a system of superficial synopsis, but it cannot be long maintained when one is using the method of synopsis in depth. This aims at distinguishing the virtual content of texts, and in this particular content it cannot fail to recognize the equivalent for an assertion of sonship. After this, there is no declaring impossible that an express affirmation could not occur elsewhere in the Gospel, seeing that it is virtual in a number of other places. The unusual novelty of the passage is not in the assertion itself but in the expression of it.

Does the passage concerning the mutual knowledge of Father and Son contain in substance any more than can be found in previous passages, particularly those concerning 'my Father' and 'your Father'? In a sense, yes, because it implies a unique and mutual familiarity. But you have only to reflect on what is implied in the relationship of 'Son of unique kind' to 'Father of unique kind' to see that this relationship, itself unique in kind, includes the idea of mutual knowledge. I suggest that in these circumstances the possibility emerges that Jesus, having *hinted* in so many ways at the sonship that was the very foundation of his being, took occasion *just once* to assert it quite explicitly.

H

V

THE RESULTS OF REFLECTION ON THE FACTS

EMERGENCE IN THE JEWISH MIND OF BELIEF IN DIVINITY: THE DOUBLE THEOLOGICAL PROBLEM

LET us take it, then, that what was virtually taught by Jesus of Nazareth was his own divinity.

To the Jew this was something certainly strange, almost impossible to assimilate, a conclusion unthinkable and yet necessary.

We could say that the idea we now express in our abstract language as 'the divinity of Jesus' was that to which the thought of the authentic witnesses was tending; it was the boundary (in the geometrical sense) of their thinking. Only this accounts for the way they acted without fully understanding what they did. But this explanation of their conduct was veiled from them at first. They could not yield to it instantly without hesitation, because they had too many ideas and beliefs that contradicted it. Perhaps experience most of all. Here was a man whose company they had shared for years: how hard to raise him above the human condition! Most of their recollections could be explained, strictly speaking, by the idea that Jesus was the Messiah. Was not the Messiah of Israel set utterly apart, foreordained to appear in the world as the 'son of God'? All these anticipations fitted the history of Jesus, his life and Passion and Resurrection.

But the idea of the Jesus-Messiah who was no *more* than the Messiah—a super-creature but a creature none the less—was bound to seem inadequate as time went on. It gave place to a new idea, one that was almost inexpressible in Jewish concepts.

The sentiments which Jesus inspired—security under his protection; divine presence, purity, and purification; the impression of being drawn into intimacy yet deprived of that intimacy; a powerful attraction, counterbalanced by feelings of reverence and awe; the idea of being absolutely good yet possessing the power to damn everlastingly—all this complex of sentiment, familiar and yet *numinous*, was precisely that which emanated from Javé. It is easy to distinguish between ideas, less so between sentiments. In the hearts of his disciples Jesus aroused the same emotions as the living and eternal God.

And yet it was impossible to assimilate Jesus to God.

These two conflicting demands were a source of mental embarrassment and inward division, the beginnings, perhaps, of acute distress.

What questions could arise, making it necessary once for all to shatter the old moulds and invent not only a new kind of language but also states of the soul such as human nature had never yet known, such as had 'never entered into the heart of man'! Was there no way of harmonizing the divinity of Jesus with the divinity of the Father? If Jesus was God, did this necessarily involve a breach of the divine unity? Had he claimed to absorb all divinity? He proclaimed himself the Son; therefore, if he was God, he could not, one would say, be God in the same way as the Father was God. To present the problem in equational form, one would have to say: However distinct in his relation of 'Sonship', Jesus is equal to a Being who can have no equal. This, at the least, introduces a dualism into the first Being, unless this necessary unity admits of some restriction. What mysteries, here, to be confronted by Jewish and then by Greek thought, then by all thought until the end of time! Mysteries not due to any lack of speculation, but present, deeply involved, like the coherent incompatibilities offered us by the sciences, in the very facts themselves.

It is not an intellectual process we have here. It is not the imagination of the metaphysician at work, inventing a second principle in the first Being, like the dialectician when he needs a second term to express the fecundity of the first or to bridge the gulf between the first principle and the cosmos. It is the realities involved in the history and sayings of Jesus that force the question: is there *duality in unity?* Plato, and a number of philosophers before him, might have declared that fundamentally being was *one and many*. Philo, and plenty of mystics before him, might have conceived the idea of a *mediator*. But these, for the moment, have nothing to do with it. Neither Jesus nor his companions philosophized like this. Here were minds without training in abstract thought, having at their disposal none but religious ideas of an extrenely concrete and positive order.

Philosophies, those of Greece and Alexandria, might later transform the primitive beliefs, but their language was a different stuff from the concrete fact to which the witnesses gave testimony. They might also be helpful to the minds of those who were strangers to the primitive Jewish background, aiding them, perhaps, to grasp and express what the earliest Christians had experienced. The more men came to recognize that the Gospel was universal, the more they had to recognize that, though expressing himself in the language of Israel, Jesus was also speaking to humanity at large; that, corresponding to the Jewish and official preparation, there was also an expectation, of an obscurer order, among all the peoples of the world. And though the elements used to express the divinity of Jesus were taken from the Messianic tradition, stretched to its extreme limits, it might be that the language of the pagans, inadequate though it was, might sometimes be more direct and effective.

A number of modern critics have sought to explain the success of Christianity in the Mediterranean area by pointing out that in the primitive Christian cult—in the theology of St Paul or in some of the ideas of St John (such as that of the *Logos*)—there were elements borrowed from the non-Jewish world. So they talk about a fusion or combination, or even a substitution of doctrines. But is this the only way of looking at it?

The religion of Jesus would never expand beyond the confines of Judaism without finding equivalent expressions to translate what could not be assimilated elsewhere, namely that factual datum which was all it professed to proclaim and adore. When we come to see (what it is impossible not to) the encounter of the fact of faith with the speculations of the philosophers on such subjects as the one, the multiple and the mediator, what we find is attempts, sometimes happy and sometimes not, to express in ancient terms the new and the unique.

To distinguish between the sphere of deep spiritual adherence and that of its expressions, even though the latter, in a sense, were foreign to the primitive Jewish tradition, is not necessarily to conclude that the tradition itself was adulterated or supplanted. In the development of ideas there can often be seen some very minute extraneous element which has proved all that was necessary to crystallize thoughts that were hitherto latent. So far from diverting the thinker from what is deepest in himself, such an influence rather makes for the fullest self-harmony.

How came the companions of Jesus to accept the idea that he was equal to the Father? We cannot tell. If we are to regard the

Johannine writings as the recollections of a privileged witness, seeking to retrace the history of this capital discovery, we may think that Jesus proceeded slowly, in the manner of a teacher, starting from beliefs already accepted, making his own contribution to their existing faith; constantly making hard, uncomprehended statements, but promising the aid to the Spirit to fertilize these seeds. There must have been a moment when there dawned on their minds the intuition of (what was to be called later) 'consubstantiality' with the Father. The account of the conversion of Thomas suggests that with some of the apostles the discovery was sudden, occurring only after a long unconscious process. The same might be said of the two on the way to Emmaus.

There are two ways of reaching one's goal. In flat country at every step you take the outline looms up constantly larger, thus giving the impression of a steady approach. So it is when, traversing the dull corn-fields of the Beauce, one sees the arrow which is Chartres first emerge and shoot skyward. But in the mountains there is no such observed proportion between the road to be trodden and its final destination. The distance grows less, but this is hardly perceptible: the final crest remains shrouded, or the slope blocks the horizon. You know nothing till the final step sets you clean on the summit. Such was the approach of the disciples to the idea that Jesus was equal to the Father, one with the Father; was God himself, as the Father was God. They were moving towards this conclusion without knowing it. One last moment could illuminate all.

Once made, whatever the process, the discovery must have seemed both *old and new*. It was in harmony with the past. But it brought with it riches that were quite impossible to assess immediately.

THE ELEMENT OF CHANCE

I have suggested how it is possible to conjecture *a priori*, going by the analogies of our nature and the development of awareness, the way in which the disciples passed from confused perception to definite belief.

But it is very rarely, one should note, that developments occur as they might or should; chances intervene to retard or hasten them. Two such chances, improbable in themselves, marked the first intellectual developments of Christianity and so enabled it to speed its history.

PAULINISM: ITS ANTECEDENT IMPROBABILITY AND
EXPLOSIVE CHARACTER

I want to consider here these two occurrences in a new way and try to decide to what extent each of these two *improbables* affected the already given seed by modifying its foreseeable and natural development.

Cournot made it a rule to distinguish events that might have been foreseen from those which occurred unexpectedly as the result of some improbable combination of circumstances. Thus the financial crisis of 1789 was probable; the rise of Bonaparte, a chance that no one could possibly have foreseen. It was the same, in her own time, with Joan of Arc.

It is useful to make this distinction between the probable and the improbable, the natural and the fortuitous, the result of causes or laws and the consequences of some extraordinary encounter or the interference of a whole series of events. They are both types of causality; but the second, when it has long-term results, and especially when these further human progress, seems to suggest the intervention of a power other than that of purely natural causality.

Several improbable conjunctions of this second sort are to be found in the beginnings of Christianity.

I say nothing here of the improbability of Jesus himself. His history (whether the Gospel version or even more the version given by the critical sceptic) strikes every mind, of whatever school, as typically improbable, if the test of improbability is disproportion between the slightness of an event and its subsequent outcome.

But I can examine what is *a priori* probable and improbable in the two remarkable intellectual events that followed so soon after the appearance of Jesus and are still largely connected in the knowledge we have of him: I mean the Pauline *preaching* and the Johannine *meditation*. I do not know whether a study of this sort has ever been attempted. All I propose to do here is to sketch an outline of it.

I am going to imagine myself a kind of demiurge, with the power to cause events and bring about rare and improbable encounters. I start with that group of apostles, the first believers in Jesus. But I require something more; there must intervene, I decide, some influence parallel and exterior to this group. My idea is a man of the same race and education whom I represent as suddenly converted. There is nothing improbable in this. After a successful revolution there often emanates from the victorious party a subtle influence which affects even its opponents: hatred may also be a cloak for admiration. As violent passions may well turn to their opposites, conversion is quite conceivable in a fervent opponent: the persecutor turns proselytizer. In the nineteenth century, Ratisbon is an example of such a conversion. But what is the probability of such an ally's being useful to the Cause? There is every likelihood of his proving a fanatic: totalitarian, narrow-minded, unamenable to discipline, one from whom to expect trouble rather than service. He would be distrusted himself, however valuable his conversion for purposes of propaganda. What is abnormal in Paul's case is that this reformed persecutor turned out to have one of the best organized minds, the best trained and most practical of any of his time, and yet had a genius for self-subordination.

That this privileged soul should have had a better understanding of the essence of the new faith is not, to me, in the least surprising, for I have taken the precaution to endow him with genius. On entering a strange house outsiders will go straight to its essential feature, often perceived only vaguely by the children of the house, the habitual disciples.

But the major improbability lies elsewhere. It is that such personal thought should have been accepted so rapidly by communities not dependent upon Paul and founded before his time, communities, too, in which an important official party, that which derived from Jerusalem, was actually hostile to him. What is so improbable is that Paul could have expressed the doctrine of the Hellenic Christians and set such a highly personal stamp on the teaching of Jesus without ever appearing to the original apostles in the light of a visionary or the first of the Reformers. St Paul, it is true, encountered opposition; it was due to various causes: to his violence and acuteness, possibly also to the asperity of his temperament; but never to his doctrine.

Is this a complete improbability?
It can be reduced to the normal scale in two different ways.
Following the mythical school one can say that Paul's message was simply Christianity: that he had no need to pay attention to an earlier tradition, which was either non-existent or else unformed and thoroughly malleable. This being the case there is no difficulty at all in effecting a reconciliation, since there are not two terms but only one. Or if there are two, one could say that the second (namely the Gospel) is only a translation, an epiphenomenon of Paulinism.

To maintain this position it is necessary to ignore those passages in the *Epistles* in which Paul refers to facts in the life of Jesus; also the whole book of the *Acts*, which shows Paul introduced to a pre-existing society. It is necessary, moreover, to swallow the extreme improbability of a religion being influenced by an intruder when it had *already* been founded by an event held divine and was *already* an institution which its faithful adherents recognized as divine. 'Christians' undoubtedly existed before Paul, otherwise he would not have been in a position to persecute them. The most important communities (those of Jerusalem, Ephesus, and Rome) owed nothing to him for their foundation and doctrine, even though in him they became fully self-conscious. Paul himself makes it clear, when telling the story of his life, that in spite of the revelation he had received he was always at pains to make his Gospel conform to that of the officials of the Church, lest the course he had taken should prove, as he said, 'useless'.

The correspondence of Paul's (subjective) strain with the (objective) strain of Peter is itself highly improbable—unless we admit that both of these strains derive from the same source, which would thus be the cause and guarantee of correspondence.[1]

My genetic explanation has the effect of reducing the antecedent improbability of Paul's intervention, since the relationship of Peter to Paul (*Peter* standing here for the Jerusalemite tradition) is that of the virtual to the actual, of facts already possessed to a more adequate expression of them.

But the coincidence of Paul's *intuition*, so sudden and flashing, with the slow *induction* of the communities and earliest propagators, the adherence, to both induction and intuition, of minds so socially and intellectually different, not to mention the mutual reinforcement of the two processes—all this amounts to an extremely remote chance.

Its consequences are so vast (since Christian theology has largely depended on it) that one can hardly help thinking it the first and most remarkable of the secondary events that were to stamp for ever the future development of Christianity. It was an event, as I have said, of the intellectual order, not necessarily involving any forces of illumination. It can be explained, strictly speaking, as an intuition of genius analogous to that of the great mystics, though

---

[1] In the same way Descartes, astonished at the correspondence between geometrical space and arithmetical understanding, which he saw as the guarantee of analytical geometry, sought the cause of it in a transcendent and creative truth.

more intense than the loftiest of all such intuitions. Genius consisted here in seeing the implications of what was already in existence.

Sooner or later, it is true, and in one form or another, these consequences would have been deduced, and what was *equivalent* to Paulinism discovered, by a succession of 'doctors' in later ages. It may even be supposed that, once the Hellenic Christians had *thought out* their existence, they would have arrived at a doctrine not very unlike Paul's. But here time is everything. For the propagation of Christianity it was most important that this explosive development should not be too long delayed, that it should even be *anticipated*. It was vastly improbable, but also an enormous advantage, that the conclusion drawn from the implicit principles should be presented with clarity, in terms that were no less Hellenic than Jewish, and without their acceptance having to depend on previous adherence to Judaism.

It is in this character of anticipation, with at the same time such remarkable energy of propagation, that the improbability of Paul seems to me to consist.

THE DOCTRINE OF PAUL

It has its setting outside time, in the eternal plan. The drama of the life and death of Jesus is a single moment in a vast design; that already contemplated in the divine predestination. On the road to Damascus God *revealed to him his Son so that he could proclaim him to the nations.* Thus he attains in an instant what for the rest had been the result of long parturition. Instead of scaling the pyramid he was—if we may so describe it—parachuted to its summit. What he was able to grasp better than the others, enclosed as they were in the time-element and perceiving Jesus according to Jewish categories very strictly interpreted, was that the 'sonship' of Jesus was an overwhelming fact which could result in nothing short of a *total* renewal of the religion of Moses. This was the viewpoint of 'Christianity'. Christ had come: with Christ, God's design (known hitherto to man only in its preparations, antitheses, and foreshadowings) was now at last discernible. Henceforth the task of thought was clear: if it would reproduce and reflect the order of being, whether stable or moving (and in fact it is both: apparently moving because it is in process of unfolding, stable because the unfolding reveals an eternal design)—if it would do this, it must first establish itself in Christ. And it is the same for the realm of action:

man's task is to co-operate in this restoration of all things in
Jesus Christ, since the aim of God is once and for ever to join All
to Christ, as to a nuclear principle, co-ordinating, ultimate, and
capital.

Thus Christ is seen as the foundation and envelopment of the
whole system of the spiritual world, as the image of the invisible
God, the firstborn of all creation, through whom and for whom All
has been constituted, who by his incarnation of obedience, which
extended even to death on the cross, pacified and reconciled All.
Did Paul say expressly that Christ was God? The fact has been
disputed, but unless he believed that he was, the fundamentals of
his thought are unintelligible.

Here is a dialectic analogous (though wholly different in form
and as opposite as can be conceived) to that which I thought I
discovered in the Synoptics and in the earliest discourses in the *Acts*.
Here, as there, the word 'divinity' is not obtruded: the monotheistic
inheritance made it impossible. But Paul cannot avoid attributing
to Jesus all the attributes of God; all, that is, except radical identity:
that would make Jesus the first Principle, which Paul, as a Jew,
could not think of as anything but unique, not communicable. Paul,
in short, a product of Jewish orthodoxy, had attained to knowledge
of God, like every Western mind, by the rational process which
ends in 'attributing' to God every high human quality, but in an
infinite, absolute, and exclusive degree. God is the sole Powerful,
the sole Enduring, the Eternal; the sole Good, the sole Just, the
sole Being. . . But it so happens that this exclusiveness, infinity, and
perfection belong to Jesus also. The necessity to admit it can be seen
operating in the discourses in the *Acts*. It can be seen in the vision at
Damascus. When Paul thinks of Christ he conceives him as possessing the same kind of power as God. It only remained to draw the
conclusion, in some sort scandalous, impossible to express. It is a
radical conclusion: one is driven to accept it. There are a number of
expressions used by Paul that are very near, almost *equivalent*, to the
assertion of divinity, though considered separately they may not
amount to so much. It is the same with love: there are avowals we
dare not make, though we make them in forms that could be interpreted as no more than expressions of politeness or civility; though
together they speak so plainly to the heart to whom they are
addressed that it scarcely matters whether the words 'I love you'
have been said. Except possibly in one passage, where the punctua-
tion has been contested (*Rom.* ix 5), St Paul does not say expressly

that Christ is God. But everywhere he clearly allows it to be understood, and his thought cannot be unified or understood otherwise.

It may well be wondered if Paul did not stamp with his own personality the conclusions he allowed to be drawn. The fact is that there are, as it were, two Paulinisms: that which is simply the immanent development of the initial data and would have emerged *sooner or later* even if Paul had never existed; this might be called the *canonical* Paulinism. But there is another, more original Paulinism, which could be described as *deuterocanonical*; it is the expression of Paul's own thought. This goes beyond what he contributed officially. The distinction is not peculiar to Paul. In all the doctors and orthodox mystics there can be discerned what can be called an official element, something that can take its place in the texture of Catholic development; but also an original element, which has not received the same approbation, and sometimes, in the case of doctors not inspired, has even been set aside.

THE JOHANNINE CONTRIBUTION: ITS IMPROBABILITY.
HISTORY AND THEOLOGY

I have laid stress on the antecedent improbability of Paulinism. Let us see now whether the Johannine Gospel shows a similar characteristic.

It is a work that appears normal enough if we see in it simply the clash of two cultures, the Jewish and the Greek; all the more so in view of the fact that the Johannine school dates from the end of the first century at the earliest; it is not, like the thought of Paul, almost contemporary with the events. But the improbability of 'John' is due to another characteristic of his writing, namely the combination, in which he is so original, of history and theology. This feature has been equally striking to ancient and modern readers and it is still an almost unexplainable riddle. The writings of St Paul are of the kind to be expected: there is nothing surprising in the occurrence so early of a Christian 'gnosis'. But what is, I maintain, strange, is the association of such a gnosis with the 'facts of Jesus', when it did not proceed from them.

The improbability lies here not in the mysticism of the writings, in all the theology they contain, but in the equal value they attach to theology and history. There is no ignoring in John's Gospel a certain tendency to stylization and symbolism, perhaps even alle-

gory and sacred arithmology. But what is remarkable is that at
many points this is a more circumstantial Gospel, more exact in its
topography; and though here more than anywhere else Jesus is
God, yet his portrait is no less human. Here he acts as God from the
very beginning. He comes straight from heaven without any description of his birth and childhood, which are represented solely by his
mother. Already his miracles reveal his glory: we feel it is immanent,
ready to appear at any moment. His parables, even his miracles,
have also a spiritual meaning linked to the mystery of his being, the
mystery of his mission, which is to lead us to the Father and to
complete fulfilment in unity with the Father. Nothing ever happens
without his permission and foreknowledge. Even in his Passion his
reign has *already* begun.

Between this and the accounts of the other evangelists there is no
fundamental contradiction. One might even say that if Christ is
really God, which is what the primitive Gospels suggest, then the
Gospel according to John has the greater verisimilitude. The real
obscurity in the others lies in the fact that a being so sublime as he
had so little to say of his own transcendence, that he should have
buried his teaching under cover of 'parables', that he should have
made himself a subject of conjecture, that his sun should have
emitted so very few rays. Here, on the other hand, though there is
even more mystery, we can understand better. Astonishing as it
seems, though the Gospel of John claims to be the testimony of a
disciple who had actually seen and felt, it has more the air of an
experience of pure faith without any personal intimacy. To us the
synoptic Gospels seem more *factual*; but they provide less life-giving
nourishment for faith. As Loisy said once: 'I use the first three
Gospels to tell me about the Saviour, the fourth to explain him.'

There can be endless speculation about the extent to which the
Johannine writings contain the actual words used by Jesus and how
much they represent a first development of his words. It is a problem that will never be completely solved. In the discourses of Jesus
there may be an interweaving of the actual words used with sayings
reported merely to give their sense, translated into more theological
language than Jesus was accustomed to use; or again they may be
the words of an editor, following those of the Master and serving as
a kind of initial commentary.

There is no contesting the fact that on the matter we are now
considering this Gospel expresses in clear and distinct terms what
the Synoptics had only suggested and implied: *My Father and I are*

one. A complete doctrine of the Church derives from this one statement. If Jesus is a man, he is only a model, a hero; we may add, of
course, the most perfect of men, of heroes and sages. But if he is God,
what there exists in common between him and his followers is
something of a wholly different order, to be identified only as the
relationship between the Uncreated and human minds. It is this
that is apparent in the 'discourse after the Supper', where the words
of a parting friend to those he leaves behind are interwoven with
expressions best fitted to define the nature of divine immanence.

Paulinism, fundamentally, tended to the same conclusion. But
John would seem to know nothing of Paul. Was it possible he was
unaware of his existence? Might he have criticized him, perhaps,
on some minor point without actually naming him? It happens
sometimes that a pair of powerful and lonely minds, desirous of
preserving the originality of their respective thought, believe themselves more in conflict than they really are. Posterity can reconcile
Bossuet and Fénelon, Manning and Newman. . . The Johannine
writings have all the appearance of a final judgement passed by a
definitive authority on the primitive traditions. Judgement does
not imply condemnation. The Johannine authority corrects only
details; fundamentally it criticizes in the purest sense of the word:
it completes and sums up. It has sublimer lights to shed, privileged
memories none other could supply, enriched by reflections to which
the Spirit has contributed. Christ's unity with his Father is here
expressed in plainer terms than in St Paul, where sometimes Christ
might be simply a mediator, unique in kind, exalted to the highest
rank by God. The title given him in the Epistle to the Colossians,
'the firstborn of all creatures', seemed to John inadequate; Jesus
Christ, for him, is the only-begotten Son. He is the Word, through
whom everything was made; he who became flesh and dwelt among
us. The words *Son* and *Word* must be taken as mutually enlighten-
ing: Son would imply a too great difference; what is more, subordination, inconceivable in equality. *Logos*, which means 'reason'
as well as 'word', would suggest too much of immanence, for our
word, and even our reason, are indistinguishable from our person.
All this would presently become clearer still, when human thought
came to study what it names, perhaps too arithmetically, the
Trinity.

Momentarily the Son has absented himself from the Father with
whom he is identified. He returns to his Father after suffering, but
only as a God can suffer, not so much by the extenuation as by the

occultation of his glory. For the Jews (perhaps for every thinking man) this was of all truths the hardest to accept, but for John it was the supreme truth, the only one capable of explaining Christ, his coming, his work, his acts of institution and sanctification. John felt that the Messiah, however sublime, was still only a man, separating us from God rather than helping us to draw near him, since his own very excellence, incapable of attaining divinity, keeps us aware of the abyss that separates us also from God. There is less fear of God than of a divine or deified being; there is none with whom it is possible to be more at ease than God. If, as John says in his Epistle, God is love, we are certainly more at ease with him than with ourselves! By insisting on the unity of Jesus and the Father, John brought the Messiah closer to humanity by that infinite distance which was yet so easily, so divinely bridged, as was proved by the incarnation of Jesus, by his history, his sacrifice and his subsequent appearances.

It is the incarnation that is the fundamental idea of his theology. It was also, and equivalently, the intuition of St Paul. But in Paul's writings the reasoning is that of a mystic who was both a theologian and an organizer. In John it is Another than John who is speaking of himself; initiating us into the mystery of his being; revealing the secrets of the Father and the Spirit; One who has not wholly left eternity, the 'Father's bosom', which is his real dwelling-place, even as man.

Though it is more or less irrelevant to the design of this book, it would be interesting to gauge the probability that what so far, following normal usage, I have called 'John' was really a person or only a school, and if a person whether he was a privileged witness. Internal evidence will never provide demonstrative certainty. One can, however, say that the earlier the date of these writings (as established by external criteria, palaeography for instance), the harder it will be to reject summarily the ancient and generally accepted tradition that identifies the author with the son of Zebedee, sole survivor of the Twelve at the end of the first century. For who else, so near the beginnings, would have had the authority so freely to deepen and complete the Gospel Tradition, in its major lines as in many details, and express it in a new way? Who else would have escaped being held as an innovator by communities so clearly suspicious of innovation? That is why, after carefully considering all the factors, I find it easier to imagine an aged Apostle surrounded by his *gnorimoi*, than a group of theologians belatedly inventing a myth of the Beloved Disciple.[1]

This, however, is merely parenthetical. To return to the relationship of John to the Synoptics: if it were not for the latter, we might think the author of the last Gospel was describing a particular revelation, analogous to that of Damascus though more circumstantial, and was expressing it in the guise of fiction. But this would be hard to maintain, even if John's Gospel stood alone, because it would mean supposing, in this prophet of a recent past, a faculty of *historical visualization* which no known mystic has ever possessed. Cases are quoted of historical visionaries like Catherine Emmerich, but she (assuming she was genuine) already had knowledge of the Gospels on which her imagination embroidered arabesques: her 'visioning' was all in the same *sense* as the Gospels. For the Johannine author, with his passion for Truth, for Testimony based on actual feeling with the hands, to create a work of that sort would be the very type of mystification, the essence of false evidence. The answer to this, I know, will be that the words 'truth', 'vision', 'testimony', have not for the mystic an historical meaning. But it is not as a mystic that John is speaking: he says he has actually *seen*, and the whole of his Gospel suggests the idea of what we now call historical truth.

We can go farther. Let us grant for the moment that for a symbolic mystic, and an oriental at that, this is not 'false testimony' but simply a literary *genre*, 'historical' only in appearance. One would then have to suppose that this mystic was in possession of very precise knowledge about a whole number of quite accidental matters that were entirely useless to his purpose. Renan, who was always shrewd, remarked on his return from the Holy Land that

[1] In a passage preserved by Eusebius, the presbyters of Clement of Alexandria state that John, at the prompting of his intellectual disciples (the *gnorimoi*) and divinely inspired by the Spirit, was the last to *make* (not *write*) a spiritual Gospel, after observing that the 'corporal things' of the Lord had been set forth already in the other Gospels.

Ph. H. Menoud, after presenting in turn all the current hypotheses concerning St John's Gospel, concludes his all but exhaustive study as follows: 'In short, John goes to work with the sovereign independence of one who might say: '*La tradition, c'est moi!*' At the end of the apostolic age there was only one man left who could have spoken thus.' Since the publication (in 1935) of the fragments known as *Papyrus Egerton 2*, which contain textual quotations from John's Gospel and are assigned by palaeographers to the first half of the second century, we have a *positive* proof, admitted even by Bultmann, that the Gospel dates from the end of the first century. See Menoud, *L'Evangile de Jean d'après les recherches récentes*, pp. 8 and 77.

the precise reference to Cana, a quite obscure village, would have been of no interest at all to Hellenic Christians, living in Asia Minor in the second century, if there had not been some memory attaching to the place. 'John's Gospel is full of indifferent, one might say irrelevant circumstances... Nothing could be less like the adventures of an abstract personification; it is not thus that India writes her lives of Krishna, or relates the incarnations of Vishnu.' Moreover, just as I did for the virtual Gospel of divinity which I extracted from the Synoptics, Renan finds 'singular circumstances without any apparent significance'. The works of Father Lagrange are a strong confirmation of this aspect of John's Gospel.[1]

The Johannine writings have very much the air of being associated with some privileged source of revelation, but not a source lying apart from the companions of Jesus. The witness makes no pretence of having heard secret words, *arcana verba*, uttered to himself alone. He boasts, though always humbly, of a special friendship which placed him closer to his subject: he was simply an intimate witness, not the depositary of a secret.

Now this complex and improbable character of the Gospel agrees very well with the conclusions I drew from my examination of the Synoptics. There were, I granted, in the teaching of Jesus a number of premises with no conclusion; but they could not fail, I maintained, to lead to a conclusion in any mind, or group of minds, with an aptitude for deduction. There is no reason for not supposing that one among the Twelve may have been abler to draw the latent conclusions, more quickly than the rest, if not immediately.

So in this light, especially at the end of the first century, the Johannine attitude looks less improbable than the Pauline preaching. It is in continuity with the Synoptics, it completes them. The improbability of the Johannine Gospel lies not so much in its matter as in its art, in the perfection of its form, so human yet so divine. But this art itself appears less extraordinary, even from the purely aesthetic standpoint, if we admit the possibility of the Incarnation.

[1] In his *Légendes hagiographiques*, Delahaye observes that topographical exactitude i no proof of historical truth: forgers are sometimes very precise topographers (p. 253) But John, as Father Lagrange seems to have established, mentioned new places, which contradicted those accepted (and very confidently) before; also that these, more probable in themselves, have been confirmed by recent discoveries made nineteen centuries after the writing of the Gospel. It is hard to see what motive a second century fabulator would have had for upsetting the faithful by modifying their evangelical topography. He would surely rather have respected the topographical facts that were already traditional (see *Revue biblique*, July 1937, p. 33).

From the point of view of faith, the art of John ceases to be one of reconstruction: it is simply an art of remembering, though to remember in such a way certainly calls for reflection and spiritual understanding. For anyone who would prolong the line of St Paul's thinking, Christ would be a 'celestial' rather than an earthly being. What John seeks to show is that Jesus is human, flesh and blood, even though also eternal and pre-existent. In this respect he adds considerably to St Paul, because he makes us touch, even feel (as it were) with the spirit, the historical *reality* of the *eternal Son* of God.

It would be possible, no doubt, in these two thinkers of the Incarnation, to distinguish other differences of the sort: differences, I mean, of 'lighting' and accent. It is always hard, when understanding depends on sensibility, to allow the same weight to two different viewpoints that cannot be associated: Paul looks more at the work achieved in time, humiliation, and mediation; John sees rather the immanence of time in sovereign and static eternity.

Moreover to me, John, though half a century later than Paul, looks somehow simpler, more rudimentary. The themes are less luxuriant; they are less developed, less logically applied; at the same time they are more intimate, more profound, more mysterious. And this is a contradiction to the law of time, according to which development should be from the simpler to the more complex, from the more germinal to the more expansive. Yet it seems to agree with what is suggested both by tradition and criticism: namely an old surviving witness, surrounded by minds with a theological bent; a witness who possibly knows the work of Paul, who does not correct him, but before his death *deposes* concerning Jesus what he himself has seen and understood.

To sum up: the improbability of Paulinism and the improbability of Johanninism tend ultimately to the absolutely improbable, which is *impossibility*—that is, when the *subject* of their testimony is kept in brackets. It is necessary, then, in the case of Paul, to regard as virtually unintelligible the success of his preaching in the churches founded before his time or independently of him; or else to relegate to the mythical every allusion he makes to the historical Jesus. And in the case of John, if his testimony is rejected and all his narrative regarded as legend, one must suppose the author of this Gospel to have had a taste for the marvellous and a faculty for fabling which took its rise in imposture.

On the other hand, the improbability of Paulinism and Johan-

I

ninism, and the infinitely greater improbability of the agreement between the two on all essential points of faith, immediately disappears the moment we admit that before Paul, as before John, there existed a *memory*, which in a latent fashion contained the doctrine common to both these theologians. Before them, behind them, there was this *x*, a mystery, something that could be translated either by a series of facts or by a system of ideas. Not only so, but behind this mystery, inextricably connected with it, there was a Person, one in whom blended, though in distinct relationships, history and thought, time and eternity, God and man.

But what is this but Christianity, and its seamless robe? So I find myself back, faced again with the same option, simple and all-embracing.

REMARK ON LATER ECCLESIASTICAL DEVELOPMENTS

Such were the earliest reflections on this synoptic datum. These almost immediate developments were part of the initial drive. Paul was in touch with the first apostles. John, whose authority guaranteed the 'Johannine writings', even though in some quarters a difference of accent may have set up resistances, was finally accepted in all the churches where the letters of Paul were already being read. In the second century these two 'theologians' were recognized as not only conforming to the rule of faith but as defining it. The first stage of development was now accomplished.

This primitive and rudimentary development had been brought about *in*, of course, but not *by* the Church. This is what is implied by the words *Testament* and *Canon*, namely a text established by law and therefore fixed for ever. The Church felt that there would be no new light forthcoming, now that the last of the First had died. 'Revelation' had been accomplished; all that remained was to collect the scattered fragments, co-ordinate their different viewpoints, and defend this body of thought against perversion or defacement.

Plenty of questions were still to arise concerning the relationship of Jesus Christ to the Father and the Spirit.

Would it not, for instance, be a correct interpretation of the texts and tradition to say that Christ, the 'firstborn of creation' according to St Paul, was only the most perfect of creatures? Arius held that it was; Athanasius, aided by the Popes, realized that the Church had never believed this. His was the wonderful formula that interprets the Gospel like a theorem: 'The Son possesses his identity with the Father, which he holds of the Father.' At the Council of Nicæa the word 'con-substantial' was applied to the Father to define Jesus Christ: even more than 'co-eternal', it excludes all equivocation. Later it became necessary to be still more exact: the Nestorians were saying that Jesus and the Word in Jesus were two separate but associated entities, whereas Eutyches was maintaining that Jesus and the Word were blended in one single 'nature'. Christian instinct perceived that neither Nestorius nor Eutyches was in the right: the one dissociated too much, the other too little. But new terms were needed to express its thought. They were provided by the Council of Ephesus, and were accepted as the most effective for excluding the errors that threatened to disfigure the original datum. At Chalcedon (451) Christ was defined as having two natures entirely distinct—a *human* nature and a *divine* nature—but *a single person* (or as we should say today a single 'ego'), which is that of the eternal Son of God. There arose later another, more subtle question: whether unity of person did not also involve necessarily unity of will. The will was then associated with the nature (in recognition, no doubt, of the fact of the Agony, where Jesus was seen to be in conflict with himself), and there was added to the definitions of Chalcedon (as against *monothelism*) that there were 'two wills' in Jesus.

It was hard to go farther, impossible to go less far, if the whole initial faith was to be 'saved' and transmitted in the terms of Latin and Greek thought, which are still, and probably always will be, our own.

PART III

RESURRECTION

DIFFICULTIES

THE difficulties to be considered are of two kinds. The first are those connected with the basic fact, local and temporal. When we talk of resurrection, are we thinking of an event similar to the facts investigated by science or history? Is it something real? Or is it a phenomenon occurring merely in consciousness?

The difficulties of the other sort relate to the common idea of resurrection. What is its content? Is it thinkable? What does it mean?

In the impression made on the modern mind by 'resurrection' there can be discerned this double origin of doubts. The first kind secretly feeds upon the second; because the cruder the idea of resurrection appears, the less interest there is in examining the evidence for it.

But the historical difficulty also influences the other. It is a more complex influence, as we shall presently see.

By rights the two difficulties should be studied together; but this being impossible the only thing to do is to examine each in turn, retaining always a remembrance of the one and a presentiment of the other.

I shall begin with what is the most striking difficulty: that arising out of the resemblance of the *fact* to a *legend*.

I

THE ORIGINAL EVENT

THE FIRST HISTORICAL DIFFICULTY:
THE PROBLEM OF ORIGIN AND EMERGENCE

THERE is no doubting that Christianity had an origin. Within the heart of Judaism, we see suddenly appear a number of communities all united in one belief: 'the risen Jesus'. It might even be said that this belief was not only the first fact but the first prism. It was due to this that Jesus was remembered. It was looking back *across* his resurrection that men came to reflect on the Gospel and re-live it. It was not till Jesus had risen that he could be *preached*. This was a fact never stated but presupposed.

Whether it was a *real fact or a subjective idea*, this fact or idea emerged. One moment it was not there, the next moment it was. Here once again we have to face that difficult problem of origin. Every origin is sudden, therefore incomprehensible. The human mind would reduce its essential character, seek antecedent states, ante-date the origin. It would like, at least, to see a continuance of earlier elements; it would like the original being, before being, *to have been*.

When dealing with the Resurrection, which there is no denying was made manifest all of a sudden, this tendency of the human mind becomes extremely active. But it is impossible here to put one's finger on sources, antecedents, or preparations. We are faced with a fact (or else an idea) entirely original in character. Nowhere, in the historical documents, do we witness a long-drawn-out genesis of the Resurrection. It was not; then it was. The utmost one can say is that before his death Jesus told his disciples he would rise again. But what proof is there that his prediction, which in any case was not understood at the time, was not added afterwards?

For the historian, it is what I propose to call a *mystic, para-normal event*. I call it an *event* without being able to say whether it is real or fictitious. Here all I mean by 'event' is the emergence of something that was not there before. I call it a *mystic* event to show that it is full of significance and can be completely meaningful only to a religious consciousness. Finally I call it *para-normal* (and not *miraculous*) so as to leave the question open whether a supernatural cause is necessary to explain it. This definition has the advantage of not begging the question, and also of fitting the first appearance of the fact.

AN INDUCTIVE RECONSTRUCTION OF THE ORIGINAL
PHENOMENON

I am now going to try to decide *a priori* what ought to be the characteristics of this paranormal historical event.

I am supposing I know nothing of the Gospel accounts of the Resurrection. All I know is the history of Jesus down to his Passion. The next thing I learn is the first development of the Church and the success of its propaganda. Between the *life of Jesus* and the *birth of Christianity* there is a hole. And I have no idea how to fill it. I am supposing always that no one has ever told me what the preaching of the apostles was all about and that I have never even heard the word 'resurrection'. So what I have to do is to decide what to make of this singular gap. How was it filled? How am I to make intelligible the transition from Jesus living, then dead, to what may be called the religion of Jesus. I am ignorant, remember, of all the latter part of the Gospel where the 'resurrection' is described. I also place in brackets everything to do with miracles. I am considering only the person of Jesus.

All I can say, I think, is what is implied by the statement that the personality of Jesus gave rise in his time to a religious movement. That seems to be the minimum: what must necessarily be accepted and cannot possibly be denied, at any rate if we are dealing with the subject historically.

Nor could a historian reasonably reject the death of Jesus, and therefore the total failure of his mission. This would stand even though the actual accounts of the Passion were all mistaken as to date and circumstances, about the authorities that condemned him, and the mode of punishment. This punishment, in itself, agrees with what we know about the customs of the age; it involves no sort of miraculous intervention; if it is doubted, is any historical fact to be believed?

But this gives rise to a by no means trifling intellectual difficulty. The death of a human being, however extraordinary, and even though he had founded a powerful party or sect, cannot possibly explain this explosion of faith, this sudden enlightenment, this rapid and fruitful spreading of belief, which is what we see in the earliest days of Christianity. Again, whether we are dealing with a fact or a myth, I cannot help observing a sudden and almost explosive emergence. An *explosion* is the best description of a strange phenomenon that is both brief, intense, and widely dispersed. The difficulty is just this, that like a firework display the explosion has been repeated time and again in Western history, causing the outbreak of new fires, the kindling of new 'set-pieces'. What could have happened? I am going to pretend ignorance. I look at the explosion, and considering this and nothing else I ask what could have caused it, what sort of a projector, what kind of chemicals.

As has been remarked by critics of the extreme school, all that can be stated with complete certainty about Jesus is that after a short career he died, and that he died by violence after a judicial process. Also that his manner of death was regarded by the Jews as infamous.

Between this death-failure and the rebirth of faith there must have occurred some mysterious fact which I want to define, as I have said, *a priori*.

If the memory of failure was not an obstacle to the spreading of faith, there must, I maintain, have been a devaluing and transfiguring of this tragic story, and in such a way that an argument against could be made an argument in favour. To use Nietzsche's expression, what was needed was a 'transvaluation of values', so that what would have been fatal to any belief in Jesus could become the principle of a new faith in this very same Jesus. I therefore conclude that the only intelligible way to explain the transition from the *death of Jesus* to the *origin of Christianity*, is to suppose there must have occurred, however we describe it, a sort of 're-living' for Jesus. To be more explicit, I would say there must have been an experience (whether it were subjective, mystic, or factual) vivid enough to leave no doubt; therefore *at least* as intense as had been the experience, so vivid in all its details, of the Passion.

I write the words *life-triumph* in opposition to *death-failure*. If I dispense with the term 'resurrection', I shall use these two words as its equivalent.

This experience of the 're-living' of Jesus, something that could impart a new value to his death, was indispensable if the original Gospel were to be usable and intelligible. I say 'usable', because if the death of Jesus were considered from the Jewish point of view it would be impossible not to see it as a curse. Was it not written in the Scriptures: 'There is a curse on the man who hangs on a gibbet'? Crucifixion was regarded by Jewish tradition as a solemn declaration that he who suffered it was condemned by God. Therefore in the eyes of the Jews, always so watchful for signs, the death of Jesus proved him a false prophet. The greater he appeared before, in the eyes of his companions and contemporaries, the more he was utterly annihilated afterwards. One may even think that the spectacle of the cross, serving in some sort to block out their memory, was a source of a real mental disturbance for those who had known Jesus. Imagine a husband, whose wife has been faithful for years, being presented with irrefutable proof of her infidelity; or a loyal lieutenant, worshipping his leader, yet obliged to conclude he was a traitor. . . After what had happened on the cross, for the disciples to recover their faith in Jesus, something must have occurred to change the negation and denial implied by his death to a meaning completely the reverse, turning it from the worst of defeats into the most glorious of victories. In such a case as this the transition is total and immediate from infamy to glory; nothing short of exaltation could redeem the scandal of the old error.

What I am suggesting now is admitted, I think, by all who have been concerned with this problem of the risen Jesus. It is a sort of initial evidence, anterior to the whole inquiry. Proudhon, for instance, no believer himself, clearly perceived its necessity. This was why he propounded the odd theory that Jesus did not die, but was taken down from the cross and was secretly present among his followers, inspiring and reanimating their faith. An unthinkable hypothesis, but it takes into account the main features of the problem.

WERE THE VISIONS OBJECTIVE?

Obviously if the Passion is a fable, if the accounts of the life of Jesus are all legends and if Jesus himself never existed, then all this reasoning falls to the ground.

But even then one would have to admit that Christianity had a beginning, therefore an unreal death followed by an unreal resurrection. And the unreality of the death presents a formidable difficulty.

Leaving aside this desperate solution, I find myself faced with two others. They are two opposite solutions, but they agree on one point. Both recognize the necessity of explaining Christianity, by a *beginning*, and one that followed hard upon the death of Jesus; but some think this initial cause was subjective, existing only in thought, others that it was objective, with an existence outside the mind.

I have not yet chosen between these rival hypotheses, but one consideration inclines me to the objective.

The event, I have said, must have had the quality of intensity. Not only so, but this intensity must have been experienced not only by a single individual but by several at least. I do not say that it need necessarily have been a collective event. That would be going too far. What I say is, that it must have been presented to several different minds.

The death of Jesus, after all, had occurred in a great city when a festival was at its height. It had been as spectacular as it well could be: the cross set up in public, the execution in broad daylight. If what we may call the 'annulling event' had been limited to the consciousness of a single person, it is hard to understand how this favoured individual could have persuaded others to share his conviction. So there has been talk in recent times of collective hallucination, of visions brought about by mass suggestion or contagion. But the more visions are multiplied, the less their value. A mystical state of any high significance is always as solitary as genius. It becomes debased as soon as it spreads and becomes spasmodic in a group. So if it is conceived as a contagious vision (and therefore of a mean order) it becomes difficult to make it the root of so great a result.

I am inclined to admit the probability of an experience produced, simultaneously or successively, in several privileged individuals: call it, if you will, a coincident plurality of visions.

But since such a coincidence of exceptional experiences, judged purely and simply by statistical chances, is a very real improbability, almost an impossibility, it would clearly be simpler (if it were possible without shaking my philosophy to its foundations) to suppose the existence of an EVENT, an actual fact external to consciousness and so explaining the similarity of the different testimonies.

When a number of different pictures represent one and the same tree, it is possible to pretend theoretically that the imaginations of their various painters have coincided; but it is more economical to say that this tree existed independently of the painters and that all they did was to reproduce it. In short, if I had not my own powerful motives for denying it, I should regard it as far easier to admit a true experience, a fact.

II

RETURN TO LIFE

THE FIRST PHILOSOPHICAL DIFFICULTY

FOLLOWING my usual practice, I want to summarize the difficulties I am faced with in this idea of Christ's Resurrection. I know I shall astonish the Christian reader, but I confess that the idea of a man 'dead and raised to life' is anything but clear to me. The faithful have been so long accustomed to these terms that they cannot realize how hard they are to believe. It is the trouble with all mysteries: what I find strangest about them is that to believers they are not mysterious.

The first of these difficulties concerns the idea of resurrection, at any rate as it is apparently understood by most believers of my acquaintance. What do they suppose it entails? The word used in the Roman creed, 'I believe in the *resurrection* of the body,' is that used to describe the *resurrection* of Lazarus. But this is clearly something different altogether.

RESURRECTION AND RETURN TO LIFE

What does it mean, *to come to life again*?

If, as in the case of Lazarus or the son of the widow of Naim, it means returning to the old life, then this would involve dying a second time. If it means being immortal on earth, eternal in time, without growing old or with an interminable old age, then it is not desirable. This is how some think of eternal life: the prolongation, the reintegration of terrestrial existence. I confess that this idea of a 'better world', if it is still a world at all, does not suggest to me a consummation to be wished.

I have no desire to see this world begin all over again, even if it should become eternal, made permanent, as many dream, at its most perfect moment. I am afraid of corrupting with cosmic images what is transcendent and incommensurable. I feel the difference to be so great that I am afraid to use the same words! If Jesus must have simply *returned*, that would look to me suspicious and too much in line with human expectations.

Not only this, but how must we understand 'the soul rediscovering its body'? When a portion of matter decays, milliards upon milliards of elements disperse; they enter into the texture of other collectivities, other bodies. It may be that in this body which is provisionally mine there are elements, lent for my transitory occupation of it, that have previously belonged to a number of other bodies. How, in that case, are we to understand the resurrection of bodies? How imagine the reassembling of those milliards upon milliards of elements that once made up my body? If God worked a miracle to achieve it, the other bodies into which these elements had once entered would have to be annihilated for the benefit of mine. There are limits even to omnipotence, which could reconstruct my body only by recreating its former elements in the likeness of their original model. I know that dogmas are mysterious, but they should not be also contradictions in terms. In the idea of a resurrection of bodies, without a new creation of matter, there is something incompatible with the very idea of a body.

I would sum up this first set of difficulties thus: either resurrection is a return to normal life, in which case it seems inadequate and spiritually unacceptable; or else it means a participation in the divine life, in which case what is to happen to my body? I shall be told that the answer to both these questions lies in the concept of the 'glorious body'. But what I want to know is, what is the relationship of this 'glorious' body to a 'non-glorious', terrestrial body? What is the transition from one to the other, and is it the same for Jesus Christ as for the rest of mankind?

RESURRECTION AS SUBLIMATION

I have a feeling that the answer lies in a deepening of the common idea of *resurrection*.

I am wrong, I think, in regarding the resurrection simply as a prodigy: as such I find it unsatisfying. The idea of a religion depending upon prodigies has always seemed to me unworthy of human beings. If it was simply a matter of those few 'apparitions' to a handful of Jews, twenty centuries ago, in an obscure corner of the Empire —no, that would not have done. A religion is not founded on an experience so suggestive of the metapsychical. If the apostles had merely seen their Master living again after his death, they might well have been moved, and even enthralled; but they would have undergone no *change of spirit* and never have promoted a faith. A prodigy cannot lead to the adoption of a new life, unless it is itself the symbol and principle of that life. And the only new life I recognize is a deeper, more interior, more spiritual life. The resurrection, in my opinion, is not to be defined in purely historical terms, as an extraordinary and memorable event. May it not also, I wonder, be the commencement of a new manner of Jesus's being present among his followers? Perhaps, too, the image, the type, the premises of a new mode of being, a new state of creation? I cannot tell—not yet. But this is the direction towards which I must pursue my investigations.

What I propose to examine today is ideas, not facts or evidence. I am not concerned at the moment with whether the belief is true, but only whether it is possible. What I want to know especially is what we are talking about.

As a matter of fact the Christian religion, properly understood, does not teach merely the survival of the soul, or even 'the immortality of the soul', but the reintegration of this concrete human being commonly called the *body*. This amounts to saying (when we have stripped the word of popular images or conceptions associated with ancient physics) that the life now present in man will be transmuted into a life of a higher order, one in which no single element of this present life will be *annihilated*, but each of them will be *sublimated*. This is soberly proclaimed in the Preface of the Mass for the Dead: *vita mutatur, non tollitur*. Life is but changed, not ended. This *mutation* without *ablation* is perhaps what is meant by resurrection.

But this being granted, much work is still to be done in the rethinking of such a dogma, because I have an idea that it is still *not completely developed*, and may never be. Christians themselves scarcely devote any attention to it, and I shall have to discover why. The expression 'I believe in the resurrection of the body' seems hardly compatible with what follows: 'and life everlasting'. Life continued everlastingly by the spirit is not that resurrection of dead bodies in order to people a new earth, even if that earth were in the heavens. Yet this traditional datum of a *resurrection of the body*, when correctly thought out, might have profound consequences in the spiritual life itself; might it not, I wonder, throw light on the real relationship between time and eternity?

Two answers are here conceivable.

One of them is crude: a temporal-eternal, an indefinite continuation of time, which is to be thought of henceforth as permanent. One might admit that by a kind of *metastrophe* time might suspend its course; that mankind, while still living on an earth and under skies and still remaining what it was, might be freed from any tendency to corruption. There would be an end to everything that hampers the functioning of life in this world, while everything would be preserved that furthers its functioning.

The mental operation that prompts this hypothesis is clear enough. It is something constant in the history of man: the stopping of time, not at any arbitrary but at the most favourable moment, so as to make infinite, or rather indefinite, the moment of supreme perfection and happiness. This is the operation that inspires the temporal messianism which is constantly recurring and is now conspicuous in the communist philosophy.

Such imagery is sometimes to be found, as it is bound to be, in biblical texts, but what is remarkable is that it is found so rarely. When it does occur, it is only in writings where the literary style is full of symbolic imagery, and even there the allusions are very few; the only quotations that immediately suggest themselves are the 'new heavens and a new earth' of the Apocalypse, and the 'reign of a thousand years' foretold for the saints. When commented on by writers ignorant of the laws of apocalyptic writing, these texts would be bound to give rise to extravagances. But tradition has not retained them in their cruder acceptation; not that it has explicitly condemned them so much as allowed them to die a natural death.

The second conception would tend to maintain that our being-in-time is simply an embryonic state of what we shall be hereafter, that this seed will later be the pattern of a new creation, in an order that will then be definitive. It is true that if we keep the language of time—and we cannot do otherwise—this restoration will not occur all at once, since an interval will elapse between our death and our resurrection. But may not the idea of such an interval be secondary? What is important is that we should have some rough idea of the restoration itself. And this makes it necessary to inquire into the nature of the body, to distinguish its various elements and to reflect on the union of soul and body.

It may be noted that it is just this last conception that is at the root of human experience and requirements. It is also that which, however much we repudiate them, inclines us to material representations of survival. He who, at the point of death, dreads that leap into the unknown, may well desire to remain clothed with 'flesh'. But if we were to put the question to a spiritual, truly 'interior' man, offering him the chance to begin his same life on earth once again, there is little likelihood of his being pleased at the prospect. He might well consent to start all over again, but it would be through fear of death, through dread of that awful solitude of a being who finds himself bereft of body, without support in the void, or in the presence of Being. Yet would he be satisfied to live again in the body, in time? His desire would rather be to eternalize what is best in his 'ego' and in his existence.

I understand how eternity, in this last sense, may be already present in time; how it might be, not, as imagination would have it, a *beyond* time, but rather, if I may put it so, a *beneath* time. It achieves, reveals, and consummates all that existed already in the form of seeds and slow maturings.

MATERIAL BODY AND SPIRITUAL BODY

If this were the kind of resurrection to look for, it would correspond better with what I should expect.

I am prepared to distinguish two elements in my 'body', the one corruptible, the other escaping corruption. It is a distinction, I dare say, that may well appear subtle; but this applies to every metaphysical distinction between aspects of being not yet actually separable, perhaps never separable, though they might become so, without absurdity, through the effect of a higher power. It is the sort of analysis analogous to that required for considering the mode of Christ's presence in the Eucharist, where the kind of question raised is whether the idea of Presence includes localization or transference. Theologians like St Thomas, philosophers like Leibniz, reflecting on the Eucharist and matching the mysteries of faith with their own concepts, were obliged to distinguish between elements or aspects of being which are combined and intermingled in common experience but are nevertheless separable: substance and accident, extension and matter, presence and unilocation. It is curious to see how modern philosophers and scientists are compelled by quantum physics or wave mechanics to make use of associations and distinctions very comparable to those formerly proposed by theology.[1] Whatever the basic value of theological speculations, i

---

[1] Thus a commentator on the ideas of Louis de Broglie and Schrödinger pointed out that their theory made questionable what had always been considered the essentia

is remarkable how often the theologians' distinctions have indirect-
ly furthered the philosophy of substance, materiality or place, of
essence or presence. It is not improbable that the paradoxical
procedure of illuminating ordinary things with the reflected light
of religious 'mysteries', or scientific 'irrationalities', will have other
applications in the future.

So in the human body we will suppose there is a properly material
part definable in terms of biology and chemistry. This is formed of
physical elements withdrawn by the vital centre from external exchanges, but beginning to become dissociated immediately at
death. These atoms of carbon, hydrogen, etc. become distributed
among other bodies; as Bossuet said, they return to circulation,
nature requiring them for other forms and new uses. These somatic
atoms, after a certain time, are located elsewhere; they may come
to form part of other human compounds. I may have elements in
my body that have already served for other destinies. Thus in a
linotype machine the actual 'types' are few; after leaving their
impress on the molten matter they are ready once more to compose
new print. That is why, as I have said, it is impossible to think of a
resurrection of bodies in which every element of a former body is
present anew; not only would it suppose a reconcentration of elements dispersed throughout the universe, but it would also require
a new creation of *doublets* for all the elements that had formerly
belonged to one body and had entered now into the composition of
another.

But I refuse to believe that the body can be completely defined
by its matter. I am inclined to think there is a second element to
define it, which is, as it were, its proper rhythm, its spatio-temporal
cadence. In music we can distinguish between the sound itself,
which is only a vibration in the air, dying every moment, and the
mode in which sounds succeed one another. The case of Beethoven,
the deaf musician, is a good illustration of the fact that the power of
organizing sounds is distinct from the power that produces them.
I am prepared to believe there is a mode of organizing the body, 'a
manner of being a body or having a body', which is not properly
the soul but necessary for the soul's insertion into the body, or rather
for the compounding of the two, which makes the soul with its body
one and the same being. It is clear enough that this *ineffable modula-*

---

attribute of movement, namely numerical identity. 'There would,' he adds, 'be no
real transference of a body across space, but the apparition at different points of a
similar image, just as radiation displaces energy without transporting any of it.'

K

tion, which is our body, can never be 'laid' in the tomb or be subject to corruption. It is impossible to bury anything but matter; but a rhythm, a modulation, or a form is no part of matter.

In this connection, to ask where this form is preserved is meaningless. We may, it is true, ask if this rhythm of the body is distinct from our soul. I said it was, even if it is not separable. It should rather be thought of as the mediating instrument of what, for lack of a better expression, one must be content to call the *unity*, which is even better than the *union*, of soul and body. What is helpful here is the analogy of a work of art, according as we consider it as completely achieved or still in an embryonic state. In the latter, what appears first is an interior 'number', an agreeable rhythm (of sounds or colours or sentiments) expressed first in the artist's own mind before being embodied in matter. This 'form' of the work of art, if the artist is incompetent, emerges at length just as a clumsy model. But if, instead of stopping short at the model, he completes the work, like Michelangelo carving his *Pietà*, he obtains the perfect harmony of matter and form.

In the case of the model, the form was still partly imprisoned in the unformed mass. This is surely analogous to what St Paul calls the Adamic or 'psychic' body. In the case of the work of art, form is given glorious mastery over matter. And if we imagine Michelangelo destroying his initial model, we should feel that the form of the statue remained to guide him when he came to reanimate the marble.[1]

SUBLIMATION

I cannot help wondering if resurrection, though a *transformation* (the mode of which transcends our understanding), has not analogies with certain remarkable processes to be observed in nature and being.

I do in fact observe that at each degree of being the lower form of existence is assumed into the higher, which embraces but does not annihilate it. Leibniz expressed it excellently when he said that

---

[1] An easier comparison would be the relationship of a *whirlwind* to the *dust* drawn up by it, which makes it visible. Our body is 'a particular kind' of whirlwind. As Adamic, it draws up dust from the earth, which it ceases to possess 'at the moment of death', when the dust disperses and 'corruption' ensues. But the whirlwind goes on. At the moment of resurrection it draws into its same eddies another kind of dust— gold dust, shall we say; dust incorruptible, impregnated by the spirit. It is now no longer an 'Adamic' body, but a spiritual body, animated by the *Pneuma*, which is the Intimacy of God.

'the lower exists in the higher in a manner nobler than in itself.' Or as St Thomas put it: *forma perfectior dat materiae quidquid dabat forma imperfectior et adhuc amplius.* Every being would seem to be destined to exist in a higher sphere; there it is assumed, without ceasing to be what it was; it continues to be what it was in an even greater degree: matter in life, life in thought, thought in that which can be designated soul, and soul in a divine life. This law of *ever retarded sublimation* would appear to be that of all nature.

The living body is made up of the same elements as an inorganic body, and we can trace, these days, all the transitional stages between inanimate molecules, crystallizable ultra-viruses, bacteria, and living cells. But at a certain moment (impossible, no doubt, to define and observe) there intervenes a principle of converging organization. It is this we call life, giving the living molecule the property of diversifying, complementing, and reproducing itself indefinitely. In the sphere of life, the elements, structures, and exchanges remain similar, but we see them entering a new order more akin to spirit. Without ceasing to be what they are, they continue to exist in a more spiritual fashion. This is what I would describe as being called to a higher life.

This mechanism of sublimation is to be found in nature at many different levels and stages.

There is a significant example in sexual life. Sexuality in man is the same as in animals, but it has not the same function. In man, who is spirit, sexuality is assumed by love. Love is nothing else but the sublimation by an idea of the confused impulses of the body.

But if its development is followed, human love can be seen aspiring to another type of existence. It seeks, surely, some other than this precarious, changing, and vulnerable state, which is the only one known to it in this temporal existence, but yet is not its real essence.[1]

Such would seem to be the meaning of the universe. Every form in it would aspire to transcendence, not as something forced upon it but as a complement both desired and unforeseeable in its modes. St Paul had this in mind when he wrote that we should not seek to be stripped of the body but rather 'clothe ourselves afresh', so that that which is mortal in us may be absorbed by life. It is not, as Spinoza said, a question of 'preserving our being' (though this would doubtless be the desire of 'matter') but, if I may so express it, of *super-being* what we are; I mean, of continuing in a higher manner,

[1] See my *Essai sur l'amour humain.*

perhaps of seeing our present nature grow ever more exalted. And this assumes that nothing of what has been will ever be *annihilated*, but that everything will super-be, at a higher level, sublimated and (as it were) recreated. No one, in his heart of hearts, can desire the annihilation of any part of being or time, unless that part of it were the incarnation of a will for evil. Even then, apart from the form that is faulty, all its matter is capable of being sublimated, as St Augustine demonstrates in his Confessions. In reality there is no past that cannot be eternalized.[1]

THE PROBLEM OF THE ULTRA-HUMAN

What I find at the root of our speculations concerning the great, I mean heroes and saints, is the problem of the superman, or rather the second Adam.

When you come to think about it, what we expect of heroes is not only to be outstanding representatives of humanity. We want them to be something more: the first members of a new kind of humanity. They are the leaders of a phalanx, a phalanx to which we belong ourselves. Even if the saints had been but a minute body, they would be enough to show that humanity has not come to a dead end, that here and there it has produced this seed of a higher life which alone is its justification. I cannot say whether such ideas are explicit when people think of exceptional men. The meaning of 'sanctity' can be translated in lay terms by something very un-Christian, the myth of the superman.

But can the saints be regarded as the actual supermen who are humanity's goal? Are they really the goal, or only images of that goal?

Even including those who are unknown, they are, I observe, very few in number compared with the multitude. I observe, too, that sanctity is only a quality of the moral being and not a transmutation of nature. So the idea of the sanctified man is something very different from our idea of a new, eternal man! But sanctity can be regarded as a kind of figure of this possible mutation. There have been instances where the body of a saint has seemed a mere con-

---

[1] It is the same with conversion, fundamentally a development understood from within. To be converted is not to turn against an old allegiance, but to continue and purify it, ridding it only of what was exclusive and partial. Everything in the old outlook that was sound and relished is rediscovered in the light and balance of the new faith.

veyor of the spirit, and wholly subject to the spirit. I have in mind those whose soul, at certain moments, has appeared to be nearly all-powerful, not merely mastering but illuminating the whole body, actually lifting it up, and having the same kind of control over it which the majority of man have only over their facial expression.

May not, I wonder, this movement, once begun, continue universally? Are we all that we shall be? And is it not desirable, if we are to be what we shall be—what we ought to be and must be—to know where our nature has its final achievement and so co-operate by looking in the right direction?

Suppose a chimpanzee, endowed suddenly with self-consciousness; would it not be bound to ask: Does not this character of intelligent behaviour, to be seen in certain individuals of my race, presage a mutation of the whole animal creation in a new direction?

I see that such ideas would have a greater probability the more one encountered, in the depths of the soul, the seed of a higher existence, as far above the psychic as psychic existence is superior to mere body; because this *vita nova*, which must reanimate and transform our present human existence, would hardly become established if we had not already some aptitude to receive it. We should have to see if we have not in ourselves, besides corporal life and self-conscious life, the beginnings of a life of another sort, a life which is to the soul what the soul is to the body.

Now it seems to me that an analysis in depth of the psychic life reveals three distinct stages or levels; which is only what has been pointed out by many keen observers, far removed from our own age. There is the corporal life, diffuse and obscure, with no need for self-consciousness, of which it is the raw material or dust: thus in sleep or torpor, in states of absent-mindedness, and in earliest infancy, a person lives without any self-knowledge; this is the first level of existence, analogous, outwardly, to animal or vegetable life. Then there is self-conscious life, attentive and reflective. But beyond this distinctively self-conscious life, and proportionately higher as this is higher than the first kind of life, is there not also a hyper-self-conscious life, what St Paul calls a 'spiritual' life, capable of standing self-revealed if only a material obstacle were removed? Is there not, as it were, a third *sphere* of existence, to which in our temporal existence we attain by accident, though we are well aware that it envelops us? The principle of this third life is to be sought no longer within us but above.

And who would venture to say that this principle of higher life would not assume the second life, just as the latter, in waking moments, assumes the first or animal life?

THE ALLEGORY OF THE FOURTH DIMENSION

If we are to believe the theory of many physicists, the real universe in which we find ourselves is made up of more than three dimensions, though these three—length, breadth, and depth—are all our faculty of perception knows, or can know. This disproportion, which we find in physics, between our means of knowledge and actual reality, might be taken to represent the disproportion, much deeper and more real, between human experience and that higher reality, of which this experience is only a part. The paradox of our present situation is very similar to that of hypothetical two-dimensional beings, transplanted into a three-dimensional universe. They would be exploring a sphere, but could never experience convexity; the utmost they could do would be to deduce it from their contradictory experience. And if some being external to the sphere stuck a pin into it, these flat beings of ours would perceive that in their world-map a wholly unprecedented event had occurred but they would be totally unable to account for it.

They would have to describe it as a paranatural occurrence, perhaps even a miracle.

This two-dimensional myth makes it easier to understand the light and shade of the concept of resurrection. We will suppose these flat beings who people the sphere are suddenly called upon to leave its surface and disperse into the surrounding air; then the moment they attained it, they would immediately understand the third dimension. They would realize then that their previous existence had been entirely paradoxical, since they had been forced to adhere to a curved surface without being able to perceive it as curved. From their new point of view, their old existence would seem a captivity, or at least a perpetual infancy. Entering the mobility of space, where henceforth they would have their whole life and being, they would feel they had been promoted to a new type of existence, that they were not so much 'immortal' as 'resurrected'.

Yet between the two-dimensional existence they had lived and the three-dimensional type they had now acquired, there is no radical discontinuity; on the contrary, a real and profound continuity, because their being has undergone no substantial change;

all it has changed is its mode and functioning. Reflecting on their past experience they would doubtless have the feeling that they *ought to have been able to discover in that experience the virtual nature of the existence they were now leading.* In any case, if this death and rebirth had been brought about by an intervention of Geometry, this demiurge had not endowed their being with new substance, but only with a new form, or rather a new condition. Moreover this transformation, this sudden mutation, was due not so much to the adding of something new to their previous essence, as to the development of a *particular* seed, already present and centred in it from the beginning: a development of which any two-dimensional genius might already have had some vague idea or presentiment.

This metaphor throws light on what I want to make clear: namely the continuity of forms of existence; the fact that our present existence is a kind of figure or foretaste of that wholly satisfying (but incomprehensible and above all unimaginable) eternal existence which is obtained by transmutation.

It also provides an interpretation of possible *apparitions.*

Among all these two-dimensional beings, promoted to the dignity, new to them, of enjoying triple space, suppose there was one privileged to enter into this new state before the rest, to be the firstborn, as it were, their predecessor and precursor. Suppose, too, that this *unique* individual wanted to give some of his former companions the proof, or at least the announcement, of their future life. Would he have any means of doing so? We can imagine one possible means: it would be to make them witnesses of his own transformation.

But how is he to give this testimony, which is itself contradictory, since there is no manifesting himself in flatness except by appearing flat himself? It would be necessary, and enough, for him who was *first transformed* to set himself deliberately somewhere in this sphere we have been considering, and submit to the conditions of the second dimension; then his late companions would see him (though without understanding his mode of entry into the texture of their own cosmos) and have the impression of his 'appearing'. He would seem to 'be among them again', though in a manner of existence precarious in their eyes and always liable to fade out. His mode of entering and leaving this present world—though in itself as simple as a word, a gesture, or an act of volition is for us—would seem to them to be utterly unprecedented, contradictory, and paradoxical. He would *appear* and *disappear*, in defiance of their laws of geometry and physics, by a process mastering space and matter.

WHAT IS A BODY?

All this reminds me that I am not quite sure what a body is.

At present my body is my complement and image, the organ of my action and the representation I have of myself. Hence the connection between face and soul, and even more between expression and soul. Of course every part of me bears my resemblance: my handwriting, the lines of my palm, the wrinkles on my forehead, even a fragment of finger-nail. Hence the attempts that are made to read character in each of these details. The people who do so are not mistaken in thinking that I am present in the minutest particles of my body. But could any but a superhuman mind discern me there?

The body is also the instrumental means of my forming part of the universe, permitting me to act and react. It is also my means of communicating with other human beings, of seeing them and of loving them.

Now these two functions of the body (that of *resemblance* to the mind, or at least of expressing the mind, and that of *insertion* in life and the cosmos) may doubtless be dissociated. When the day comes that the cosmos is no more, or when it has at any rate been so transformed that it will bear no analogy to 'matter' and 'life' as we experience them now, its function of *insertion* will cease to serve any purpose. What use would be organs, capable of receiving and transmitting movement, when movement is no more? What advantage to possess germinal cells, the apparatus of reproduction, when life has ceased to propagate itself by means of corruptible organisms, when the vital urge, its very essence, has either disappeared or finally become fixed and sublimated for ever?

At the same time, if the body has ceased to be an *instrument*, it may still continue as the *complement*, the symbol (as it were) of life and soul, perhaps even *as a medium of communication between minds*. Here we face something quite unimaginable. The body, for us, is a mass of animate matter, united to the soul, or having the soul for its form. But these ways of representing the nature of the body are not without drawbacks. The first, which is Plato's, is unacceptable. The soul cannot be regarded as an essence merely lodging in the body

It is the very texture of it; it has been wholly *made into the body*. But the idea of the soul as the form of the body, pushed to its logical conclusion without stopping half-way, leads to the total merging of the soul into the body, because one can no more think of its subsisting after death than of the subsisting of the shape of a statue once the statue is broken. It may be that the body is less dependent on the soul than we think, and at the same time less material than we imagine it is. It may be a kind of face which the soul turns to other souls.

In this way I can understand how the existence of a 'sublimated' body may be included in that communion of beings with God which makes God 'all in all'. To be still *oneself* in eternity, one would have to retain some basic memory of one's temporal history, know what one has done, or rather desired or neglected to do. But it is hard to conceive what memory could be without a sublimation of the body. There might, it is true, be what Bergson called a *pure* memory, a *pure* remembrance; the interval between death and resurrection would seem to imply a memory of this sort. But such *pure* memory must be regarded as abnormal: it calls for an achievement, a complement. The permanence of the self, formerly temporalized but now historicized in the *vita æterna*, is required for what the Gospel calls the servant's wages, inconceivable if the person recompensed forgot he had ever existed. It is a problem to imagine the kind of existence enjoyed by souls between the 'particular' judgement and the 'general' judgement. But the Christian faith represents it as provisional. The subsistence of the self seems to imply a *reintegration* (however that may happen, *Deus scit*) of what we call 'the body'.

Thus when we try to go deeper into this idea of eternal life, we see in it no annihilation of the body, but its sublimation, its rediscovery. 'To have a soul,' says Paul Valéry, 'and to be nothing evermore except that soul, is a strangely pallid desire compared with the possession of a body and duration.'[1]

Are the ideas of space and time, of volume and mass and life, necessarily associated with the idea of body? They certainly are, if

---

[1] Quoted in Biancani, *Le Mystère de la Vie*: an invitation to reconsider that idea of R. Ruyer: 'Suppose—what is not so arbitrary after all—that the death of a plant, an animal, or human being, instead of leaving behind a body similar in aspect to the living one and decaying only very slowly, was manifested by an immediate shower of fine dust (the result of an abrupt suppression of all the connecting forces that constitute the body's form); this would give us far juster ideas about structure and form, death, and life.'

the body is only matter. But if matter is assumable by spirit, which we see it is even in our present existence, does it depend fundamentally on space-time and biology? Can we not conceive the possibility of the body's being no longer subject to space, no longer submitting to it, or treating the physical world as an instrument? We can go further than this. Is not the idea of this supreme possibility the idea we form when we try to conceive the incomprehensible union of soul and body, which of all mysteries is the most familiar and most obscure? I will to raise my arm, and my arm rises; I think, and the word takes form. How absurd to suppose all this could be possible—if it were not a fact. Guardini was right: 'We need the Resurrection and the Transfiguration if we are to understand truly what the human body is.'

OBSCURITY

My views have undergone a curious change. The idea of a possible sublimation of the body seems no longer something to be rejected. On the other hand, the idea of an immortality of the soul alone appears to me somewhat obscure. A soul once separated from its only means of expression and presence could hardly be said, properly speaking, to enjoy a life at all.

It is just this that makes the spectacle of death so strange. What nature appears to rob us of in death is not the soul and the mind, which we divine are incorruptible, but the language, the sustaining power, the support of this soul and mind.

This was the difficulty that struck the Jews of old; hence the soul, according to them, merely slept while waiting for the resurrection of the body. It would not wake till the last day. As for the first Christians, they believed the Resurrection so close, the interval between death and rebirth so short, that they were little concerned with such negligible speculations. The Lord would soon be coming; those who saw him and went to meet him, those who would be still alive on the last day, would have the good fortune to by-pass death.

But since the resurrection still tarries, we now devote more attention to that provisional state, so extraordinary but so long-lasting, of the separation of soul and body. It is true that we reason in the light of *human time*, and for us even a century is long. . . But in the light of divine time, or it would be better to say *eternity*, there is no slowness in the unfolding of events, nor any length in intervals of time. Besides, as mankind is one with Jesus Christ, the reintegration, which started with the head, has virtually begun already in the members.

SUMMING UP

So I cannot tell yet whether the Resurrection is real or not. All I have been doing so far is examining the idea to see whether it involves either crude imagery or contradictory concepts. And I must admit there are real obstacles: it is hard to avoid the image of the resurrection of a corpse. But I am now convinced that the vulgar idea of the resurrection of the body is one that may well be purified. I would even say that so far from seeming absurd it corresponds to a reasonable aspiration of the mind in regard to the total development of our nature.

IS IT POSSIBLE TO HAVE EXPERIENCE OF A SUBLIMATED BODY?

Let us see now where I must investigate next and what are the positive results so far.

In the first place, I can no longer bar the event of resurrection with any initial impossibility. In the ordinary way I strongly suspect any narrative that professes to tell of a total revivication, whether it be in a dream or awake in broad daylight, as when Aeneas relates meeting his mother in the wood. But may not the Gospel be referring to something else? What I have to ask now is how we are to represent a 'fact' or 'experience' of sublimation. It is a difficult question. I touched upon it just now, and here I must return to it.

Suppose, shall we say, a person so metamorphosed, in possession of a higher life wholly removed from the conditions of our own life and world, wanted to enter into relations with us, not merely to send messages but to make us aware of his mode of existence. How could such an experience occur?

I see quite clearly that an experience of resurrection would not be identical with experiences that occur in physical nature, not even with interior or historical experiences, nor with what are called (rightly or wrongly) metapsychical experiences. In all the cases known to us, in all that can be imagined here, experience is of one and the same stuff. Experience is never more than a *part of the whole*. Upon this whole we project artificially a specially keen light, in order to see what exists outside us but evades our inspection. Experience is the isolating of a phenomenon in order to observe it better. Every apparatus (including the electronic microscope) is to all intents and purposes a magnifying glass, which helps us to see better but does not alter the nature of the phenomenon; the latter is always a part of nature, subject entirely to the determinism of law. Indeed the whole purpose of experiment, as practised by scientists, is to discern in some particular case how the universal mechanism works.

But here the process is different. A sublimated and spiritualized body belongs to a universe wholly different from that which we call *nature*. This extra-cosmic body is removed from the conditions of time and space. Suppose for a moment that such a body were trying to make itself known to human beings, trying to instruct them, I mean, not merely cause them astonishment. If it were to enter into the texture of this world, become once more a prisoner of time and space just as we are, it could never be known as a spiritual body. Therefore, in human eyes, it would lose what it essentially is. It would not be distinguishable from any ordinary body. By its very insertion in nature this glorious body would necessarily be misconceived. Its *intrusion*, if brought about by force and violence, would destroy the stability of the universe: what was intended to be *instruction* would be sheer *bewilderment*. So neither insertion nor intrusion seems to be a suitable way of experiencing one who is beyond experience. There lies a difficulty. How, in a natural universe, could a praeternatural being get itself known and recognized for what it really is?

III

THE DEVELOPMENT OF THE TESTIMONY

IMPROBABILITY OF THE DOCUMENTATION

THE first thing to do is to examine the earliest documents. The Resurrection of Christ, whether fable or fact, must have an origin: there must be written remains capable of being dated.

Here, as anywhere else, historical judgement must have texts to work upon. But here, much more than elsewhere, there is an almost tragic disproportion between the paucity of sources and the seriousness of the choice before us. Yet the existence of even these rare remains must be regarded as a fortunate and improbable accident. The early Christians might have preserved no written attestation of their faith beyond the condensed and laconic summary in the creed: *The third day he rose again according to the scriptures.* The Gospels too—as we see their tendency was—might not have thought it necessary to refer to the apparitions. This may have been the case with Mark's. Or the Apostle Paul might not have described the apparitions, or only alluded to them, since they were events admitted both by himself and his correspondents. It was a mere chance, in itself improbable, that Paul should have quoted at such length a statement of faith, which the people of Corinth knew as well as he did. Besides, at the moment of dawning faith, who thinks of noting details? There is so much else to do.

Now for an inventory of these remains.

If the three synoptic accounts are set side by side (and *Mark* contains two), together with the Pauline and Petrine discourses in the *Acts*, the professions of faith preserved by Paul and Paul's own testimonies, the documentation of the Resurrection will be found to contain a number of different points of view: a dozen in all.[1]

---

[1] See Schmitt, *Jésus ressuscité dans la prédication apostolique* (1949) and its bibliography.

A. *The First Phase: General Affirmations*

THE PRIMITIVE PROFESSIONS OF FAITH
(1 *Cor.* xv 3–8)

This passage occurs in one of the earliest and most accurately datable documents of primitive Christianity. The *Epistle to the Corinthians*, from which it is taken, was written from Ephesus about the year 55; at a time, therefore, when the Gospel had already spread in Judaea and also among the pagans (*Acts* xxi 20; *Rom.* xv 19). The verses we are considering were not a message from Paul himself: he is quoting a doctrine he has *received*, not 'perpendicularly' (so to speak) by way of revelation, which would have been something peculiar to himself, but 'horizontally', by way of tradition. In this year 55, some twenty years distant from the Easter happenings, this doctrine was already old; its formulas were *already* stylized and stereotyped. Paul would have received this tradition on the occasion of his first visit to Jerusalem (about the year 46) when he first compared his message with the apostolic teaching. This was fifteen years after the event and the principal witnesses were still alive. We are therefore as near to the event as it is possible to be in any development of the religious type, where the first textual outcrop is bound to take the form of a simple profession of faith, not a reporting. It is remarkable to see how, even at this very early period, the statement of belief was already fixed in its major lines. These are factual assertions, not left to private judgement but always repeated in the same order. And the order is historical, involving narrative connections: *And then, and then, and at last.*

Now take the profession of faith quoted by Paul.

It is in two parts.

In the first it recalls the various apparitions officially recognized and *confirmed* by the first and responsible Church, that of Jerusalem. This down to the fifth verse.

Paul next goes on to list other apparitions, not confirmed: those to 'five hundred of the brethren all at once, most of whom are alive at this day'. Then comes the apparition to James, then one to 'all the apostles'. The appearance to the five hundred may correspond to what we call the Ascension, though seemingly to Paul it was not the last. The apparition to James has nothing corresponding to it in the Gospels. That to 'all the apostles' might be the one recorded in *John* xx 28. Paul finally speaks of Christ's apparition to himself alone, that on the road to Damascus, the details of which we know from the three accounts in the *Acts*.

Paul uses the same words ('he was seen by') to describe the Damascus apparition and the apparitions to the apostles; which shows that in some respects at least they must have seemed to him equivalent.

He makes no reference to the empty tomb; but the profession of faith which he quotes presupposes that the *buried body* of Jesus is that which *rose* from the tomb *on the third day*, and therefore that after the third day the tomb was empty.

This is not the only profession of faith. Embedded in Paul's Epistles there are other passages which had, we must suppose, already become fixed by the middle of the first century at latest.[1]

Romans x 9

'Thou canst find salvation, if thou wilt use thy lips to confess that Jesus is the Lord, and thy heart to believe that God has raised him up from the dead.'

There is no disputing that what we have here is a technical 'profession of faith', one implying the idea of divinity (Jesus is *kurios*), but also asserting that it was God who caused him to come out from among the dead.

Ephesians v 14

'This is the meaning of the words, Awake, thou that sleepest, and arise from the dead, and Christ shall give thee light.'

There is general agreement that this is the text of a hymn in the primitive liturgy, almost certainly for baptism. One might also mention the hymn quoted in the first *Epistle to Timothy* (1 *Tim.* iii 16). But the date of *Ephesians*, and still more that of the *Epistle to Timothy*, being still open to discussion, I will not press these two passages.

---

[1] There is a suspicion about verses 6 and 7, which could in fact be omitted from the development without altering its essence. But it is odd that something *unnecessary* should have been *added* to the account! Besides, even if the apparition to 'all the apostles' were a reiteration of that to 'the Eleven', it would simply corroborate the opinion we had already formed of the multiplicity of the sources. It would have come from a different source from Paul's, which a (no doubt very early) copyist wanted to keep in the old text and harmonize. These are idle arguments, because proof is impossible and the point at issue does not affect the essence of the problem.

THE DISCOURSES IN THE ACTS

The professions of faith are not the only ancient remains. We have also the discourses in the *Acts*. If these had been invented when the book of the *Acts* was compiled—whatever the compiling process may have been—one would expect them to be coloured by the developed faith of the Christian communities. The messiahship of Jesus would have been shrouded in his divinity. He himself would probably have been shown as the contriver, not merely the subject, of the Resurrection. The end of time would not have been represented as likely to occur almost immediately.

Now when considering the discourses of Peter, whether at Jerusalem (ii 14–36; iv 8–21) or at Caesarea (x 34–43), or those of Paul at Pisidian Antioch (xiii 16–41), I notice that, so far from this being the case, the themes are rather contrary to the subsequent development of Christian thought. Jesus is represented, not as God equal to the Father, but as his Servant, exalted, avenged and crowned by God. The point insisted upon is that the Messianic age has arrived.

Not only so, but there is no cutting out, in historical duration, distinct apparitions, separate and discontinuous. It rather seems that history before and after the Resurrection belongs to one and the same continuity of time; it is on this that the whole weight of the testimony bears, a continuous period from the Baptism to the Ascension. Here, as there, what it comes to is an intimate community of word, love, and life: that which consists in 'eating and drinking together'. For 'eating together' and 'partaking of the cup' were Jewish expressions for community life.

B. The Second Phase:
Narratives, Circumstances and Answers

In the first period there are no narratives of the Resurrection. It is asserted; it is also given its place in God's eternal designs. The apparitions have already been listed. At their first entry into history, though they emerge so near the event (only fifteen years away) they are already recognized as old.

Now for the developments in the second period. These are *narratives*. They tell a story, which has its beginning, its unexpected turns, its conclusion. Being narratives, they are bound to be more precise about spatial and temporal co-ordinates; they have to bring in characters, describe the reactions of various minds to events, provide details in order to make memorizing easier when the accounts have to be passed on; they must also contrast and simplify.

Finally, since the event proclaimed by faith has awakened doubts and provoked denials, the development of this second period had to provide answers to the objections of unbelief. These objections, it will be seen, had not been overlooked, even in the earliest stages, and the replies anticipated them.

MARK'S ACCOUNT

(xvi 1–8)

Mark's original Gospel breaks off at verse 8 of chapter xvi. It is generally admitted that verses 9–20, a summary of the apparitions, were added later. Was their breaking off intentional? Or has Mark's Gospel lost it original conclusion? It is a debated question, but fundamentally not important. If Mark ended with the words in verse 8 ('Trembling and awe-struck, they said nothing to anyone out of fear') his Gospel would still have a deep significance: the tomb is empty, Christ has therefore risen. He will be able to appear. . .

Mark, according to tradition, was Peter's interpreter. The impression produced by the whole Gospel goes far to bear this out, not least the final chapter. The contents are primitive, abrupt, summary; Peter has a primary place in it. 'Go and tell Peter and the rest of his disciples. . .'(xvi 7).

MATTHEW'S ACCOUNT

(xxviii 1–20)

Matthew's account follows Mark, or Mark's source. But it shortens it. Repetition occurs, surprising in so short a narrative, as when Jesus (in verse 10) repeats the words of the angel (in verse 7). In verses 11 to 15 the Gospel of Matthew gives the incident of the guards. In so sober a context, this passage strikes a somewhat discordant note; it is rather suggestive of the apocryphal manner. However that may be, it is not without interest to a critical mind: the evangelist is arguing here against Jewish objectors, who pretended that the body of Jesus had been secretly removed by his disciples to gain credence for his resurrection (which in time to

L

come was to be the theory of Proudhon). This suggests that at the time he wrote the Jews were aware of the Christian preaching concerning the empty tomb. Doubtless therefore, from the very beginning, there was a 'scientific' opposition based on a denial of the evidence.

In verses 16 to 20 Matthew sums up the essentials of the Easter message. His conclusion may be said to throw a flash of light upon past as well as future. The scene is in Galilee, on a chosen mountain. As elsewhere in this Gospel (iv 8; v 1), the mountain is not named. It is the Sinai of the Resurrection, the high place where Jesus founds his Church and all his teachings are condensed. The circumstances are given very briefly. It is mentioned that some doubted. Jesus shares God's power on earth and in heaven.

It is impossible to prove that the liturgical usage, of baptizing in the name of the Father and of the Son and of the Holy Ghost, had no influence on the writing of this Gospel, or that the Gospel gives the actual words used by Jesus without subsequent development. In the *Acts*, the four baptisms there recorded are performed in the name of the Lord Jesus alone. It is hard to believe that this abbreviated liturgy could have been possible if Jesus had solemnly *fixed* the trinitarian formula.

However that may be, the message of Jesus in *Matthew* has pastoral and liturgical import; it recalls the two essential phases of Christian initiation, catechetical instruction and baptism in the name of the three Persons.

LUKE'S ACCOUNTS
(*Luke* xxiv 1–23; *Acts* 1)

Luke's writings differ from Matthew's and Mark's both in sources and themes. The resurrection, in *Mark* and *Matthew*, bursts like a storm, astounding men's minds and seeming to interrupt the whole course of history. They stress the rupture, the discontinuity. But discontinuity, of whatever sort, is a pointer to deeper continuity. It is this deeper continuity that Luke reveals to us.

If the supreme art of the historian is a free treatment of the rhythm of time (like the heart, alternately dilating and contracting) then Luke may be said to be inimitable here. He dilated the time of the Emmaus incident, just as though he could foresee that, in twenty centuries' time, minds more curious than his own would seek to understand how, in the development of an apparition, the human mind actually works. On the other hand he condensed, like the historians of Greek antiquity, the course of events regarded as official.

He wanted, also, to satisfy the Jewish mind, with its craving to find a place for partial history within total and divine history. The resurrection is presented to us as the accomplishment of a very ancient and serene plan (verses 7 and 26). The ancient times are peacefully accomplished; now comes the peaceful commencement of new times. Luke seems to 'engage' the Resurrection in its context; he explains how consciousness gradually became aware of it; he makes it possible for the human mind to assimilate it. The *event* becomes an *advent*, surprising, wonderful; but capable, afterwards, of being conceived as something normal.

Thus the account of the women at the tomb is here retold in a more human light. The angels are men. Their words, on the apparent death of all who die, are sublime in themselves: 'Why are you seeking one who is alive, here among the dead?' There is a recalling of what Christ said in Galilee, but no prophecy of an appearance in Galilee.

The women relate what they have seen to the apostles, who disbelieve them. Yet Peter runs to the sepulchre and is dumbfounded.

Then Luke relates the Emmaus incident, an explanation of the apparitions; it is an explanation, psychological, scriptural, and theological, all in one. The disciples, having recognized the Lord in the 'breaking of bread', return to Jerusalem, where they learn that the Lord has already appeared to Peter.

What is transparent in this account is the trouble which is taken to answer objections, such objections as might have been made by that very Theophilus to whom the Gospel is addressed, and might have weighed, we feel, with the Corinthians to whom Paul had addressed his Epistle. Might not the risen Christ have been a ghost? (1 *Cor.* xv 35–49). Luke makes us sure that the risen Christ was no spectre. Jesus offered his hands and feet to prove he was one and the same as the Crucified. But this was not enough; it might still have been a vision. Jesus asks his disciples to *feel* his limbs. He does more: he actually eats in their presence. Thus he presents his body as an object of experience and at the same time as an object testifying to his resurrection. And since, in spite of all, their bewilderment remains, he explains his Passion-Resurrection by showing them the meaning of the Scriptures.

What Luke does is to incarnate the risen Christ in history—as far as he can, as much as any Jew could wish, perhaps as much as a modern man would require.

Yet Jesus, while linking his manifestation to past history—which he sums up in himself, fulfilling what was told of him by Moses, the Prophets, and the Psalms—also proclaims future history, the evangelizing of all nations, 'beginning at Jerusalem', where he is now—Jerusalem, the hinge of space, as the Resurrection is the hinge of time.

He then tells them he is going to send, he *is sending* them, the gift which was promised by the Father, and that in this same city where they must now await it.

Afterwards he led them out to Bethany and blessed them: 'and even as he blessed them he parted from them, and was carried up into heaven.'

All these events are represented here as happening the same day, that first Sunday.

In the *Acts*, which is a kind of sequel to the Gospel, the Resurrection is assumed. It was for the first time, what it always would be in the Church, the all-enveloping Reality, a kind of new mental eye, something not merely to *see* but to *see by*. I have called attention to the passages where the Resurrection is set in place in the eternal design. In the *praxis* of the apostles, their 'acts', their experience of the Resurrection provides the motive power.

It was in fact a *completed* experience, in the sense that the *Acts* state explicitly that there was one last and definitive appearance, an end to the whole series; consequently that if any similar phenomenon occurred it could not be regarded as belonging to the same order. St Paul, when he talks of *his* apparition, also conceives it as the last, completing the series a second time. The question is: how is this appearance of Christ to Paul to be reconciled with the other appearances?

More questions still are sure to be asked.

The events which the Gospel assigns to a single day—the apparition, the entrusting of the mission, the disappearance—are here said to have occupied *forty days*. Moreover the last words of Jesus are less concise than in the other Gospels. They make no reference to the past triad—Moses, the Prophets, and the Psalms—but to a triad to come, the scenes of the apostles' future activities which the author himself had doubtless witnessed: Judaea, Samaria, and the ends of the earth. Having opened these three vistas, Jesus was lifted up and a cloud hid him from their sight. And while *they* were watching his passage heavenward, two men in white brought them down to earth by announcing that Jesus would come again in the same fashion as they had seen him ascend.

Here the historical evidence may be said to impinge on theological explanation. The significance of this last passage I shall have to examine later.

The idea I am left with is simply this: that for St Luke there was a last and solemn apparition, indicating to the apostles that a new historical order was now to begin, one in which the presence of the risen Christ would lie concealed in the texture of history, in missionary activity, in the daily life of the Church. In the *Acts* this apparition included a kind of levitation, full of symbolic teaching for the Jews. Holding as they did, and in their own peculiar manner, a tripartite division of the world—hell, earth, and heaven—the raising up of Jesus and his disappearance on high impressed on their minds that he was *finally* leaving the land of men, that his dwelling, from now on until the end of time, would be the kingdom of the heavenly Father.

JOHN'S GOSPEL

It is a unique document. In its description of the Resurrection it would seem that the Johannine Gospel represents a tradition of testimony distinct from the synoptic, particularly from Mark and Matthew. Was he ignorant of the earlier tradition? It looks more as though he were making it more precise, touching it up, as a direct witness might do after reading the accounts by indirect witnesses, working on sources: accounts of an event which only he had actually seen.[1]

From the point of view of fundamental significance, these adjustments of detail serve no purpose. They are useless, too, for general attestation. But personally I find them valuable: they make it possible to apply the criterion of comparing the event with what might have been expected. One would have expected, in this theological Gospel, the effects of a reconstructing imagination; these are certainly to be found, but all mingled with the working of historical and concrete memory. Moreover this Gospel contains a

[1] Compare the Johannine text xx 1–2, 11–18, on running to the sepulchre, with *Mark* xvi 1–8; or xx 3–10, on the empty tomb, with *Luke* xxiv 12; or xx 19–29, on the first appearance at Jerusalem, with *Luke* xxiv 36–49.

number of particulars of place, time, and circumstance, of little
relevance to the central theme and important only to the person
relating them.

Unless the fabulator be allowed the gift of second sight, so as to
foresee the requirements of nineteenth-century criticism, and nothing short of a genius for hoaxing, there is no conceiving how he
could have come to invent these trifling and perfectly pointless
details—verified, as it happens, twenty centuries later, by archaeological research.

So we have every right to conclude that the evangelical tradition
depends on two independent historical sources. One, the earliest
gathered, but already capitalized and stylized, was the Mark-
Matthew, drawn upon by Luke. The other, collected much later
and not stylized, consisted of the memories of a privileged and
spiritually minded observer. It is true that the Johannine memories
are (as it were) transubstantiated into a doctrine, in the sense that
John's final criterion of historicity is significance. But the fact is, this
tendency to sublimate *fact* in *meaning* is less noticeable in the account
of the Resurrection, which reminds one more of the factual manner
of the synoptic Gospels.

John tells us that on the first day of the week Mary Magdalen
came to the sepulchre, saw the stone had been taken away, then
went to tell Peter and that beloved disciple who is the narrator
himself. One has only to substitute 'I' for that disciple to get a first-
personal account by the witness. The Synoptics are less direct, with
the possible exception of *Mark* (if we take it that Mark's was really
Peter's Gospel).

Peter and John run to the sepulchre. 'I outran him', says John;
'Peter went in; he saw the linen cloths lying there. I also went in,
and saw this, and learned to believe.'

Then Jesus appears to Mary Magdalen and bids her tell the
others. The evening of the same Sunday, when all the doors are
closed, Jesus reveals himself. He makes his disciples touch him, and
appoints them a mission, conferring on them the Spirit. Thomas,
who was absent, doubts. Jesus presents himself the following Sunday, when he gives Thomas tangible evidence of his pierced hand
and open side.

A development has been added: the account of the apparition
(called 'the third') in Galilee. It consists of a description of the
miraculous catch of fish, when Jesus is recognized by John, and

then by Peter; Jesus takes bread, and also fish, which he gives them to eat. After the meal, Jesus entrusts Peter with his mission as universal pastor.

Whether John knew the other Gospels or not, his own has the effect of reconciling the other three by presenting a more probable sequence. It makes a firmer connection between the apparitions to the women and those to the apostles by giving the official verification that the tomb was empty. It sets the Galilean apparitions side by side with those at Jerusalem. It reconciles the idea of an apparition (something to be seen and even touched) with revelation given to faith alone. It agrees with Mark about the women at the tomb; but in typical fashion these women are represented by the person of Mary Magdalen. It agrees with Matthew for the final scene of bestowing the mission on the apostles; but the eleven are represented by only one of them, Peter. It agrees with Luke about the Sunday apparition to the eleven at Jerusalem; but the doubters are represented by Thomas alone.

It therefore *confirms*, but it also *sublimates*. Mary is *more* than the women; she does more than see, she touches, she loves; Christ makes her his messenger, reveals to her his coming Ascension. Peter does more than rule; he loves more, he sacrifices himself. Thomas does more than doubt, then believe; he adores God in the person of Jesus.

C. The Third Phase: Harmonizing and Summarizing

Finally we have a third type of development, which seems fairly late. After the intuition, grasped in all its initial energy, after the explosion of the rocket, it is a sort of final summing up, a synopsis of what has already been told. There are no new fireworks. It is only a matter of making an inventory.

There are two ways of unifying a subject. The first has its origin in the depths of memory: we have seen this in *John*, a unity reminiscent of a work of genius. The other way is the commentator's. The first is harmony, the second is harmonization.

Chapter xxi of *John* is perhaps an intermediate stage. Some have noted a deliberate effort to present the facts fully: the chronology appears to be stressed more than usual (verses 1 and 14).

At any rate the conclusion to *Mark* (xvi 9–20) presents us with the final stage of these summarizing developments. A number of sources are used. The editor is trying to connect them together in a certain order; at all costs he must reduce them to a synthesis. We are now at a period when the Church has become clearly aware that no new evidence will come to light. It must be content with what there is, piece it together or sum it up. The tendency is not to invent; rather to 'disinvent', to reduce; it was, so to speak, a scholastic age, one that gives the impression that inspiration has dried up. The primitive fire has died out; all that is left to do is to gather up the cinders; the story can now be summarized.

Thus the conclusion to *Mark* combines different traditions: the apparition to Mary Magdalen, from *John*; that seen by the disciples on the road to Emmaus, from *Luke*; the apparition to the Eleven at table, from *John* and *Luke*. The words of Jesus recall the conclusion to *Matthew*. It adds an announcement, which appears to be a commentary, about the miracles that will accompany the preaching of the Gospel.

Next comes the Ascension, which is made to occur immediately.

IV

THE CHARACTERISTICS OF THE EVIDENCE

THE CONTEMPORARY ATTITUDE TO THE DOCUMENTARY
EVIDENCE: ITS SUBJECTIVITY: ABSENCE OF
PRIMITIVE VERIFICATION

I HAVE just been examining the documentary position, trying to connect the texts with the law of development followed by the human mind when becoming aware of an event. The question now arises: does this development suggest the existence of a real source external to the mind?

I want to consider first the chief difficulties experienced today by critical minds.

One objection, raised by many, is based on an initial denial. It amounts to saying: 'I would believe in the Resurrection if I could see it authenticated by an observer who was not a believer; only such authentication would be *objective*.'

Turn it as you will, this requirement really means: 'I will never believe, whatever the pretended proofs.' For verification by an unbeliever, *who remained an unbeliever afterwards*, by definition could never be favourable. It is just what we see in political trials, when witnesses for the defence are eliminated on principle; suspect as 'unreliable', they may even be condemned along with the accused. But it is in times of 'terror' that the condemnation is obtained beforehand, and the machinery of justice is no longer the *cause* but the *effect* of the verdict.

Being resolved to resist this powerful temptation, I may say that for my part I would be intellectually horrified if ever I found myself begging my own questions.

But after saying so much I still think it true that at first sight the evidence of the texts seems an insufficient support for the degree of certitude necessary to faith. So what verges upon the tragic is that in a matter of such importance for humanity (really a matter which it ought to regard as the only one of moment) there would seem to be no more room for argument.

In a positivist age, when knowledge must needs be founded on experience, there are seemingly here no means of examining the question for ourselves; we must rely on the assurances of the original witnesses. This, it is true, is what we invariably do in all other matters; but in the sciences we rely on those who attach as much importance as we do to caution, verification, and self-distrust. All faith in another depends on our regarding him as the same sort of person as ourselves. But had the apostles, so morally superior to the mass of men and perhaps even to the most eminent, that critical prudence, in matters like this, which minds of our day regard as indispensable?

INCREASING TENDENCY TO THE CONCRETE

A secondary objection arises in the type of mind that is all for arranging documents in chronological order.

What confronts it here, as I have said, is a tendency to make more *concrete*, to 'historicize' the original tradition. This has often been pointed out in recent times, and there is no denying it. The earliest professions of faith, the earliest discourses, all make general assertions about the appearances of the risen Christ. St Paul speaks of 'visions', and he appears to class together the appearances of Christ to the apostles and his appearance on the road to Damascus. The conclusion to *Matthew* reduces all to a single discourse. In Luke's Gospel we see a Christ who converses, who takes a meal; in John's, a Christ who eats fish, who allows himself to be touched. There is no avoiding the impression that all these details, so eagerly sought after by the contemporary mind, were reduced to writing only very late. We may suppose them to have been preserved in the memories of witnesses; but the critical mind inquires: was historicity really regarded as so necessary at the earliest stage? May it not have been due to later development?

These are questions it is impossible to ignore.

FAITH AND HISTORY: OPPOSED STANDPOINTS:
THE CHARACTER OF THE GOSPELS

This brings us back to the crucial question, whether the Gospel is historical. But here the first principles of rationalist criticism join forces with the first principles of orthodox criticism to confuse the issue and create a darkness of quite exceptional density.

Believers generally hold that the Gospel, having God himself for its author, permits no liberties with the historical narrative. Such a narrative cannot contain what a modern historian would call error, confusion, repetition, or inexactitude. It is just what it would have been if it had been written by a Mommsen or a Fustel de Coulanges.

For anyone committed to this idea of inerrancy it is quite impossible to admit that one writer contradicts what another asserts, that one of the accounts is mistaken in some particular of time or place, that any saying is attributed to Christ which was not actually uttered as it stands, in the place and at the time alleged. The believer, as such, is not concerned with exegesis but with the spiritual life. To defend the general and simple truth of the evidence, it is much safer (at any rate for the piety of the masses) to canonize the literal truth of every portion of the sacred text. When a divergence occurs, it will always be possible to find a subtle explanation that will reduce it to harmony. And fundamentally faith is in the right. In the hierarchy of practical values, the general truth takes rank above detail. And even in the human scale we should never get anywhere unless we were willing to ignore minor historical truths in order to grasp the major rhythms of the subject, the statistical laws and ultimate convergences. To describe minutely, simply for the sake of precision, the zigzags of innumerable molecules, instead of neglecting the inessentials and observing only the phenomena of heat and gravitation, would be to make impossible not only ordinary perception but technical science and human life itself. Harmonizing is an operation that takes place everywhere: it is a scientific law. There is more reason for it still in the moral life, in the way we must needs judge others and ourselves. The scrupulous who neglect this law are tortured in consequence.

The place for exegesis is a laboratory, closed to the public. Many problems connected with exegesis (such as the 'movement of the earth' in the sixteenth century and 'human origins' in the nineteenth) were badly handled because the pastoral standpoint, so legitimate in those responsible for the consciences of all the faithful, took precedence of the standpoint of positive research, which is of interest only to a handful of intellectuals.

Sceptics, on the other hand, have tended as a rule to put historical truth on a par with that kind of *verification* which belongs to the sciences of description, such as 'natural history'. Their idea of historical truth is that it should be something objective and impersonal, divorced from practical utility and significance. In their eyes any intention of proving something is itself a sufficient reason for doubting.

Obviously this frame of mind would involve treating as legend almost all the contents of the Gospel. How could these fragmentary writings with all their divergences, writings produced in an atmosphere of religious zeal and simply to promote faith, have ever for the scientifically minded the least guarantee of objective precision—especially when the testimonies they contain refer to an event which statistically speaking is as improbable as it well could be? There is such disproportion between the momentousness of the event if true, and the slenderness of the proofs offered by the documents of faith, that sceptics, lacking faith to bridge the gap, must regard these narratives as the product of mere belief.

These difficulties, it is true, have diminished not a little during the last fifty years. Important work has been done on both sides.

A more exact knowledge of literary styles, of oriental mentality, Semitic history, and the earliest state of the evangelical tradition, has made it possible to reduce a number of these misunderstandings.

The Gospels are not purely historical documents, as we now understand the word 'historical'; they were written to confirm faith, the faith of communities or chosen individuals, like Luke's Theophilus. Before the Gospels were written there were already traditions about the various events in the life of Jesus; these, differing in detail but fundamentally identical, circulated among Christians orally. They were not by any means facts pure and simple, but facts charged with religious significance. Though facts were its foundation, it was this religious significance that was held more important. The evangelist had to gather his traditions and make his choice among them, which meant rejecting this and retaining that, in accordance with his general design. He never intended to tell all he knew. As a believer, who would be at the same time teacher and artist, he wanted to give a coherent account, unified, symphonious, and self-sufficient. It is praiseworthy on our part, and also a temptation we can hardly resist, to seek in these different accounts, put together for instruction, agreement in all their details and viewpoints. The greater our awareness of the importance of Jesus, the more we wish to know *everything* that concerns him and the more reluctant we are to accept a lacuna, more still a contradiction. But it is clear, on deeper reflection, that we are bound to have regard for our means of information and that it is vain to try to impose on them the forms we would like them to take.

As for those who regard these gaps, and the catechetical nature of the documents themselves, as a reason for denying their value as evidence, they forget that the very essence of the Christian testimony is its being founded on a *fact* which is also a *sign*. To reject the fact, because faith sees it a sign, is to answer the question before grasping what it is. Besides, even the most objective of facts may possess a secret significance. The most 'scientific' criticism of a sceptical thinker is as full of human significance as the Gospel is of religious significance.

Having said this, we can see these accounts in a new light. Each is self-sufficient. It would therefore be sufficient for anyone who was not in possession of the others. Each asserts the real death, each asserts the entombment, and that transition to a new life which implies the disappearance of the body.

It would have been natural enough if the fable-making element (which had free enough play in the apocryphal gospels) had also its place in describing an event which is not, in some respects, without a certain affinity to it. There are isolated verses, particularly in *Matthew*, which it would be hard to defend, if one applied the critical tests I employ, and considered them, apart from their sacred significance, as merely statements of fact. This may be a source of embarrassment for believers, if they hold that inspiration is a sufficient guarantee of the historical truth of *all* the recorded circumstances. In my opinion this is impossible, for there are times when the Gospel presents us with radical divergences.[1] In any case it is highly improbable, to say the least, that a fact so unheard of as a resurrection would not have given rise, in certain minds, to a flood of marvels and prodigies. It is a phenomenon that occurs regularly in all heroic history. Granting that the resurrection, after Christ's, of certain saints is a wonder recounted without evidence to support it (though it is impossible to prove this), the fact is merely accessory, without consequence for faith, and cannot be compared with the resurrection itself.[2]

[1] For instance the four accounts of Peter's denial.

[2] From the point of view, that is, of the inquiring free-thinker. But anyone convinced of Christ's Divinity and Resurrection would never reason quite like this. *Before* this conviction, the antecedent probability of the Resurrection's being accompanied by

As for chronology, there are certainly statements it is impossible to reconcile; but we know, from comparing the conclusion of *Luke* with the beginning of the *Acts*, that the same author thought nothing of distributing the same events either over a few hours or *forty days*, without any notion of this being likely to trouble the faithful, and prove baffling or deluding. His was a different mentality from ours.

In regard to topography, there is one important difficulty for the modern mind, though no doubt it would have been barely perceptible to that of antiquity. Matthew and Mark appear to know nothing of the apparitions in Jerusalem, whereas Luke seems ignorant of the apparitions in Galilee. One conjecture is that the apparitions occurred only in Galilee, but that later it seemed appropriate to make them occur in Jerusalem. Alternatively, they may have taken place only in Jerusalem and it seemed more fitting to place them in Galilee. But this last hypothesis is the less probable. One might also admit that Christ appeared in Jerusalem *and* in Galilee, and that some of the evangelists omitted the apparitions which did not fit their plan. John, who came last, places the first apparitions in Jerusalem and adds the Galilean apparitions afterwards.

Whatever the answer, these questions do not touch the heart of the problem. Quantity here carries no weight at all. One single proved appearance would be a sufficient guarantee for faith. Topography, in my view, is only important to the extent that its erroneousness might throw doubts on the genuineness of the basic testimony.

It is strange, too, that silence about a fact should be taken to prove its unreality, as if *to say nothing* were the same as *to deny*. An historian, these days, tells you he is careful to omit nothing. This was not the way of the ancient historian, who was more interested in *meaning* than *exactitude*. If the same theme (that, for example, of the women at the tomb) has undergone variations of greater or less detail, if the sayings of Jesus have been differently reported or the order of times and places modified, none of this alters the essence of the testimony. So on points like these, it seems to me, orthodox scholars can safely afford to make generous concessions.

---

some prodigy is very slight; the probability of fabulation very strong indeed. *After* this conviction it is otherwise: it would seem quite possible that so cardinal an event would be accompanied by paranormal phenomena, which would be seen as a kind of fringe or halo to it.

What appears to me fundamental is that Jesus appeared to the assembled Eleven, most probably on Easter evening, in Jerusalem (*1 Cor.* xv 5; *Luke* xxiv 36; *John* xx 19), and that he bade them preach the Gospel to all nations (*Matt.* xxviii 19; *Luke* xxiv 47; *John* xx 21). This would be enough: it includes everything.

Critics are eager to point out discrepancies, to call attention to interpolations and joins in the narrative. Their method is bound to lead them to *pulverize* the texts, to attach more importance to *genesis* than *content*, to their *content* than their *value as evidence*. These are professional, good craftsman's habits. Critical craftsmanship tends always to prefer the negative interpretation, just as the judicial profession has a propensity to believe the guilt of the accused.

Again, what astonishes me is that the points on which the disputants tear each other to pieces are generally of quite secondary importance. Most of the corrections demanded by criticism would modify the customary presentation of the facts but make no change in what is essential. In the same way, the conclusions drawn from the physics of Galileo have modified our ideas about Scriptural inspiration; this has become deepened, better defined, restored to its authentic pattern; but the blunder committed by the Holy Office made no difference at all to the problem of the transcendence of the Judaic-Christian Scriptures. What I would say to the critics is this: 'Granting this passage is not by St Paul, but by a commentator who borrowed Paul's name, Paul's manner and style; what of it?' To object that a text has been wrongly attributed has only a certain polemical value; it irritates your opponent. If he has made the attributed authorship the test of authenticity, you have successfully floored him. Suppose we admit that Christ never appeared in Jerusalem, but that the Galilean apparitions have been transferred to Jerusalem in order to make their significance more striking; or again, that the later accounts of the apparitions contain details put in to emphasize more vividly an idea present from the first, namely that what the witnesses saw was not a ghost. Personally, being free to think, to weigh fundamental reasons for believing or not believing, I am scarcely worried by this at all. My mind is sufficiently ventilated and free from prejudice, strategic enough, too, to distinguish what is of capital importance and what is not. I do not confuse the stained glass window with the stone ogive. My faith rests on the arch, not on the glass.

So though the problem has many aspects, and contains some

highly personal implications, it is yet very *simple*. It calls for no answer but YES or NO, without, alas, any midway positions. As with the problem of God—so closely akin, logically and ontologically, with the problem of Jesus—the proposition is one which we are bound to deny or affirm in its entirety; there can be no *via media*, no agreement to compromise.

From now on we must inquire with redoubled care whether the original event was of the subjective type or really historical. In itself it is a problem independent of dates, of details and document-ary homogeneity.

It is true that if the documents were far removed in time from the initial moment, then the negative probability would be all the stronger. It would be stronger still if in the documents themselves there were clear traces of late compilation or fable. Therefore if criticism were to stretch the gap between the documents and the fact, or by studying their form discern evident traces of legend, it would then be necessary to reconsider the question. But it may safely be said that the labours of the last hundred years have produced a number of positive results, which have made it necessary to revise the positions taken up by the critical extremists. The interval be-tween the event and the writing of the texts is one that has been tending to diminish.

HISTORICITY AND ATTESTATION: FROM THEMATIC
TO CIRCUMSTANTIAL ASSERTION

There are difficulties of another order. These arise, as I have said, out of classifying the documents according to their order and seeing the emergence of an increasing tendency to historicize.

To answer this difficulty we must see how it is that the mind comes to perceive a significant event.

When I first learnt of the death of Péguy, in August 1914, I knew nothing of either him or his work; an article by Barrès was the only information I had. All that was impressed on my young mind was: *Poet, killed in action*. It was a *theme* rather than a *countenance*; much as would have been '*poet executed*', '*consumptive poet*', '*poet in exile*'. There are not many possible poetic destinies. For the child I was then (as for the mass of contemporary Frenchmen) to have perception of Péguy's death meant unhooking from its peg one of these fateful epithets and applying it to this unknown personage, Péguy. *Poet who died young, Poet killed at the front*. In 1939 the same thing happened in the case of Patrice de la Tour du Pin, whose 'wound in the head' was announced by Mauriac. With Péguy, the initial theme was enriched by another of the prophetic order. People remembered the line in *Eve*: 'Blessed are those who have died in a just war.' So Péguy became one who had died 'according to the scriptures'. It was not till twenty years later, in the four biographical 'gospels' of Halévy, Romain Rolland, Johannet, and Mercel Péguy, that we were given historical details of Péguy's death, the final phases of his life, and his last words.[1]

One might well argue that if twenty centuries hence this man Péguy were to become the subject of heated debate, the most probable solution would run something like this. First, a legendary theme, the poet-who-died-young, the poet-killed-in-battle, the poet-who-was-his-own-prophet. Critics would then produce the following hypothesis: 'People started with the line "Blessed are those who have died" etc., and then proceeded to invent the story of this happy hero's death; they imagined him killed in the opening battle, face to face with the enemy, with a bullet in his forehead, all as it should have been. For a long time the public was satisfied with this. Then, as curiosity grew concerning this Péguy's personality and the circumstances of his life, there were forthcoming several contradictory accounts, the product of learned fabulation, more or less consciously so in the case of the authors Halévy and Rolland.'

Yet we know that this hypothesis is false. The initial absence of an historical account, the presence in the narrative of poetic themes, are neither of them proof that the event is a fable. The absence was not a radical absence; the narratives existed, at any rate virtually, in the memories of the few witnesses of Péguy's death; but these witnesses, busied with their wartime preoccupations, had no leisure to record in permanent form what they knew. Not being questioned, they had no occasion even to give thought to the subject. But their narratives were ready to appear. When they came to be put together, twenty years after 1914, there would naturally be many deficiencies to be found in them. But this would not affect the basic facts: Péguy did in fact die, he was killed in action at the

[1] I was a prisoner of war with La Tour du Pin, and he showed me an account of his own funeral in Belgium: a case of patriotic and poetical fabulation carried to its final conclusion without any regard for historical precision. Here I was able to measure the distance between reality and fable. But the fictitious fate of La Tour du Pin was suggested by Péguy's; he merely made the mistake of not dying.

M

Battle of the Marne. And one could go into more detail: he died in a particular field, in a particular way.

If the first knowledge was not of the narrative type, it was not because contemporaries would not have liked to have a narrative; it was because owing to the war the writing of such an account was impossible. All that was known was the bald and indisputable fact, announced in the casualty list. But just because all that was known was the unadorned fact, it could be seen at once in its deep significance as 'patriotic martyr', 'poet-prophet'. So what was given first, by a kind of reversal of the normal process, was the thematic significance, not the detailed narrative.

This comparison, I feel, may help us to understand how knowledge of the Resurrection came about.

The first knowledge of it was *thematic*. In this case it was not due to the impossibility of gathering detailed evidence, but to the fact that the witnesses did not dwell upon the circumstances (as moderns would have done, with their passion for dating and verification), but rather upon the meaning of the facts. In this case it was a religious meaning, manifested in the phenomena of the outpouring of the Spirit, the behaviour of the apostles and the life of the community. For the Jewish mind, the victory of Jesus over death meant necessarily incorruption and a corporeal reappearance, in a manner, therefore, other than that of a vision seen in a dream. This victory was asserted in virtue of the fact itself, just as the fact of his warrior's death was asserted in the case of Péguy. In the earliest period, this was enough.

Naturally, to this assertion, there had to be annexed some rudimentary theory: pronouncements, that is, not subject to verification, such as 'dying-for-our-sins'. Death could be verified, but not 'dying-for-sins'. Here we have an element of faith. It is the same with the idea of dying out of love for someone; the 'out of love' is not verifiable by the senses.

The Resurrection on the third day, conceived as emergence from the tomb, and the appearance to Cephas and the Eleven—this was all that was required. The rest could have been the result of later additions. The fact was established in the first official verification, made by a body of witnesses officially constituted.

Last came the narratives. That these became increasingly circumstantial is explained, among other things, by the way everyone, when he starts to tell a story, searches in his memory for the little facts he knows to be true, facts which as time goes on become more and more prized. The stress laid on the palpable element in the apparitions is also due no doubt to the desire to refute any ghostly explanation.

For the first disciples the Resurrection was of such cardinal importance that it was a statement of fact before becoming a narrative, a dogma of faith before a narrative supporting faith. Hence so many gaps in the surviving accounts.[1]

It is probable enough that the rapid stylization of the event tended, in those early days, to allay curiosity, which could have been satisfied, then, by interrogating witnesses about all the particulars. When these first witnesses had died, and the Gospel came to be written, it was too late to collect the details we should have valued so highly. This cleavage between fact and narrative occurs almost everywhere in history. When the witnesses of some momentous event are with us, when they relive it and recount it interminably till they bore the whole company (as do old soldiers and ex-prisoners of war), no one takes the trouble to make notes. Later, to compensate for lack of proximity, what is wanted is a written text, the little fact that paints the whole picture; but then it is too late

THE RESURRECTION AND MENTAL EXPECTATIONS

The method of analysing developments structurally, the principle of which I indicated in connection with divinity, suggests inquiring here how far the experience of Christ's apparitions corresponded to the 'mental expectations' of those who heard the testimony or composed the narrative.

The conformity of a testimony or narrative with previous anticipation is no proof of authenticity, because it usually happens that one does in fact see what one expected to see, hear what one expected to hear. But when there is a *divergence* between the anticipation of the event and the subsequent account of it, then the critic

---

[1] The Gospel gives us a historical picture of Our Lord. One could go further in this same concrete sense; one can imagine, for instance, a *logion* which said: 'At that time, Jesus went forth, wearing his white mantle. His face was sunburnt. He still bore the scar of a wound on his left cheek...' But what more would we learn from this? Those who came first had no need of such descriptions; all the less, in that they had so many already. The impression we moderns get, when we see a film on some historical subject (and how remote it looks, with all that detail and colour!), they had still more. It was not a Gospel they needed then, but a Definition. So we, when we have buried one who was dear to us, would have inscribed on his grave that word which tells all. The essence condensed into a single word, that is what we want.

sees this as a sign of authenticity, for such a divergence makes improbable the hypothesis of fabulation, which would have projected into the account its own expectations and images.

So the question is: did the Jews, contemporary with Jesus, expect a resurrection of the Messiah? And if so, did they expect it in this form?

It is not an easy question to answer. The idea of a *general* resurrection was present in the minds of many Jews. It was not so much a universal hope, part of their mental patrimony, as an intellectual conclusion reached after long spiritual labour. Since the Jewish mentality, being thoroughly factual, could never imagine a soul separated from body, death seemed to them more revolting than it did to the Greeks, who were accustomed to distinguish soul from body and willing to admit its survival after the body's corruption. Confronted with the fact of death, and unable to conceive a purely spiritual state, the Jews could not but doubt whether the just, once they were dead, would be capable any longer of praising Javé. The only solution was to affirm that the whole being would be reconstituted, 'raised up again'; then it could live with God and receive its reward. In the second century before Christ the sufferings of the Jewish martyrs in the persecution of Antiochus Epiphanes rendered it intolerable to think that God, who was master of life, could have left annihilated those bodies that had suffered so much for his sake.

But this was a late development. One might say it had hardly begun when Jesus appeared.

There were prefigurations of it. Isaias had spoken of death as being 'engulfed for ever' (xxv 8), of the dead having 'fresh life'. Ezechiel had talked of the tombs being opened and God raising up the house of Israel, reanimating it, rather, for a new life on earth, complete with sinews, flesh, and skin, in the valley of carnage (xxxvii). But it is a communal reanimation that is always envisaged, a whole people's return to existence. The famous passage in *Job*, 'This at least I know, that one lives on who will vindicate me, rising up from the dust when the last day comes,' is clear enough when interpreted, as it is by the liturgy, according to the faith of the Church; but taken in its literal sense, and interpreted in the spirit of the *Book of Job*, it implies no idea of corporal resurrection. Daniel sees the awakening of those who lie sleeping in the dust of earth, 'some to enjoy life everlasting, some to be confronted for ever with their disgrace'; but here again, it would seem, it is an eternal life of the temporal or historic order (xii 2–3). Finally, we know that resurrection, in spite of these hints, was actually denied by one official school of thought, that of the Sadducees.

But the chief point to remember is that, before Christ, 'resurrection' was hardly distinguishable from earthly and temporal restoration to life. It was communal and eschatological, something that would come about simultaneously for all.

For the aspect of it which concerns me now, namely the probability of the story's being invented, this is a very important characteristic. Not only was resurrection a theological doctrine restricted to certain schools, but in the Jewish mind it was so closely connected with images of the end of the world that it could hardly have given rise to what we meet in the Gospel, namely the idea of the resurrection of one single person, and that in historical time; especially as this historical time was not brought to an end nor even interrupted. On the contrary, it proceeded on its way; one might even say that, with the birth of the Church, it begins.

The Bible also contained accounts of assumption (that of Elias, for instance, in *2 Kings* ii 3, 11–12), or reanimation, like that of the son of the widow of Sarepta (*1 Kings* xvii), or the son of the Sunamite (*2 Kings* iv 33–6). The Ascension, in fact, and also the resurrection of Lazarus were prefigured, but not the forty days' *convivium*, a historical reappearance confined to the Messiah alone, without an ending to time and with no final judgement.

To sum up, I would say that the mental expectations here were of two kinds.

The first arose out of the Jewish way of thinking about the human compound. This was fundamental; one sees it in the earliest biblical documents. So deep did it lie that it had hampered the development of belief in eternal life. It made all but unthinkable the existence of the soul, once a person was dead and the soul no longer had bodily support. It laid down in advance, as far as the Jews were concerned, the conditions that would be required if any preaching of the Resurrection was to be accepted: such a resurrection would imply the removal of the dead body and the substituting of a new and identical body. To preach this involved very serious risks, for all that was necessary to refute it was a very simple piece of evidence, of decisive importance in Jewish eyes: the production of the body or the testimony of those who had concealed it.

The second mental expectation was more localized and also

vaguer. It was that of a general resurrection on the last day.[1] This would favour any vision of the eschatological type, but certainly not an historical narrative.

One might sum up by saying that these sets of ideas contained an element that was useful, perhaps even necessary, for understanding the event *after it had taken place*, but they were too weak and too vague, too unsubstantial to produce the event by fabling anticipation.

[1] Cf. Martha's words to Jesus concerning the dead Lazarus: 'I know well enough that he will rise again at the resurrection, when the last day comes' (*John* xi 24).

V

APPARITIONS AND MYSTICAL EXPERIENCES

THE RESEMBLANCES

I HAVE before me here a very arduous task: the hardest, I am sure, I have so far undertaken.

I have to decide what is the nature of an event that has never recurred and has had the most extraordinary sequel. There are, as I have said, two possible explanations, one subjective, the other objective.

The method I have followed up to now suggests the order in which I should tackle these alternative theories. On the analogies of history, which is the more probable? Obviously the subjective. It is extremely improbable that one who is dead should be recalled to life. Even granting there is a God, who can 'raise up' a dead prophet, there is no indication in history of his ever having done so. But what would seem to be most conclusive is this: the human heart protests so violently against death, needs so badly to believe in survival, and accept a proof of it as proof of God's goodness, or even of his existence. It is so easy, too, for faith to produce accounts of survival; and, for those still living, there are so many confused experiences that give the impression that the dead still exist, that natural explanations, calling for no unique exception to the human lot, look very probable indeed.

All the same, when I am trying to account for the beginnings of Christianity I must always remember, not only the uniqueness of the fact, but its spiritual value and importance in the history of the human race on this planet. This leads me to reject without hesitation the common eighteenth-century explanation, namely fraud and imposture. Nor could I defend very long the theory of love-illusion, adopted so readily by Renan, though it is questionable whether he believed in it very seriously himself. It was his way of saying: *Ignorabimus*.

What I must try to discover first is an explanation which takes into account the quality of the original faith, without obliging me to bridge that yawning gap which separates me from faith; an explanation, in short, which would leave the event subjective while retaining all its spiritual substance.

Therefore, if I can, I shall try to explain the apparitions of Christ as mystical experiences.

This is an explanation that preserves a golden mean, almost exactly midway between the two extremes of faith and non-faith, though it certainly inclines to the side of non-faith and could never be accepted by the orthodox Tradition. One might call it ambiguous. It avoids committing itself strictly to one side or the other; for mystical experiences, in the opinion of many, furnish no real knowledge; all they reveal is the state of the subject, the depths of his subconscious, or rather, perhaps, his dialectical genius for representing to himself what is at work within him.

Mystical visions, it should be noted, are no longer treated as maladies of the mind. Phenomena of the kind are met with conspicuously at the founding of great religious undertakings. So there is no need now for the sceptical hypothesis to go so far in the negative direction and devalue the propagation of Christianity by making it rest on neurotic conditions. All it need say is that mystics, like those it was to produce in its later history, are also to be found at the origins of Christianity. This hypothesis, of course, has to reject the theme of the empty tomb, at any rate in the form in which it appears in the Gospel, because a mystical vision, having no foundation in reality, is wholly unrelated to the *body* of the person who appears, and for its justification it requires no real removal of the body.

SOME CHARACTERISTICS OF MYSTICAL EXPERIENCES: THE SOCIAL BACKGROUND

It is not uncommon for mystics to 'hear voices', or see figures, which appear to them to be external to themselves; they may be so, in their true causes, but they have no substance in the exterior world of matter. What leads one to think that their visions are related to their own inner selves is that they see celestial beings according to the norms and categories of their own social background. Thus the persons seen and heard by Catholic mystics are those who are known to Catholic tradition. Such mystics perceive, in a new form, beings whose images they have already seen in church: Christ, the Blessed Virgin, and the saints. If Joan of Arc saw and heard the archangel Michael, St Margaret, and St

Catherine, it was because these three heavenly beings were then the objects of popular devotion in France and along the borders of Lorraine.

THE IMPRESSION OF REALITY

It should be observed, too, that mystics cannot control their states. Their visions come and go of their own accord; they themselves can do nothing about it. These voices and lights, these sensations of touching, are more vividly real to those who are favoured with them than are real people and things to a normal person. The light they see makes the sun appear pale; for neither things nor persons nor the light of the sun so penetrate the inward man as to sublimate and transform him, as the mystical visionary is sublimated and transformed by those beings who 'have appeared'. In telling their experiences, what mystics always insist on is the subsequent impression they have of the unreality of the physical world. When her saints left her, Joan of Arc wept and kissed the ground where their feet had rested. The reason is that we endow the people we see with greater substantiality in proportion to the warmth and peace they bestow on our inner life. In the lower order of art, the characters in a novel have more reality, for those who possess an aesthetic sense, than the people who eat at their table and share the same house. No wonder, then, that *visions* are more than *ordinary* experiences.

SPIRITUAL MISSION AND MESSAGE

What should be noticed, lastly, is that visions are not barren, things seen or contemplated without any meaning. They have an object, and they instil into the person enjoying them a certitude of what it is, together with a lively desire that others shall share his faith. They are therefore an inspiration to propagate faith. As Bergson rightly pointed out, the mystical state, when complete, normally results in some act that inspires imitation, in a truly creative humility, in utterances that are also seeds, and in the founding of enduring communities. True, this might be said of any generous intuition, imparted momentarily, as it would seem, to one individual in solitude, so that he in turn may transmit it to others. But how much more in the case of mystical visions! These are pregnant with action, and all the more so in that they have first been longer experienced in secret. It might even be said that all the churches, nations, and parties, the very institutions and ordered modes of living that sustain our existences in this twentieth century, all derive originally from some sort of vision.

Here is an example, close at hand and therefore easy to study: the Lourdes pilgrimage. I perceive analogies here between the apparitions of the Blessed Virgin to Bernadette and those of the risen Jesus to the apostles. In both cases the same word 'apparition' is used spontaneously. A number of aspects are similar: an intense feeling of presence; a sudden appearance giving rise to perplexity; an equally sudden evanescence; the apparition's independence of any desires on the part of the subject; appearances following one another discontinuously like separate events; a co-ordination between them; one apparition supplementing the other, then all of them ceasing, never to recur in a lifetime—and a lifetime all intent on experiencing them again; a state of certainty on the part of the mystic, who in spite of persecution never denies what has been seen; a message resulting from the apparition, one that allows complete freedom either to accept or reject it, and one gradually imparted to an ever widening circle of people, drawn, for the most part, from the poor, the suffering, and the humble.

THE APPARITIONS OF CHRIST AND PERCEPTIONS

This theory, which would relegate the Resurrection to the category of mystical experiences, is one I must now examine with some care. It would seem to reconcile the requirements of faith with what is demanded by science.

My training in criticism is against having recourse to the paranormal unless I am driven into a corner and can do nothing else. I must be as economical as possible with this kind of hypothesis, which is a desperate resort and yet at the same time over-hopeful. Both faith and the analogies of experience require seeing Christianity as divine in origin. But whereas it is impossible, in my view, to explain its sudden birth by hallucination, what appears at first sight to be an adequate explanation is some sort of initial mystical experience. What seems to me to be required primarily by faith is not so much Christ's physical triumph over the laws of biology as the conquest and diffusion of a new supernatural life.

For the mass of the faithful, it is true, the realist conception of the Resurrection would appear to be indispensable: it is important for them that Christ should have truly resumed his own body and with it entered a life of glory in heaven. In other words, for the majority of Christians the dogma of the Resurrection seems to imply the material reality of the body of Jesus and its physical identity with the corpse which had hung upon the cross. But it may well happen that a belief, which has long been expressed in realist terms, may come to emerge from the trappings that enveloped it. For instance, in the earliest times, Christians interpreted in a local and geographical sense the expressions 'ascended into heaven', 'descended into hell', and they would doubtless have been scandalized to be told that heaven was a *state* rather than a *place*, and that the Father was not to be sought in the sky, nor hell in the depths of the earth.

The safest course would be to proceed in two stages. I am going to inquire first what the difference was between the apparitions of Christ and the perceptions of our senses. This will bring the apparitions more in line with mystical phenomena.

I notice first that they have not the character of perceptions given by the senses.

Exterior objects are perceived by all present in the same spatial circle, irrespective of their private dispositions. Take, for example, the statue in the Louvre known as the *Victory of Samothrace*. It will be seen by all who stand in front of it. Suppose, among the visitors to the Louvre, some dull individual who has no appreciation of the Greek idea of beauty. He will see the statue as clearly as anyone else. The image on his retina will be similar to that enjoyed by an admirer of the *Victory*. Of course the sentiments produced by contemplating the statue will vary according to the observer. In the marble draperies, the attentive will seek details that had passed unnoticed, and the artist's final appreciation would have little in common with his first impressions. But the mental operations thus involved make no difference at all to the perception of the statue; they simply help to reveal aspects that were always present but not detected by the casual glance. Even if the artist had doubts about the presence of the *Victory of Samothrace*, they would be banished at once by a few simple operations. All he needs to do is to go up to the statue and see if he can touch it; if necessary he can ask his neighbour, and we know very well that our neighbour *sees precisely what we see*. It might also happen that the contemplation of this work of beauty might give rise to an artistic vocation, perhaps in some young man who had entered the Louvre out of mere curiosity and left it to be an artist for the rest of his life. But in this case the bare perception of the statue could hardly be considered the cause of the vocation, it was merely the occasion that made him aware of it.

It is very different with the *apparitions* we are considering. It is remarkable, in the first place, that the risen body of Jesus was perceived only by those who already believed in him and were his faithful followers. I am fully aware that these disciples had no idea of one solitary resurrection. I know very well that after the death of Jesus, all unexpected as it was and so very humiliating, they were a prey to bewilderment and doubt and despair. Yet in spite of this they had latent belief; before their Master's death they had made bold acts of faith; these there was no going back on: they were binding on their consciences for ever. They believed in Jesus, at least humanly, and the extent of their disappointment was the measure of their faith.

Jesus appeared only to those who believed in him, and whose belief gave rise to a kind of impulse of welcome. He showed himself first to the women; and the reason, no doubt, is because it is woman's nature to be more completely possessed by faith. When the tomb was found empty, it was John (if we accept the Johannine account) who was the first to see it so, because the faith he represents is that which is activated by love. The Emmaus disciples, as they trod their long road, had minds dulled with a cloud of questioning, but they were ready to believe. If they did not see until *afterwards*, it was because faith is better manifested in its purity when the reality has disappeared. Thomas, who declined to believe till he had seen and touched, was judged less 'blessed' than those who believed on the strength of the word alone. The fact is, Jesus appeared only to those who were willing already to see what they saw, to hear what they heard, touch what they touched. Jesus never appeared to Pilate or Tiberius. So here again, in this last characteristic, the apparitions have no resemblance to sense-perceptions.

THE STRANGENESS AND AMBIVALENCE
OF THE EXPERIENCES

There is another aspect, too, in which these perceptions differ from ordinary perceptions. This is the alarm, the doubt and fear they caused, at any rate at first.

Nearly all the Gospel accounts present a very odd feature, and one, incidentally, that would be difficult to explain on any fictional hypothesis, because it would call for considerable subtlety in the inventor. It is the fact that the disciples fail to recognize their

Master *immediately*. Some of them believe, others doubt. Peter did not recognize the Lord, though he had lived with him in very close intimacy. Mary Magdalen mistook him for a gardener. Others thought he was a ghost. The Emmaus disciples did not recognize him either, after conversing with him all that time. Seemingly it was only after a period of perplexity, which varied in different cases, that the apparition became identified with Jesus. It is nowhere stated that this difficulty was due to lack of goodwill or just to surprise. It is true that Jesus reproached his disciples for their slowness and incredulity, for the tardiness of their faith, but he also admits the difficulty of *recognizing* him, for he presents himself afresh and in different circumstances; he tries to convince them (as on the road to Emmaus); he increases the reality, the substantiality of his presence by eating in their company and allowing Thomas the test of touch. On other occasions one gets the impression that he has adopted a disguise: that of the gardener or casual wayfarer, of the stranger standing on the shore. One might think he desired to remain anonymous. Are we to regard these accounts as extremely clever fiction? Are these difficulties to be surmounted put in simply to keep the reader in suspense? Personally I prefer to think that this impression of strangeness is due to the difficulty felt by the human brain in adapting itself to such novel experiences; and the reason, I am sure, is that these experiences, to be fully understood, call for an exceptional degree of tractability. A certain amount of light is shed upon this by the analogy of mystical experiences. We find that mystics, too, are perplexed in the presence of an 'apparition'; they ask for signs and assurances; when they are simple souls like Bernadette, they ask the apparition's name and offer pen and paper to have it written down.

Here was no evident perception, no sort of photographic record, no direct communication with a person such as exists in ordinary human encounters. Compare the Gospel accounts of the Passion with those of the apparitions and you will notice this curious difference. In the one case a collection of facts that develops without any ambiguity, in the other an experience that raises problems, provokes an attitude of criticism.

It was not an event that constrained belief. The evidence was not of the incontestable sort, nor was the vision something in the ordinary sense 'seen'. Therefore there was room for error and illusion; the Gospels describe the mental effort that was necessary on the part of the witnesses before they could attain to certainty.

Theirs was a process of testing, similar to that we make when we try to verify, in a case of doubt, the data of one of our senses, comparing them with the data about the same object provided by another sense, one supposedly more reliable; testing, for instance, a visual sensation which we fear is illusory by touching or feeling the object before us. What the apostles wanted was to touch Jesus, or test his reality by watching him take food.

Whatever the reality of these episodes, what seems to be certain is that the witnesses' awareness of it deepened with the passing of time and subsequent reflection. It was a matter of assimilating a fact which was part of the witnesses' experience, but not wholly satisfying from the cognitional point of view. It presented them with the question of its reality.

It was a fact, too, that called for something more than what a philosopher would call an act of reflection, more than a purely intellectual operation. It also required adherence of the will, a preliminary trust, in other words an act of faith. This adherence of faith did not account for the phenomenon, but it was a condition morally necessary for its cognition. In all probability the apparition would never have occurred without it.

THE APPEAL TO EARLIER TRADITION AS A TEST
OF AUTHENTICITY

What is equally remarkable is the way Jesus seeks to dispel his disciples' doubts: to convince them of the truth of their perceptions he appeals to Scripture.

This is seen quite clearly on re-reading the episode of the Emmaus pilgrims. There Jesus prepares their minds by expounding all that had been said on the subject by the Law, the Prophets, and the Psalms. The visions of Isaias were clothed in Jewish imagery; those of the seer of Patmos conformed to the apocalyptic structure, those of Joan of Arc reflected the popular devotion to St Michael and the statues in the church at Domrémy. But here there is something else besides.

The disciples, surprised by a unique experience, would want it confirmed by the experience of others. But the Jewish soul was profoundly religious, and what a Jew would expect, before a particular experience could be sealed with its full meaning, would be to see it related to *official* experience, to the *condensed* experiences of past generations, gathered together and guaranteed in the inheritance of Israel.

I was considering just now the reactions of a person looking at the

Victory of Samothrace. He could, as I remarked, perceive it quite well without any reference to earlier tradition. Yet if he had never heard of Greek art, and did not know that this was an example of it, might he not, perhaps, have hesitated for a moment? The apparitions of Jesus were totally different. It would seem that in order to remove doubts he appealed to Scripture. In what sense? Were there passages in Scripture where the Resurrection of the Messiah was distinctly *foretold*? Possibly; but interpretation was needed to throw light on these passages.

To find anticipations of the Resurrection in Jewish Scripture it is necessary to be already convinced of it. I am inclined to think that when talking to the Emmaus pilgrims Jesus did not quote any particular text in isolation (as Jewish and modern readers, with their somewhat scholastic mentalities, would have us believe), but rather imparted to them—one might say, inspired them with—an interior and general knowledge of the Scriptures. He made them understand the meaning of divine history, as related in Scripture, from the first Adam to this new Adam, with the Suffering Servant as intermediary, a sublime link between the two, summing up all and announcing more to come. But the apostles, with their rabbinical training, had been taught to distinguish, in the mass and flux of Scripture, some particular passage, clear enough as it stood, yet capable of prophesying what they themselves had witnessed and thereby giving it a divine warrant. In the Old Testament, that inspired and canonical collection of documents, they searched for verses that might appear to proclaim a resurrection for the Messiah 'on the third day'—which was what had happened. The account of Jonas' imprisonment in the sea-monster had to be interpreted as a figure—if Jesus did so interpret it during his mortal life—a figure presaging the Resurrection.[1]

But it is, as I have said, also possible to think that it was the whole history, related in Scripture—not this or that fragment of it, this or that detail hitherto overlooked—which presaged, which actually *taught* the Resurrection. The historical experience of Israel, that of the Adamic human race, was an alternation of deaths or torpors

---

[1] At the present stage of my progress I cannot decide definitely whether the predictions of the Resurrection contained in the Gospels were inserted after the event. That is why I here leave the question open. It is one of the many questions that arise in this study which are seen in a different light according as one is commencing the inquiry or nearing the end of it. Obviously, if Jesus is God, the probability of the Resurrection's being foretold is much stronger.

and unforeseeable revivals. Time and again God had caused his people to arise out of the shadow of death. Was not Javé he who *raises up*, who *raises up again*? In Paul's speech at Pisidian Antioch, reported in the *Acts* (xiii 16–41), we see him at one time using particular passages in a symbolic sense, at another basing his argument on the idea that God was acting through Christ as he had previously acted through Israel.

We may also conceive that Christ reminded the Emmaus disciples, in a moment that really summed up all, of the many lessons he had given them by act and word; all this, I suggest, came to final achievement at that unique moment, and served as commentary and context to the manifestation that was to occur later.

Thus, when once it occurred, this manifestation would take its place in the spiritual history of the past. It would be the rounding off of that vast spiritual area presented to the mind by the Old Testament (now, though the disciples could not know it, closed), in that line of duration starting with Abraham and going back to the very first day of creation, which was that of a first *surrection* of being. In this way the event was guaranteed true by its conforming with what was already canonized as divine truth and prophetic history.

In this respect too the apparitions of Jesus have a certain resemblance to mystical apparitions; for these are never fully certified by the experiences themselves, however vivid they may be, till they have been confronted, not so much by Scripture in this case, as by that living Tradition which is the earlier authentic experience of the Church. Till this approbation is given by the representative of Tradition—firstly and provisionally the director of conscience, then the bishop and finally the Holy See—the Catholic mystic, though sure of *having seen*, may still be doubtful whether his experiences really come from God. The agreement of his experience with Tradition is what gives him complete certitude. If the analogy is sound, I would say that to have a complete vision of Jesus as risen it was not enough to have the senses alert; it was also necessary, with an effort of the whole soul, to supplement the present memory with Tradition, the memory of the Church.

THE PRESENCE OF A VOCATION AND A MISSION

There is one last respect in which the apparitions of the risen Christ could be compared with mystical states. I mean the presence in their very content, of a vocation, a mission.

Sense perceptions, as I said just now, are hardly ever charged with a message; they have no power by themselves to bestow spiritual energy. But here we have perceptions that convey power and are somehow reminiscent of creative intuitions. An inventor, once he possesses in germ form the whole sequence of his work and is already transformed by it, foresees in a flash the way to realize it. How much more so, one who receives from God, by special favour and as a special trust, some exceptional certitude, judged to be useful, perhaps even necessary, for the salvation of mankind!

It is a commonplace of Christian apologetics to show from the Gospels and the Acts how the apostles were transformed after the events of Easter and Pentecost. Indeed this changed state of mind is the one historical fact that can be seen at the outset as unquestionable. It is more certain than the historical existence of Jesus, which some people have contrived to deny. A handful of Jews underwent a psychological change which led to the propagating of a cult—this is something it is impossible to contest. So we may say—what is admitted by all historians—that the apostles, after the death of Jesus and the mystery which followed it, began suddenly to show not only enthusiasm and zeal, but also patience; and not only patience but a sense of the possible, even the art of government. Possessed by the divine Spirit, they controlled with great prudence the explosive manifestations of that Spirit. Theirs was peace even more than exaltation. But in this also the visions may be compared with the states experienced by the great Catholic mystics, which produced in them not only spiritual energies of an altogether exceptional order, but (stranger still) a genius for patience, a genius for prudence and even tactics.

INVESTITURE

It is very remarkable that no one was ever favoured with an apparition in order that he might enjoy his certitude alone. Every apparition contains a kind of investiture.

Jesus revealed himself to bestow mandates as well as powers. Sometimes these were limited to a particular mission. This was the case with the private apparitions, as when Jesus showed himself to the women, to Mary Magdalen. If the Emmaus apparition appears to be an exception to this rule, it is because it was a preface to the account of the collective apparition, when the two from Emmaus rejoined the assembled Eleven. When Jesus appeared to the aposto-

N

lic college it was to give them commissions to bear testimony, to impart to them the Holy Spirit, and send them on a mission that would occupy all history. When, in the conclusion to *St John*, he appears to the fishermen at Tiberias and eats with them, it is again to invest Peter: 'Feed my sheep! Feed my lambs!' Here we find again an idea that was fundamental in the Old Testament: no perception of God without a divine calling to some mission of salvation. The Easter visions were no exception to this law; they too were calls to a definite work, the most universal it is possible to conceive: nothing less than the founding of a society of the Spirit vast enough to include 'all nations'.

A vivid feeling of reality, a state in some sort more than real, yet none the less strange and capable of being doubted; a seeking for support in the past by referring to official religious Tradition, which is nothing else but capitalized experience; an urge towards the future, the desire to transmit a message to a privileged few, and through them to all people—such are the three aspects of these mystical experiences which principally linger in my mind.

I have encountered them again in a preliminary description of the facts given in the Gospels concerning the appearances of Christ.

VI

HOW THE APPARITIONS DIFFER FROM
MYSTICAL EXPERIENCES

SEEMINGLY, then, this explanation of the Easter experience
by regarding it as a mystical phenomenon makes it unnecessary
to admit a real miracle or a genuine physical perception, yet at
the same time it allows the Easter event to retain its religious value.
We may well believe that some such explanation will continue to
be given in the future by minds solicitous for science but reluctant
to be unduly disturbing to faith.

THE APPARITIONS TO THE APOSTLES
NOT MYSTICAL VISIONS

But though it professes to be a positive explanation, it has against
it one initial experience, which is the testimony of the only witnesses.

If the apostles intended this explanation of their behaviour, there
is reason to think they would have regarded it as a negation of
what they held fundamental, namely that their contact with Christ
was objective, historical, and real. And even from the scientific
point of view it is embarrassing to have to admit that the only observer is fundamentally deluded. Why admit the truth of the vision,
when the veracity of the witness himself is denied? Why not reject
the whole story *en bloc*? Why this distinction between the authenticity of the vision (which is rejected) and its subjectivity (which is
accepted as a mystical *phenomenon*)? You come and tell me you have
seen the devil. It would be reasonable to conjecture that you have
seen nothing at all. Why say: 'You have actually seen nothing,
there is no devil; but all you tell me about him is deeply significant.
I have complete faith in you, your moral worth, your sincerity, your
religious genius, everything—except what you tell me'? In short,
to reduce the visions to purely mystical phenomena is to remove
their main characteristic in the eyes of those favoured with them,
which was the fact that they were *not* mystical phenomena.

The reply will be, that the contemporaries of Jesus were unable to distinguish between interior visions and objective apparitions, those, that is, where the subject is in some relationship with external reality. But it is very noticeable that that such a distinction was in fact present to the Jewish mind. Though they knew very well what they meant by the word 'vision', the Jews never applied it to the Easter experience.

Anyone who has even a superficial acquaintance with the prophetic or historical books of the Old Testament can see this distinction already being made.

God might communicate with men by means of dreams, suspending their faculties so as to carry them above the temporal order. He might also reveal himself through historical events which would serve as divine signs. These means can be seen at the very beginning, in the ancient account of the creation of Eve. Adam falls into an ecstatic sleep, during which he has one of his ribs removed. And the author assumes that this rib was missing when he awoke. In the experience of Israel we see the intervention of dream-theophanies and prodigy-theophanies. Sometimes the Eternal acts by means of visions, in ecstasy or sleep, and (in Israel) more often still through the hearing of a voice; at other times he acts historically, by signs visible to all. The former phenomena are outside history and wholly individual. But as the God of the Bible gradually reveals himself in time, the missions enjoined in ecstasy have historical effects. From the ecstasy of Abraham emerges all Jewish history. Yet it still remains true that for the biblical authors there was a vast difference between ecstasy of this sort and such cosmic events as the 'suspension of the waters' or the 'standing still of the sun'. Ecstasy, one might say, is able to *historify*, but can never be *historified*.

These ideas, as we see in the Gospel writings, continued under the new dispensation. Though Jesus was conceived by the evangelists as the Son *par excellence*, he for whom the heavens were always open, there is only one passage in all the Gospels where he is shown testifying to an ecstatic vision of his own: 'I watched while Satan was cast down like a lightning flash from heaven' (*Luke* x 18).[1] The cases where he may be supposed to be in direct, non-historical relationship with the Father can be reduced to four (the baptism, the

---

[1] The other passages which show Jesus in direct communication with heaven (*Mark* i 10; *Matt.* iv 1; xi 25; *Mark* ix 2) are not ecstatic in character. See Kittel, *Theologisches Wörterbuch*, II, p. 454. Yet the enemies of Jesus, in a passage as little open to suspicion as any, represent him as being out of his senses (*Mark* iii 21). Fabulation might easily have got busy on this point, were there not memories to counter-balance it.

temptation, the transfiguration, and the triumphant jubilation). These exceptional incidents accentuate by contrast the non-ecstatic, objective, and therefore historical character which the writers saw in *what was capable of being told in narrative form* and was imbedded in the texture of time common to all.

The apparitions of the risen Christ were never conceived as occurring at night, in a dream. They were neither dreams themselves nor revelations imparted in a dream, such as those we know in Matthew's Gospel (in the accounts of the Infancy) and in the *Acts* (ix 10, etc.). They are never represented as theophanies or angelophanies. The risen Christ never speaks in visions, which was the regular Jewish way of representing and translating a divine communication.

St Paul, describing the manifestation on the road to Damascus, distinguishes clearly this experience of Christ's presence from the 'vision' of Ananias (ὅραμα, *Acts* ix 10; the same technical term is used of Moses' 'burning bush'). He also draws a distinction between this experience and his own visions (ὀπτασία) and revelations (ἀποκάλυψις).[1] For Jewish writers a 'vision' did not imply what we call historicity. For instance, when the *Acts* tell how Peter was miraculously released from prison, they say: 'So he followed him out, unaware that what the angel had done for him was true; he thought he was seeing a vision' (*Acts* xii 9). In spite of the difficulty presented by Paul's assimilating his Damascus experience (to which I shall have to return later) to the official appearances of Christ, I cannot help noting that the contemporaries of Jesus made a virtual, and even technical distinction between the subjective and the objective, the personal and the historical. Tending though they might to regard themselves as visionaries of a heavenly Jesus, they yielded submissively to another fact: the evidential and historical character of these appearances of Christ.[2]

Mystical experiences always remain enigmas even to those who experience them. St Teresa of Avila declared that although numerous masters (she mentions twenty-two) had assured her that God was acting in her soul, yet she was never so completely convinced herself as to be ready to take her oath on it. She protested that she never allowed herself to be guided solely by what she heard in

---

[1] He had experience of *visions* (*Acts* xvi 9–10; xviii 9) and esctasy (xxii 18).
[2] The texts are collected and described without interpretation by Kittel, *Theologisches Wörterbuch*, articles: Ἀποκάλυψις; Ἔκστασις; Ὁράω.

prayer. If that was true of the most self-possessed of mystics, how much more for someone who merely hears what the mystics relate? He would need signs at least, such as improbable achievements brought about with consummate ease. At any rate, the authority whose function it is to transmit the deposit of faith has never officially guaranteed the historical reality of any particular vision, or its objective truth. This belongs to what is private and interior, non-historical and non-evidential; here certitude, however likely, cannot be established by the convergence of public and independent testimony. All the Church does, therefore, is to judge the spiritual fruits of the vision and its dogmatic content.

Moreover, if the Resurrection were only a mystical experience it would be no more miraculous to the well-informed faithful than any other mystical experiences, which are always ambiguous owing to the impossibility of making any exact demarcation between what is subjective and what is objective. And there would no longer be an *event* at the origin of Christianity, but only a state of consciousness, of the prophetic sort, such as had been present so often in Israel. This has never been the Christian feeling about it. What Christians see in the *Easter fact* is an historical reality, not limited to the consciousness of those who witnessed it; for them it is a 'miracle', and the guarantee of all other miracles, of all those events in which the Creator acts personally, beyond what is expected or recognized as possible.

But it is not enough that the founders of Christianity, applying Jewish classifications, make this clearly marked distinction between the apparitions of Christ and subjective visions. We must see whether the impression they had was really justified by the accounts they allowed to be given of their experiences. Was it historical, this fact which we divine behind their testimony?

There are various tests of historicity: the convergence of independent testimonies, the continuity of events, the multiplicity of circumstantial aspects. But the most striking, perhaps, is what may be called *insertion*.

INSERTION IN THE TEXTURE OF HISTORY

In these apparitions we see Jesus making himself perceptible to the senses. He lets himself be touched. He takes food. He travels from place to place; he talks; people answer when he questions them. Much more than this, the events, as they unfold, take their place in the texture of history, 'engage' (as it were) in common-to-all duration. Everything seems to suggest that they are of precisely the same nature as the events that had gone before.

This point was emphasized at the very beginning (*Acts* i 3; x 41–2, 'we ate and drank in his company'; xiii 31); then later, when the narrative of the events appeared, this always stressed the homogeneity of the life of the risen Christ with the life of Jesus: the Gospel is continuous. The second generation insists on this again: the risen Jesus is shown using the same gestures, speaking the same words, teaching the same doctrine. Thus throughout the first century we see developing not only the historicity of the event but a homogeneity of circumstances, those of today and those of yesterday.

Here again the apparitions differ from visions. Visions, though they profoundly affect the subject's interior life and even bring it renewal, are only *parentheses* in his historical life. While the phenomenon of ecstasy lasts, he is ravished; momentarily, but completely, he is 'taken out of himself'. He seems to undergo some marvellous kind of distraction, to be completely disengaged from this physical world, to which he will return almost immediately. Moreover the object of his vision is outside time and space; he himself is drawn into its essential *unhistoricity*.

In the Gospel narratives there is no *ecstasy*; rather (if we may invent a word) an *enstasy*, in that some reality of a higher order is 'inserted', as it were, into the familiar experience of a small group of people. True, this *sacred history* is history only for this little group; it was not witnessed by others. But by virtue of the testimony, first *personal* but very soon *institutional*, especially by virtue of the 'breaking of bread', understood as a sign of recognition and thanksgiving (a remembrance of the apparitions as much as a memorial of the Lord's Passion), and by the institution of Sunday, the subject of the testimony becomes inserted in universal history: it was to be the Church itself, occupying the whole duration of time.

THE IDENTITY OF THE CHARACTER OF JESUS

The character of Jesus is the same as it was before, I mean the human traits of his nature. We find him as he always was, showing the same consideration, the same patience in teaching; kindly, tender, a lover of holiness in women; yet firm, severe, sometimes even hard; a leader, too, master of the future, ordaining laws for his Church; loving, appealing, consoling, a worker of meaningful miracles, the friend of all, but always with special friendships; recognizable also in the same manner of teaching, with the poet's use of hiatus and repetition, and the same familiar gestures, that raising of the eyes as he broke bread. Ordinarily so serious, he now gives us a glimpse of something like a smile. All these various features are indications of an historic human existence: here is movement and variety, adaptation to circumstances, the need to ask and answer questions, the need for adjustment to circumstances, feeling the way, assuming a given place. A visionary object does not behave like this; its symbolical image merely presents its *essence*, not its *existence*.

AN OBJECTION TO CORRESPONDENCE

Here an objection occurs to the critical mind, that which always suggests itself when what it is sought to establish is the improbability of a correspondence between any two series. The correspondence, it will be said, between the risen Jesus and the Jesus of the Gospels is due, not to unconscious fabulation of the mythical sort, but to a deliberately constructive and systematic fabulation. To answer the contention, on the part of Jews and Greeks, that the risen Christ was simply a ghost, it was necessary to make the apparition narratives follow the lines of the earlier narratives in the Gospel. And it will be pointed out that in fact the correspondence grows more precise in the later narratives, those of Luke and John.

There applies here what I have already said about the argument from prophecy. It is ambiguous in itself, and all the more so as it claims to be more perfect. It can always be supposed that the cause of the correspondence between the *old* and the *new* is not the presence of divine *simultaneousness*, the eternity of divine action, but simply the work of the fabulator, whether he makes up his story on the basis of an earlier text, or invents the prediction after the event. That is why the correspondence argument has more *critical* value when it is less precise, when it is not circumstantial but broad and general.

In the present case, what strikes me is not identity of detail, because from any given one it is possible to derive two contrary impressions, according to whether one inclines towards faith or doubt. A too strict resemblance would be a reason for mistrusting it. But I see a *general* resemblance between the risen Christ and Christ as he was before. Here again, if a fabulator had been at work, what he would have imagined, I think, would have been a celestial, super-human Christ, a kind of King-of-the-ages, similar to the Lamb of the Apocalypse, giving utterance to oracles—not a so humanly similar Jesus. The evangelists would have been quite capable of inventing apparitions that bore no traces of *insertion* or *historicity*: one has only to remember the Father's voice at the moment of the Messiah's baptism, or again at the Transfiguration. In both these cases, the voice, the light, were not 'inserted' in duration; they were not the voices, the lights, the persons of this world. The evangelists must have been greatly tempted by accounts of this 'uranian' type. If they did not yield to it, it was due to the 'resistance' they encountered in memory.

The experience attested by all the documents, even the earliest, is of Jesus *reliving*, though in a new mode of existence. The essence of the testimony bears on just this point: 'We ate and drank in his company after his rising from the dead' (*Acts* x 41).

It is possible, obviously, and even probable, that in narrating one of these appearances the writer had before him the text of an earlier Gospel and would naturally have been influenced by it. But from this it is a very big step to declare that he made up the story on the lines of earlier accounts. To assert pious fraud is a summary solution of what is really an extremely complicated problem, and it leads one to suspect some deep inhibition that has its origin somewhere else.

THE APOSTLES' DOUBTS

I come back now to the doubts of the apostles, and the question I ask is this: To what extent does the *ambivalent* character of the apparitions suggest that these Gospel narratives were, or were not, the work of legendary fabrication?

One may suppose, as I have said, an exceptionally astute fabricator, who would have invented these states of doubt in the witnesses, these processes of verification, so as to make their testimony look more convincing. From the point of view of criticism, the credibility of a story is all the greater when the narrator admits he had himself doubted its truth, but afterwards contrived to overcome these doubts and reach a state of conviction. A good legend-maker should have had the imagination to stuff his narrative with doubts overcome.

So I put up this objection: suppose the evangelists were highly ingenious storytellers. But this, it seems to me, is to think of them as modern historians, or better still novelists, sitting at their desks, with all the leisure, intelligence, and skill that would be necessary to invent the details they required. But all we know goes to suggest that the Gospels were written by believers, and written in some haste. Is there any probability that they had the knowledge and freedom for the subtle and by no means easy task of altering a tradition they regarded as sacred, especially since for them the bearing of false witness was the unpardonable sin?[1]

I am therefore inclined to believe that these doubts of the first witnesses were original facts. I see no point in the narrators' inventing them. If what they wanted to do was to confirm the faith of these primitive and fervent communities of Christians, they would have done much better to invent clearer and much more significant apparitions. As Jews they would have had no difficulty in this; they could have drawn on their prophetic and apocalyptic tradition for examples of visions that left no room for doubt. Given belief in the divinity of the Saviour, it was surely derogatory to think of his appearing to the original witnesses in forms that might well be regarded as dubious.

This, it seems to me, is another element that conflicts with the theory of fable and rather indicates a convergent primitive tradition.

THE JEWISH IDEA OF OBJECTIVITY

When we are dealing with a unique event, incommensurable with any other, the quest for analogies can yield at best only very remote images. Adequate expressions are wanting, and will always be wanting.

To translate the *reality* of the Easter event, a modern mind will contrast it with purely interior states: ecstasies, mystical experiences, hallucinations. The words that suggest themselves are rather *historicity, objectivity, eternal-temporal,* or *observed, recognized and testified fact.* The Jews of the time of Jesus were bound to raise the same questions, but they lacked the critical concepts with which to translate them.

The fact is, there are two ways of evaluating a spiritual event: according to its importance in the scheme of salvation and according to its capability of being witnessed. These two scales need not necessarily coincide. For instance the temptation of Jesus, so im-

---

[1] See on *Pseudomarturia* Kittel's dictionary under μαρτύριον; and also I *Cor.* xv 15; *Matt.* xv 19.

portant for the understanding of the inner nature of the Messiah, could never be the subject of historical evidence. On the other hand, the three denials and their circumstances, the episode of the young man who ran away naked (*Mark* xiv 51–2), the behaviour of the women at the tomb, these are historical but without spiritual import. The first chapters of *Genesis* tell of events that could not be amenable to historical verification, yet their doctrinal value is unique. The books of *Samuel* relate events that might partly be subjected to historical tests, but their doctrinal value is indifferent. It would seem that under the old dispensation spiritual substance, at times, was in inverse ratio to critical security.

Every temporal development, in process of being accomplished, can always be observed from two points of view, and these a whole infinity apart. First there is the divine perspective, where the future is also a present, the design unfolds without any breaks, known in its entirety, all its failures and deviations enlightened by the final goal; this is divine history, sometimes obscurely revealed to man, something that might be described as the *historial* aspect of time. Then there is the human perspective, always falsified by the fact that the temporal observer must always assume the present as his viewpoint, must reconstruct the past segment of time with the aid of scanty remains and records, and so work on discontinuous sections of duration: it is what may be called the *historical* aspect. Modern existentialism has rediscovered this deep-lying distinction between total, integral, and real history and the history of historians, made from a shifting, subjective, and provisional viewpoint; but it corrupts it when seeing it in an atheist context, which means inevitably assimilating man to a demiurge whose function is to create the future.

To a modern, trained to the requirements of criticism, a Jew might have said this:

'You of the twentieth century are chiefly concerned with critical verification; we are chiefly concerned with spiritual content. But we are not so very different after all. You do not deny that for the spiritual life the *meaning* of an event is more important than its *matter*. We do not deny that human beings, being rightly distrustful of sacred manifestations for the very reason of their ambiguity, must ask some guarantees of the divine.'

The disciples would have readily accepted such precautions. In an age that was far from critical, they distinguished very clearly between the event experienced in solitude, incapable of being confirmed by a second, independent testimony, and the public event which was capable of being checked. So Luke's solemn opening to the public Gospel refers to Roman and Jewish chronology (iii 1). The apostles, when proceeding to replace Judas, looked for a witness of all that was public in the life of Jesus, from the Baptism by John to the Ascension (*Acts* i 22).

This shows the Resurrection to be the intersecting point of two entirely distinct axes of thought: it is a *historial* mystery known *historically*. It is, as it were, an *advent* in the divine life (the exaltation of the incarnate Son), and an *event* in the life of a handful of human beings. The Resurrection is a mystery whence all else flows, and it is reproduced in the liturgy, which is, so to speak, a repetition of divine history on earth. But the Resurrection is also a fact, a fact which can, and should, be ascertained by verifiable evidence.

It has the values of mystery and the values of testimony; no wonder, then, that it impressed the disciples as something superobjective.

Not only did they rank it above 'visions' and 'revelations', as we see in the cases of Paul and Stephen and Peter, but they also endowed it with a higher historical value than that of previous Gospel history. The whole weight of their testimony rested upon this, more than on the earthly events that had gone before. The speeches of Peter make it clear that the testimony of the apostles, that which it was their mission from Christ to bear ('You are my witnesses'), concerned the Resurrection. It was the testified reality *par excellence*, the reality that increasingly shed its character on all that conditioned and preceded it, the Passion and the events before the Passion. The thing they 'must tell' was what they had *seen* and *heard* after Easter.

And yet, for Peter, the tenor of life with the risen Christ was the same as that with the terrestrial Jesus. The public period, on which his testimony bears, goes from the Baptism by John to the Ascension (*Acts* i 21–2). He sets the two epochs on one and the same plane: there is no breach, for him, in historical continuity.

A DIFFICULTY: THE DAMASCUS APPARITION

Yet the Resurrection, in Paul's eyes, as he describes it in the earliest document on the subject—the most official too, and the most certainly dated—must seemingly be likened to a *vision*. Strauss insists on this difficulty, and it is by no means negligible.

In the first Epistle to the Corinthians (xv 3–8), Paul recalls the *tradition*, which was already fixed, twenty years after the event, and says that Christ *was seen by* Cephas (Peter), then by the Eleven, then by more than five hundred of the brethren at once. . . . And he adds: 'And last of all, I too *saw* him.' We know from the three separate accounts in the *Acts*, and in some detail too, what the apparition had been on the road to Damascus: it was a vision of Christ in a dazzling light from heaven. Paul had not strictly seen the Lord. He had heard a voice. He was dazed. He rose up blind. There is no doubt at all that Paul thought he had *seen* the Lord, for he made this his qualification to be an apostle. In his own view, then, his experience was comparable to that of the Eleven. It was certainly the last of the apparitions and belonged, as far as he was concerned, to the series of Christ's apparitions.

It would be a serious difficulty if the official apparitions had to be judged in the light of Paul's, and his made the type and measure of them all. So this is the question that must be examined first.

The experiences might be analogous without being the same. It is true that the Damascus apparition was extra-historical, it was that of Christ in glory, whereas in the other apparitions he had appeared in human form, 'inserted' in history. But in both cases the Lord had *been seen*, if we take the expression to imply, as it does in the New Testament, a deep religious experience. This is what Paul asserts, and it is no good contesting the point with him. But his experience, however fruitful as a creative vocation, could never be regarded by the official Church of the Eleven as the grounds of his message and faith. It was never to find a place in the Church's professions of faith. And it is precisely thus that Paul himself regarded it, which is why he went to Jerusalem for his investiture as an apostle.

It would seem, too, that Paul, who had a genius for discrimination rather like Plato's, was careful to establish a hierarchy of values among the ways of knowing the glorified Christ.

At the lowest level he set rapture and ravishment. He makes an intellectual distinction between *incommunicable* and *communicable* values. Heavenly rapture belongs to the first class. Just as he had distinguished between 'speaking with tongues', something incomprehensible and therefore not edifying, and 'prophecy', which was both intelligible and edifying; or again between a faith that in itself was barren and all-efficacious charity; so here the *sight*, which transformed his existence and founded his apostleship, is not placed on the same level as the various 'ecstasies' which had given him strength and consolation. These last, for him, remained purely private, of no official value.

As for the Damascus incident, it had been the source of his vocation, which he regarded, not only as the complement, but as the counterpart of that of the Twelve. For him, the Gentiles; for Peter, Israel. It is therefore understandable that the amazing sequel to the Damascus vision led him to place it, although it was the last, on the same level as the apparitions that were already canonical; especially as the technical term used to describe them, in spite of their being of such a special order, was simply the general biblical term: 'He was seen.' From the point of view of efficaciousness—apostolic and missionary—Damascus might seem richer than all the other appearances put together.

Moreover Paul was primarily concerned, in the Epistle to the Corinthians, to get his apostleship recognized in the Judaic-Christian circles where it was contested. Now there was general agreement that in order to be an 'apostle' it was necessary 'to have seen' the risen Christ. Paul bore witness that he too had *seen*.

THE 'METAPSYCHICAL PHENOMENON' EXPLANATION

As a possible explanation of the apparitions one might suggest those telepathic or metapsychical phenomena which have attracted so much attention, particularly in 'Anglo-Saxon' countries.

We possess reports—and considering the quality of the witnesses it is difficult to suppose them all illusory—of the newly dead, *at the very moment of their death*, appearing to friends still living and knowing nothing of their death. The documents collected by Myers seem to show that sometimes the recently dead give exact information, unknown to the subject but afterwards verified. Bergson, who admitted that the evidence was well founded, was impressed by the shortness of the interval between the time of death and that of these ghostly apparitions; this led him to think that what was perceived was not 'ghosts of the dead' but 'ghosts of the living', in the sense that the subject emitting them had *not yet* departed from the space-time world. In Christian terminology, one would say that the dead person had *not yet passed to the other world*, had *not yet* been judged. He would be in that unstable state described by Newman in *The Dream of Gerontius*, where the soul, detached from the body, is not yet attached to God.

But we may say at once, of these manifestations of the recently dead to minds still incarnate, that whatever their truth they have no direct bearing on the Gospel fact. This would certainly have to be extenuated not a little before it bore any resemblance to spirit manifestations. The official apparitions of Jesus were not produced at the moment of his death. They were not communications received in a state of semi-consciousness; rather they implied a consciousness very fully awake; a familiarity, too, which took many different forms.

This is not to say that metapsychical experience may not provide us here with a kind of rough pattern. Nothing authentic is to be condemned *a priori*, or dismissed out of hand, in this universe where everything is linked up together, and where the humblest of things may contain a vestige or caricature of something most sublime. We know of people, highly endowed intellectually, who claim that tele-pathic experiences have brought them liberation from the spiritual blindness of nineteenth-century materialism—and idealism. *Tantae molis erat!* The idea of a possible experience of the future state of the body led them to consider the Gospel texts on the Resurrection as a record of experiences which a free thinker had no business to neglect. But the occasion is not the cause. In the story of a conver-sion, one must distinguish between the shock that removed the obstacle and the actual light that came afterwards. To pass from a spirit to the spiritual it is necessary to rise above an ambiguous, uncertain, and terrestrial order to an order of spiritual reality that engages the whole soul.

VII

THE SIGNIFICANCE OF THE EMPTY TOMB

A S I came to realize yesterday, it is about the empty tomb that the battle finally develops.

If that problem were solved it would be possible to decide between the two explanations of the Resurrection, the *mystical* explanation and that which (for want of a better name) I propose to call the *existential* explanation. If the apparitions were only mystical phenomena they had no existence outside the mind; they have therefore no connection with the body of Jesus which was laid in the tomb. It was not the body of Jesus that appeared, but an image, a talking photograph of that body, something that left the body in the tomb completely unaffected.

But if, in these apparitions, it was really the body of Jesus that allowed itself to be seen and touched, then, since it could not be in two places at once, it could not be still in the tomb. It was present in the cenacle, and on the shore of the lake: therefore it was not in the sepulchre. Belief in the emptiness of the tomb is involved in the realist character of the apparitions; consequently, too, their purely subjective character would tend to be excluded by evidential proof that the tomb was empty.

SIGNIFICANCE OF NEGATIVE EXPERIENCES

Here it will be objected that it is a very big jump to conclude from the fact that the tomb was empty that the body of Jesus was no longer on this earth. I often discover that an object is not where I expected it to be; I never conclude from this that it has been completely annihilated, I merely assume it is somewhere else. This, according to St John's account, is the way that Mary Magdalen argued. There is no experience that can give certitude of annihilation. The experience of the empty tomb, assuming that it was a true experience, is similar, in some respects, to the famous experiment of Michelson, which gave such an impetus to Einstein's theory of relativity: the discovery that light does not move in relation to the ether. Taken by themselves, Michelson's discovery and that of the 'holy women' are both purely negative, they give no result; but the very absence of result, *given the question at issue*, is highly significant and positive.

On the morning of the third day the disciples were able to verify the fact that the sepulchre, where they had laid the dead body of Jesus, no longer contained it. The first hypothesis that must have presented itself to their minds was that it had been removed. And this, as I have just said, was precisely how the Magdalen reasoned: 'They have carried away my Lord and I cannot tell where they have taken him.' But the removal hypothesis has always been difficult to maintain. If it was the apostles who removed the body, if they made up the legend of the empty tomb to authorize the legend of the Resurrection, then it is impossible to understand the courage of these impostors; on any estimate of human probabilities, the origin of Christianity becomes a riddle. If it was the Jews who caused the body to disappear, they had every interest in producing the remains, which would destroy, once and for all, the fable of the Resurrection. There is no sign of their having done so. On the contrary, if we are to believe Matthew's Gospel, the rumour was put about in Jewish circles that the body had been taken away by the Christians.

The whole sequence of events and ideas looks probable. On the morning of the third day the apostles satisfied themselves that the tomb was empty. It was a fact they were unable to explain. What was to be done? Nothing except *wait*. The apparitions, when these began to occur, awakened the memory of the empty tomb. Then each experience threw light on the other. The facts about the sepulchre suggested that Christ might have come to life. The apparitions confirmed the emptiness of the tomb; above all, they transformed the experience of the tomb's emptiness to a certainty of the body's assumption.

But does not all this fit together too well?

A SUGGESTED EXPLANATION: THE EMPTY TOMB AS THE FINAL STAGE OF FAITH'S MAGNIFICATION

The problem of the empty tomb is highly important, for it is this that determines the true significance of the Resurrection.

Is there no means of eliminating the episode altogether, and explaining it simply as the work of fabulation?

As long as men pursue exegesis there will be an easy way to make
o

this theory look plausible: it is to make the empty tomb, not (as the Gospel chronology indicates) the origin of the Easter event, but an incident that served to crown the apparitions. By transferring the event from the real to the mental, from the historical level to the theological, it would be possible to see the empty tomb as a development of belief in the Resurrection. It would indicate, in fact, the final phase of this development: that which interpreted the apparitions as the glorification of Christ's body, caught up from this earth by the power of God. Similarly, one could add after 1950, the Assumption is the final development of Catholic belief concerning the Virgin, which began with meditation on the virginal conception as related in the Gospels of the Infancy.

This hypothesis assumes a *magnification* in the accounts of Christ's appearances. It therefore implies the possibility of determining, according to their dates, different levels in the narratives, as it is possible to do in the case of the Pentateuch. It implies also the possibility of proving that the Resurrection, from being purely spiritual in its origins, as time went on became materialized.

One of the most constant themes in critical works is that tradition transformed the primitive account of the Resurrection, and that it is possible, in the texts themselves, to see how imagination was at work to make more and more palpable, and more and more miraculous, what had been at the beginning no more than a vision. Obviously, if one could really prove that there had been several stages in the belief in the Resurrection, and that these stages follow a law of realist amplification, this would certainly indicate their subjective character. When the imagination gets to work, it regularly invents embellishments as it goes on, adorning an originally commonplace narrative with more and more poetic details, till the story, which had at first resembled the event, in the end resembles the mind that conceived it.

If we start with this principle, that fabulation *materialized* the apparitions, when we come to the last stage we can discard the empty tomb. It is an indication that once faith in the Resurrection was established and secure—having found its support in the prophetic past, and having seen in the Church's early triumphs the future that now lay before it—it *had* to conclude, when it came to being precise about time and place, that Christ had risen at the first possible moment when in Jewish opinion the soul could be independent, namely on the third day. But if he had risen on the third day, and only on the third day, then he was not in the tomb.

Therefore the first witnesses *could* have seen the tomb 'empty', they *should* have seen it empty, they *really did* see it empty.

Then again, as good Jews, the disciples could not rise to the idea that spiritual life was possible apart from the body; therefore it was impossible that Jesus should really *live* if his body was still in the tomb. For them the apparitions, without the afterthought of the empty tomb, would have been only ghostly phenomena, like the visions of *doubles* commonly experienced by the pagans, which were regarded in Israel, if not impossible, as unholy and unlawful, something that went with idolatry.

But does all this justify my drawing from these hypotheses a law: an evolutionary law, according to which belief would have progressively *materialized* the apparitions by inventing scenes of eating and touching, culminating in the episode of the empty tomb? From the critical point of view I consider this method unsatisfactory. I know too well how modern dialectics (a subtle equivalent to the myth-making of the ancients) is always ready with a convincing chain of ideas to reconstruct an historical sequence, which looks a most impressive intellectual achievement. I agree that if I start with an *a priori* law of magnification—'apparitions must develop from the spiritual to the material, from the individual to the social' —then it will be easy to describe as 'first' the purely visual apparitions; as 'second' those which include contact, familiarity, feeling; and set in the 'third' and last place the episode of the empty tomb. But this seems to me a vicious procedure, for it assumes as a principle what remains to be demonstrated. When it is a question of determining the dates of documents, of arranging them chronologically, one must use indications that have nothing to do with tastes and fancies, but such criteria as style, the state of the text and the allusions contained in it, not some philosophical theory about 'stages'.

Nor does the criterion of *a priori* impossibility apply to the case of the empty tomb. There is nothing miraculous about people not finding something where they expected to find it. As Strauss saw clearly, of all the facts related about the Resurrection, that which is the least contestable, for anyone applying modern criteria, is the discovery of the empty tomb.

Finally, from the point of view of fabulation, if there was one 'event' that demanded to be told (*legendum*), it was the emergence of Christ from his tomb. In time to come, apocryphal gospels and popular imagery would not miss describing this scene of triumph.

But it has no place at all in the official Gospels. The prolixity we observe in the description of incidents which, from the point of view of faith and the Jewish mentality, serve no conceivable purpose, is in strong contrast with the almost complete absence from the narrative of that 'celestial event' which, from the point of view of faith and the apocalyptic mentality, was the one expected above all others. The abundance in the one place and the absence in the other seem to be due to the resistance of some initial fact. The abundance derives from the convergence of early Jerusalem traditions; the silence about the apocalyptic event is due to the absence, in those earliest times, of any witnessed account or even of any imaginary vision of this triumph over the sepulchre and death.

A psychologist might add that nothing looks more humanly probable than this account of the women on their way to the tomb, running as they went, on the morning of what was to be Easter day. It all seems so natural to anyone with experience of woman's devotion, of that love which prompts her to despise possibility, and even propriety.

This train of considerations inclines me to postulate a primitive x, and it must have been something very potent. We still, even now, feel that shock of surprise, the memory of which has reached as far as us: 'He is not here!' This rings so true that historians, even those least tolerant of the miraculous, have never thought of denying, *till comparatively recently*, the incident of the empty tomb. Far from it: they fairly leapt upon the narratives that described this episode: here was a 'scientifically' verifiable fact, established by witnesses who all agreed; here, they thought, was the original priming of that mental operation which was bound to culminate in the idea of the Resurrection. The Gospel itself suggested its refutation: the victim's body had been removed almost immediately, and new-born faith concluded that it was in heaven.

DIFFICULTIES IN THE WAY OF REDUCING

Whereas the school of thought we associate with Strauss seizes on the empty tomb as the one historical fact, according to the mythical school it was the *idea* of the Resurrection that eventually engendered it, so as to support itself with pretended facts. Here again, in this very visible conflict, I see confirmation that these two schools of thought correspond to two distinct classes of minds.

Here, as everywhere else in the problem, there is clearly an underlying choice. Is this a legendary story based on a minute element of fact; or is it a narrative, modified perhaps in certain details by the compilers, but resting on fact, a real fact supported by evidence? It stands to reason that the problem will appear in an entirely different light according to the presupposition with which one starts.

But as far as I am concerned, after a lengthy examination, I am now rather against the idea of fabulation.

I recognize the plausibility of the mythical explanation, but what seems to need stressing is a serious misunderstanding on both sides. Believers tend to ignore any development of belief in the Resurrection. The sceptics take their stand on certain incontestable developments which they take to be a proof of fabulation. Here again the misunderstanding is due to not distinguishing between *mental evolution*, implied in the process of fable-making, and *real development*, which appears to me to be the condition of all temporal evidence.

Suppose we take it that *Matthew's* conclusion is the earliest document, that *Luke* must come next and finally the conclusion to *John*. It is noticeable that at each of these stages the faith becomes more explicit. In *Matthew* what is given is the essence of the fact: the Resurrection, the mission of the apostles. In *Luke* the fact is enlightened by earlier Scripture, and there may also be a connection with the Eucharistic liturgy. In any case there are now no more doubts about the reality of the apparitions, for Jesus breaks bread, allows himself to be touched, eats roasted fish, and a honeycomb. Finally, in the Johannine Gospel, the experience goes further: Thomas not only touches, he thrusts his hand into the side, an inward touching; Jesus prepares a meal of bread and fish; the mystery of the Church's foundation, summed up in the investiture of Peter as its head, is linked up more closely with the paschal mystery. But this development, if it stresses the reality of the apparitions, the communal and organized character of the apostles' mission, introduces nothing new, nothing that was not there already, and there from the beginning. This, in the sense in which I have often defined it, is development without magnification.

Moreover one certainly has the impression that if the oldest professions of faith do not expressly mention the empty tomb, they at any rate presuppose, if not the verifying of its emptiness, the fact that it was empty. They all insist on the burial (whether of 'rite' or 'honour' makes no difference), and the quitting of the tomb on the third day, or 'after three days'. It must be remembered, in

this connection, that according to the Jewish idea it was not till
the fourth day after death that the soul left the body and the body
began to corrupt. 'The soul,' says the Jerusalem Talmud, 'remains
three days beside the body, seeking to re-enter it; it departs when
the body's aspect begins to change.'[1] To go by appearances alone,
the idea is understandable: to those who watch, the dead themselves
seem to be present, witnesses of their own sleeping. In John's
Gospel, Martha seems to think that it is impossible to recall Lazarus,
since he has been dead four days (ix 39). It has been pointed out,
too, that in the East a guest should not stay more than three days.
The fourth day indicated that he was staying for good. Jesus had
visited the mansion of death; he did not remain there.

But it is possible to give two completely opposite explanations of
this agreement between the episode of the empty tomb and Jewish
ideas about the soul's life in the body and the exact moment of the
Resurrection.

It can be maintained, with the myth-theorist, that it was precisely these ideas which imposed on faith the apparent 'materiality'
of the Resurrection, namely a bodily resurrection of a Christ
identical with the crucified Jesus, the conception and the image of a
Jesus resuscitated with the same body he had had before, which
would therefore necessarily leave the tomb empty.

Alternatively there is the hypothesis of faith. Remembering the
Incarnation and all God's gracious condescension to mankind, one
might suppose that if Christ wished his Jewish contemporaries to
believe in his resurrection he would adapt himself to their mental
expectations; that in the same spirit of charity he would provide
for the verifying of the identity of his glorified with his mortal body,
and that at the first moment when an authenticated disappearance
would have any meaning for a Jewish mind, namely at dawn on the
third day. For Christ to fulfil our mortal condition completely, for
him to assume all its burdens, it was necessary—according to the
ideas of his contemporaries to which he wished to conform—that
he should be 'three days' in the tomb. If he had risen any sooner,
he would not appear to have truly risen at all, for he could not have
been thought to be genuinely dead. From this point of view, the
waiting for three days would seem the final concession made to
mankind by God's most gracious Incarnation.

Viewed from this standpoint, everything assumes an entirely new

[1] See Schmitt, *op. cit.*, pp. 122 and 171, and Sir Edwyn Hoskins, *The Fourth Gospel*,
pp. 199–200.

meaning. The Jewish mentality is no longer seen as the cause of fabulation: it becomes the instrument of revelation.

On which of these two positions is adopted will depend, to a large extent, the solution given to the problem of the tomb.

DISCUSSION OF THE PROPHETIC ARGUMENT

We know that the prophetic argument, which Pascal found so convincing, is really ambiguous. Prophecy of any kind, according to the mythical theory, is not the miraculous foretelling of some future event but the first stage of a fictitious narrative.

In the affair of the empty tomb, the mythical school dismisses lightly deductions drawn from a text supposed to be prophetic; as when Peter and Paul, in their speeches in the *Acts*, quote as proof of the Resurrection that Davidical text which they consider decisive: 'Thou wilt not allow thy faithful servant to see corruption.'

But here again, in my opinion, both sides are responsible for obscuring the issue through an equal neglect of the way minds work. There is no denying that for the Jewish mentality, and especially the rabbinical (which was that of Peter and Paul), the hall-mark of historicity was a fact's being in conformity with a divinely inspired prophecy.[1]

That being so, a critical mind could not accept as valid proof the vague image presented by some isolated verse; an unbeliever could well describe it as a pure piece of artifice. On the other hand, this particular verse, uncertain as it is and unique, could have a very profound significance for faith. Revelation may declare it an inspired announcement of the Resurrection; and no one can deny *a priori* that God in his eternal design, having determined an event that was to bring salvation, could have caused to be traced beforehand by prophecy some enigmatical hint of the forthcoming event.

But the question I am concerned with at the moment is not the possibility of a prophetic announcement of the empty tomb or the absence of corruption. What I want to decide is whether the authors of the Gospels, on the strength of a few uncertain texts which they

[1] There is a certain very deep insight in this idea. The whole of history is in itself phenomenal; an event is a dream, passing like human life. To guarantee its stability it must therefore bear an eternal meaning. And what more perfect guarantee, in the eyes of faith, than the fact of its having been foretold or prefigured? This desire for a final justification, founded in God, might be compared with the procedure adopted by Descartes, who declined to accept the evidence of his senses till he was able to base it on divine truth.

judged to be prophetic, could have actually made up the events they relate. Probably they could, if they had regarded a 'figure' as the *foundation* of historic truth. But what we know of their mentality makes it impossible to suppose that they went on this principle. For them the 'figure' served as guarantee and confirmation, it was never a cause and foundation. This is proved by the fact that no such guarantee might be forthcoming. This happened frequently. How many facts in the Gospels have no such guarantee! Moreover it would have no value as proof, except for those of the faithful who had been born in the Jewish tradition and accepted the inspiration of the Scriptures; it could not be offered to converts from paganism. That is why the scriptural argument, characteristic of the earliest catechesis, takes second place in dealing with ex-pagan Christians.

Apart from this, the agreement of prophecy with attested fact is a *general* agreement, like that of a parable with the lesson it is meant to teach. It is not circumstantial, not an exact and detailed conformity, like that between an allegory and the thing it represents in real life.

For instance it might be argued with some force that the account of the Passion is simply an illustration of the texts in *Isaias* about the Suffering Servant, if it could be proved that the *details* of the prophetic text coincided with the *details* of the Gospel narrative; if they did, one could hardly avoid the supposition that the 'narrative' was only a tracing-over of the 'figure'. But the details in *Isaias* are too sibylline and ambiguous to inspire the compilation of a whole *sequence* of events, each arising out of that which precedes it yet telling us something new and unforeseeable. And even in the correspondence there are conspicuous divergences. Isaias, for instance, says the Servant had burial with the wicked, and with the rich in his death (liii 9). But in the Gospel, Jesus, when dead, was not cast away with the wicked; and if his sepulchre happened to be that of the 'rich' Joseph of Arimathea, his body was never with Joseph's.

The famous passage in Psalm 16: 'Thou wilt not leave my soul in the place of death, or allow thy faithful servant to see corruption,'[1] was too vague, taken by itself, to provide a circumstantial narrative of the death and burial and Resurrection.

This is not to say that these scattered anticipations in Scripture were without any influence on the compiling of the narratives: the insistence on the 'third day'—the reason for which I sought in the

[1] *Acts* ii 24–32; xiii 32–7.

Jewish ideas about death—would seem to have been due to an intention of verifying the prophecy of incorruption: *He rose again on the third day according to the Scriptures.*

Much the same might be said of the Johannine account of the Passion. John refers to prophecies on more than one point; but there are very notable differences between the elliptical passages he takes from Scripture and the precise historical details he claims to have witnessed. It is the prophetic message that looks more like an illustration, a confirmation inspired by the Spirit.

THE GOSPEL EVIDENCE CONCERNING THE EMPTY TOMB: ITS VIRTUAL PRESENCE IN THE EARLIEST PREACHING

Those who regard the empty tomb as a reconstruction, fictional or dialectical, have one very serious difficulty to face.

The episode might well have been mentioned *in passing* by one of the sources of the Gospel tradition, and yet been missing in all the rest. What we find is nothing of the sort. Of all the traditional facts, this particular episode seems the best attested by all the historical criteria that we moderns appreciate. In itself there is nothing miraculous about it. If we are to take as a guarantee the convergence of the different accounts in substantial detail, this incident can claim it, quite as much as the denial of Peter. In fact we would gladly do without the twenty-eight verses in which the four Gospels talk of the empty tomb if they would only have told us rather more about the apparitions.[1]

We can certainly admit that by the end of the first century the argument from the empty tomb had become a necessity, to give the lie to those, Jews as well as Greeks, who said: 'We don't deny that the witnesses saw Jesus, but it was only a ghost.' Therefore the only thing to do was to invent this historical legend of the empty tomb.

But the objection presupposes that the accounts of the empty tomb are late, or at least that they are not developments of a seed already present in the earliest *kerugma*.

Here I return to the idea that resurrection implied for the Jews a reunion of soul and body, which could not occur before the fourth day after death. That being so, the article of the primitive creed, *He was buried, he rose again on the third day*, implied the existence of an empty tomb, otherwise the claim would never have been made.

[1] For instance in *Matthew*, out of twenty verses devoted to the Resurrection, eight are about the empty tomb.

Paul, writing to the Corinthians about the year 55, considers all resurrection as the germinating of a body laid in the earth. It would be going too far to say that the earliest preaching included the account of the empty tomb, but it implied at least the belief that it was empty.

Since we see this 'discovery' was so present in men's memories during the second half of the first century—there are four distinct accounts of it—it is not going to be easy to deny *a priori* that it was an accepted fact from the very beginning. Nor, seemingly, did the anti-Christian Jews ever deny the fact that the tomb had been found empty. They assumed as much when they declared that the apostles had made away with their master's body.

ITS PLAUSIBILITY FOR THE GENESIS OF FAITH

In any case, if the episode of the empty tomb had not been known, any historian who wanted to explain how everything happened would have had to invent its equivalent, so as to account for the fact that the apostles, *a few days* after the death of Jesus, were able to preach his Resurrection in Jerusalem. And the argument would still stand even if the 'few days' had to be extended to a 'few weeks' or 'few months'. Such a preaching could not be conceived practicable if any remains of Jesus still existed. It would have been so easy to produce them, or bring forward witnesses to say they had hidden them or buried them elsewhere. After all, the interests at stake were considerable—religious, national, and political interests—all of which made it very desirable to confound and destroy this newly born sect. That is why the negative school is so tempted to dismiss all the difficulties *en bloc* by asserting that *originally* there was no preaching of the Resurrection, which was a legend that came later under the impetus of faith.

This problem of the empty tomb is an excellent example of the eternal conflict between minds of different casts. The three types of thinking, which I have already distinguished, are to be seen here very clearly indeed. The *critical* mind (represented by Strauss) admits the historicity of the empty tomb, but sees it as a germ later developed by fabulation. The tomb was found empty because someone had taken the body away: hence the legend. The *mythical* school offers the contrary hypothesis: that the Resurrection was an Idea, which eventually, for the sake of greater consistency, gave birth to the theme of the tomb being found empty. Finally the believing type of mind (or the *historical*) grasps the sound arguments of both of these schools, which each uses against the other for their mutual weakening. It accepts, in my view, the total experience; it admits the empty tomb and also the Resurrection, each supporting and warranting the other.

VIII

THE NATURE OF THE APPARITIONS

SO, whichever way I turn, I find myself confronted with what I would call the ontological structure of the apparitions.

This, like every structure, consists of two closely connected and inseparable elements. The first of these is the reality of the manifestations: they were not dreamed or merely thought; they were not visions, for the empty tomb is an historical experience occurring at the very outset. This experience is like the *key* of a piece of music; it seems to have been recorded at the beginning with the express purpose of keeping the mind from wandering off on a path that looked all too tempting. This is the first element of the structure.

But this must not lead us to forget the other, which is that the Christ of the apparitions is not the mortal Christ, once more alive, nor even an immortal Christ enclosed again in this physical cosmos; he is a Christ who has 'ascended to the Father', who is glorified at the Father's side.

And it must always be noticed that, real as the apparitions were, they cannot be likened in any way to ordinary experiences.

This is made clear in the Gospel of John. Its mysterious author, the last of the four, informed by direct experience yet more of a theologian than any of the others, endeavoured to explain, by significant incidents, the fundamental nature of these apparitions. It might have seemed that Luke, in his wonderful account of the Emmaus pilgrims, had already suggested a theory about the apparitions themselves and their genesis. He had shown the spiritual conditions of the experience. But the meeting between Jesus and Mary Magdalen in John's Gospel contains a theory perhaps even profounder still. Mary, at that first instant when she made to touch him (which is a gesture of testing) sought a concrete knowledge of Jesus who had just addressed her by name. Jesus replied that she must not touch him (or go on touching him) because he has not yet 'gone up' to his 'Father's side'. Mary wanted to enter into her old relationship with Jesus, an earthly, sensible, historical relationship; but this was no longer possible, because now he had entered into a new kind of life (or was to immediately). And Mary was bidden to tell the apostles that now, if they would see the Master, they must understand first that it was a glorified Lord they would see. The condition of the apparitions, according to John, was the ascent of Jesus to his Father's side, his exaltation at the Father's right hand.

THE RESURRECTION-IN-ITSELF AND
THE RESURRECTION-FOR-US

What follows naturally from this is the distinction to be drawn between the *Resurrection-in-itself* and the *Resurrection-for-us*: the first could well have occurred without the second.

One should also, I think, distinguish between a 'revelation' of the Resurrection and a 'proof' of it.

The Resurrection could have occurred without the apostles' being informed of it. What is more important, they could have been informed of it by means other than those described in the *Acts* as 'manifestations'.

The Resurrection, considered as fundamentally an act of God's power—the raising up of Jesus to the Father's right hand—is a reality independent of the knowledge we have of it. It could have happened without our knowing it. Or it could, again, have been made known to men by some other than the historical and evidential way: by a revelation, for instance. The apostles seem to have regarded those historical 'manifestations' of the risen Lord—which, since they were privileged to witness them, could be made into narratives of evidential value—as gracious condescensions on the part of Christ, *who had deigned to make himself visible*. In themselves they did not constitute the Resurrection; they were signs making for faith in it, the most natural way of proposing it to human conviction, the way that best respected human dignity and freedom and conformed best with the general economy of history.

The apparitions were not necessary to the Resurrection, nor *a fortiori* was the finding of the empty tomb. Christ quite conceivably could have risen without 'appearing'; no one need have found that his body had disappeared. One may think of the 'apparitions' and the 'empty tomb' as 'accommodations', as God's concessions to human weakness. For how could the Resurrection, without the apparitions, have been presented as a real occurrence, otherwise than as a truth of pure faith and without that human testimony, on which, *in fact*, the Church was built? Without the ascertaining of the empty tomb, how could Jews—persuaded as they were of the unreality of a soul separated from the body—be assured that the apparitions were not those of a ghost?

There are—no doubt there always have been—two tendencies at work in interpreting the account of the apparitions and the Resurrection. Those interested in showing the coherence of divine events are inclined to see them as necessary consequences one of the other, the aim being to emphasize the harmony of God's work. The other tendency, which I think is more in conformity with the essence of revelation, is to stress the contingency of supernatural facts. It seems more probable, in a divine work which is essentially gratuitous, that every stage should have been unforeseeable.[1] In this latter view, the apparitions would have their origin in the benevolence of God, deigning to manifest to men invisible realities by way of history. This seems to me to take better account of the divine transcendence and the divine freedom.

To say that the manifestations of the risen Christ served to fortify faith is far from implying that they were the product of faith. It rather suggests the contrary, because it is an insistence on experiences anterior to faith, which are not its *effects* but its *conditions*. It distinguishes between the divine fact of the Resurrection and its human-divine signs. The proofs and signs of the Resurrection are not the Resurrection itself. They are necessary only as a means of bringing it into the category of the historical and the witnessed. The *mission*, which is the work of witnesses and human faith, seems to have been the means in this world chosen by God for propagating the divine faith.

Differences of mentality explain why the work of criticism—necessarily of concern to a believer today if he is to reply to scientific objections—was less important to the Jews than knowledge of prophecy, which takes you at once to the very heart of the eternal designs.

But, taking a broader view of the Resurrection experience, one can see how the two requirements, of the *sacred secret* and *critical verification*, ultimately converge and become one. The Resurrection satisfies all that is required by both the ancient and the modern mind. In the first place it is a divine fact, concerning only the Son

[1] In Mariology, it has been remarked, theology respects even more than elsewhere this divine consideration, because here everything is 'gratuitous'.

and the Father, and in this aspect we could have learnt it by revelation. In the second place it is a human fact, understood as such and transmitted by witnesses.

It is not a late philosophical distinction, this between the *in-itself* and *for-us*. It is presumed from the beginning. Imagination could have fixed so easily the exact moment of the night when the Messiah emerged from the tomb. It never did so, because in the apostles' minds there was doubtless the conviction that this was a mystery in some sort nuptial, belonging to the intimate life of the Son and the Father. A sacred and numinous act, arising out of Love and Power, had taken place at a moment determined by God, for us indeterminable except by its limits: it happened as soon as possible for the Jewish mind. It was not on the Saturday evening that it happened; it had happened by dawn on the Sunday. When? How? It was impossible to say. It was not a subject for speculation.[1]

The distinction appears also in the professions of faith: the 'He rose again' is distinguished from the 'He appeared'. One is the necessary foundation; the other the contingent and gracious consequence. Suppose there were other beings in this present cosmos, beings belonging to the moral order, saved by the same Incarnation uniquely accomplished in this world of ours: then the Passion and Resurrection might be made known to them by means of divine testimony, owing nothing at all to the testimony of men.

In the Ascension there can be seen this clear distinction between the event hidden in God, occurring unwitnessed, and its manifestation to men.

The raising of Christ to the right hand of God is closely associated with the Resurrection. Resurrection and Exaltation are two aspects, as it were, of one and the same mystery. The Resurrection is the fact perceived more temporally, in the historical universe of men. The Exaltation is the same fact perceived more eternally, situated in the divine rather than in the human sphere. But just as the Resurrection was graciously made manifest by apparitions, that which completed it, the Exaltation of the Son, was graciously manifested to the eyes of the apostles by the symbol of a visible ascension, which was also the last apparition. This ascent, momentarily visible, is not a central fact in the testimony: in the account in the third Gospel,

---

[1] Only one evangelist has given particulars of the manner, mentioning lightning, fear, and earthquake. But these are not so much historical facts as biblical symbols of the Passing of God (cf. Schmitt, *La resurrection de la chair*, in *Lumière et Vie*, April 1952, p. 37).

Luke barely mentions it. John just alludes to it. Here again, it would seem, we find resistance to the marvellous, a submission to fact.

The great difficulty I have found in writing this book has been to say only what I know. The danger has been so great of being drawn over one of the two precipices on either side of me: on the one hand premature faith, on the other *a priori* rejection and denial. It is tiresome to be restricted to ordinary language, when I really ought to create new words, in order to reflect a state of mind midway between doubt and faith, or to describe the subject I am studying— this Resurrection, which if true is something wholly unique in kind.

It is now time to face the final question. What are these 'apparitions'? What is their nature, their degree of reality?

For reasons I have already given, they are not *perceptions* in the sense that they were granted to everyone. They were given only to those who were already disciples; their effect was a new faith, a spiritual life more forceful and more expansive. The being that appears, though actually in this world, is independent of space, perhaps also of time.

On the other hand the apparitions are not subjective projections, like hallucinations. They confront the apostles with a being that possesses historical characteristics, whose words, acts, and behaviour enter into the events of their lives, when they travel from place to place, when they eat, when they go fishing.

We could say they are PERCEPTIVE in type, but a special kind of perceptions.

PERCEPTION AND PRESENCE

The idea of perception implies two distinct elements, which generally occur together but would seem to be dissociable:

Firstly, perception is an interior fact not willed; it is something imposed on us, in spite of our efforts to banish or lessen it; to perceive by sight is to be unable to see anything except this object: once our eyes are open, we see it. In this respect the apparitions were perceptions. It is this that makes them matter for *historical* verification, which would never be the case of even collective visions.

Secondly, perception is the effect of something outside the mind, something bounded by space, affecting the different sensory organs whatever the subject's moral dispositions, whatever the depth of his

spiritual life. From this point of view, in that they were not granted
to every passer-by but only to those whom God found ready for
them, the apparitions were not open to everyone's experience to
perceive.

PRESENCE AND BODY

But how to explain the fact that the subject appearing seems
somehow to lead a normal life, have part in the history of a group of
people, if he is superior to the laws of earthly space?

Of course there are various ways of being present in a place. We
assume that the 'density' of presence varies with proximity. We
describe as *present* one who lives in the same space with us. But
suppose a third dimension. One who inhabited *depth* might well
make incursions into 'length' and 'breadth' without being subject
to them. From this point of view a 'phenomenological' study of perception might possibly open new vistas; free us, at any rate, from
old-fashioned mechanistic conceptions, which reduce the act of
perception to a mere contacting or photographic operation, as if the
mind were only a passive spectator.

As a matter of fact, every perception implies the grasping of a
presence. This is its essence. It is possible to analyse the mechanism
of perception; it is possible to describe how it occurs. But this will
tell us no more of the essence of the act of perception than a study
of its physiological mechanism, or its psychic origins, will tell us
about the act of loving. Human perception, when it is the perception of a subject by a subject, not of an object by a subject, is analogous to language. It is an incarnate mind's being set in the presence
of another, equally incarnate, mind; then the two minds communicate through the medium of their bodies, the whole of which are
signs. Perhaps it was wrong to begin the study of perception with
the experience that seems at first the most elementary: the perception of an inanimate object (a piece of wax, a tulip, or a cube), then
to transpose this procedure in order to explain what happens when
John perceives the presence of Peter. When the body perceived is of
another sex we know very well that, if the flesh has sometimes a
presentiment of the fact, it is the mind that divines it as part of the
cosmos containing a being capable of loving. The way a mother
perceives the body of her child, a husband his wife's, are two typical
cases of this communication of minds through the medium of
bodies, bodies that have now become silent words.

One might, it is true, apply to the appearances of Christ the

P

ordinary mechanistic explanation, and say that Thomas set about perceiving the risen body with the aid of his sense of touch, as one does in the case of an inanimate object: wax, cube, or tulip. But Thomas's case would seem to have been exceptional: he was given an opportunity he did not use; so he was permitted the touch refused to the Magdalen, the touch that was not necessary, nor even the normal way of perceiving a real presence.

As far as one can judge of a unique phenomenon, one that transcended all analogous experience, it was not a question of sensory-motor adaptation, not a 'recalling', nor even a 'recognition', so much as the establishing of an *I-and-he* relationship, one in which the body's function was not so much instrumental as mediating, just as the word—the word of a perfect poet, a triplet of Dante's—serves as mediator for thought. For a 'glorified body' is not opaque to the spirit, and one must doubtless conceive it as, more than any other, one with the spirit, which it animates, which it actually is. This suggests a *body to body* knowledge, if we give the word 'body' (*corpus*) a more intimate meaning than the usual sense of 'flesh' (*caro*): one that approaches nearer to what we call 'heart' (*cor*). Hence Newman's motto: *Cor ad cor loquitur*—'Heart speaks to heart'; meaning that it is the bodily intimacy of our being that directly awakens that of another. And we know there are two ways of perceiving even the simplest of objects: one is to project its shape on the background of space, the other is to hear its rhythm and resonance in ourselves.[1]

This brings us back to the analysis of the idea of body. Just as speculation on the Trinity has deepened our knowledge of the human soul, as speculation on the Eucharist has taught us the meaning of substance, speculation on Grace the meaning of freedom, speculation on the Blessed Virgin a knowledge of womanhood, sublimation and time, so reflection on 'resurrection' (or on 'assumption', which is a preparation for it) will teach us perhaps the nature of a body.

What we call 'body' is that portion of living matter which we animate, love, and *are*. But our intimate relations with this symbol and mainstay of our being are disturbed—is this the consequence, perhaps, of some initial catastrophe? If the body weighs heavily, it is not (so it has been said)[2] because it is united to the soul, but be-

---

[1] In this connection it might well be worth investigating certain illusions of perception, as in the case of lost limbs, asomatognosis, heautoscopy, etc.

[2] By J. Mouroux.

cause it is not united enough. A state is conceivable in which the body might become an 'instrument of expression, action, and communion', its own vital element being sublimated, not destroyed. Art gives us a hint of such a metamorphosis; so does the vision of childhood and virginity. Joubert remarks that a painter of the Crucifixion should not merely show us a body that is to be buried, he should let us glimpse beyond it 'the beginning and seed of a supernatural and approaching resurrection'. But in certain bodily states, especially in perception, we seem to see with our own eyes the possibility of sublime transformation.

MESSAGE AND EVENT

I meet the same kind of difficulty again when I visualize the *historical* character of the apparitions, a question which is at the very root of faith.

If the apparitions were only an object of faith, analogous to visions, then the Church is founded on the mystical revelation of a reality not *inserted* in history. In this case, as I have said, the testimony is not an attestation, strictly speaking, but only a declaration, a message.

But if, besides being objects of faith, the apparitions were realities, admittedly without a place in the texture of public history, but known by processes which make an event what we call 'historical', then the Resurrection must be held to be a real fact, not merely a fact for a private state of consciousness. We must use the customary word and say it was a 'miracle'. And not only a miracle, but the bedrock and foundation of all other miracles: according to the thought of St Paul, the final guarantee of their credibility. It was the conclusion of a long historical development, and the origin of a new one; the sign of signs, and the archetype, too, of what man would become when parted from time. As the Sign of signs, as Pledge of pledges and as a possible subject of study, it could not but fascinate any mind concerned for the interests of humankind. Hence the importance of discovering what sort of knowledge we can have of it.

If the apparitions were lies, their only reality is of the pathological order.

If they were mystical phenomena, their only value is for believers.

But if they were really manifestations of a body withdrawn from the cosmos and truly 'risen', then—even though they were offered only to the privileged among believers and in a mode of presence hitherto unheard of—they were facts fully attested and belonged to the basic history of the human race.

It is clear that from the beginning, and even with Paul, it was in the last sense that the apparitions were understood by Tradition.

But this is where the serious difficulties begin. The apparitions, it would seem, were not made in circumstances to be witnessed by normal *historical* observers. They appear to have been confined to disciples and those called to be such, and the grace of faith follows them. There is no record of their being granted to 'scientific and impartial' observers! The risen Jesus never took his place, as Lazarus had done, in his old surroundings. So can one describe the apparitions as *historical*? Can the 'account' which is given of them be strictly called *evidence*?

TWO MEANINGS OF HISTORICITY

If an *historical* event is one that is verifiable universally, the apparitions do not belong to history. Though their object was one who had been known before his death by a vast number of contemporaries, the risen Christ never presented himself publicly to all, as he had done during his trial and Passion. History, in the strict sense, knows only events that are verifiable by any normal man and call for no privileged means of knowledge. A conversation, for instance, between Napoleon and Bertrand at St Helena could be described as historical, even though the only witness was Las Cases, because anybody who happened to be there could have heard the same words. In this sense even the most private history is virtually public. But it would seem to me that if Tiberias or Tacitus, if Philo or Pilate or Josephus had happened to be present in that room where Jesus appeared, none of these would have seen anything at all. (This is *meaning A* of the historical.)

The above definition, though strictly correct, is in my opinion rather too narrow, for it excludes events which might well be *real* but not therefore (if I may so express it) *universalizable*. Certainly in most cases (perhaps in all but one) it is adequate. But the whole question presented by the Resurrection—the logical and metaphysical question—is whether there are not temporal *realities* of a higher order, perceptible only by privileged witnesses.

I must therefore adopt a definition of history sufficiently broad not to prejudice the question I am asking. So I will simply say that what history looks for is the *temporal in everything attested*. From this point of view it is *individual*, rather than *universal* attestation, that must characterize the essentially historic (*meaning B*).

I therefore call historical what has really *happened* in the world exterior to the mind, anything that is *eventual* and not merely *mental*. And in another and deeper sense, I also call historical that which, though not in a normal sense *eventual*, nevertheless did happen and has been really attested by reliable witnesses.

Finally I call historical, in a deeper sense still, what has been affirmed by different witnesses independently, in such conditions that the agreement of their testimony can be explained neither by chance nor by mutual influence.

It is, I think, in this last sense that I can say the Resurrection has every appearance of being historical. What I have said already about the apparitions and the empty tomb (and especially their mutual relationship) leads me to think that here is a reality with the character of an event, even though it be rather a TRANS-*event*: I mean an event *in* this world, but not only *of* this world. After considering the evidence, I am bound to think its origin does not lie in interior states, but that it consists of *judgements of reality*, asserting the subject-object relationship and presenting 'that mixture of the ordinary and the extraordinary' which I have noted already to be the characteristic of the Gospel testimony. My conclusions on the mutual relationship of the narratives, their agreement, and divergence, makes me think it would be very difficult to explain this agreement by mental contagion or coincidence.

The idea of resurrection has come to synthetize for me a number of very different and very complex experiences: that of the empty tomb has all the characteristics of historicity in meaning A; that of the apparitions is historical only in meaning B. Yet it was the historicity of the empty tomb which no doubt prepared the witnesses for the extraordinary experience of the apparitions and guaranteed for us the objectivity of their vision. I admit that the witnesses, in order to interpret what they had seen and touched, had needed light of a higher order. But the inclusion of the act of verification and attestation in the higher sphere of an act of faith would not, in my opinion, destroy its historical character or its value as evidence. An act or state of a lower order of reality is not weakened by being incorporated in an act or state of a higher order.

Just as the risen body contained the temporal body, sublimated in a higher order of existence, so the act by which the disciples recognized Christ, though prompted, sustained, and consummated by a special illumination, contained a testimony which I assign to the historical order, and not to the mystical, since in its essence it is analogous to the ordinary testimonies on which history always relies.

Here language begins to fail me all round, for I cannot define with any distinctness either the *reality* which is now at issue or the *mode* of knowledge we have of that reality. It is not hallucination; neither is it a vision or an ordinary perception; but it is infinitely more of a perception than a vision. It is not an interior phenomenon, nor yet an ordinary historical phenomenon, but it is very much more of a fact than a message. What we have here, in other words, is a *trans-reality* known by *trans-historical* cognition; a transreality, but reality; transhistorical, but based on evidence. And this transreality, considered as the type of other-world reality, has an enormous hypothetical interest. This *trans-attestation*, gathered solemnly and officially by a collegiate body, was the rock upon which Christianity was founded.

Though transnatural, this reality is the type of many natural realities; perhaps the type of the union of mind and body. This evidence, though the object it bears upon is *trans-spatial* and *trans-temporal*, is the 'type' of all testimonies given by the human mind on serious matters that concern it. And this event, though transcending time, is the 'type' and 'limit' towards which tends every event that has to do with vocation, personal destiny, and irrevocable choice.

THE SIGNIFICANCE OF EMMAUS

I believe I can detect these same ideas in the account of the Emmaus pilgrims.

Like a slow-motion film, this episode divides into separate moments what was no doubt all but instantaneous. Yet at the same time, like certain critical moments of existence, like a testament, it gathers into a swifter impetus what for slower minds calls for long and arduous toil, sometimes even a lifetime of research.

I described the testimony we are concerned with here as a linking of the ordinary with the extraordinary, the normal with the paranormal. The Resurrection took place in a context of perfect normality; the narrative of the Passion, the entombment, and the empty sepulchre. In the accounts of incidents anything but normal (such as the miraculous catch of fish) the normal, the common-place, and the familiar occupy a conspicuously prominent place. But the familiar note was perhaps never stronger than in the Em-maus incident: the conversation along the road, the meal taken at nightfall. Yet it all had to do with someone who no longer shared the human condition. Here the character of the testimony bears out well this inherence of the paranormal in the normal. And we could say, of course, that this mingling together of the familiar and the sublime, so noticeable in human life, so visible in the Gospel itself before Easter, increases still further when we come to the appari-tions, where a glorified Christ is seen sharing in the common life of men.

But time presses. I cannot dwell too long on the Origins alone; I must touch also on the other extreme, so as to grasp the whole course of things in one and the same view.

As the Jews ate the pasch in travelling garb, since it was 'the passing of the Lord', so the mind must be attuned to the passing of time, which is the way to all knowledge.

IX

EXPLANATORY DEVELOPMENTS

ATTESTATION AND EXPLANATION

IN the seamless robe of the testimony, I have so far distinguished two aspects: attestation and explanation, namely the fact and its significance, the thing and what the thing was the sign of.

What I was investigating before was how the evidence developed; what I did not consider was the development of its meaning.

The two aspects should never have been separated. No fact is understood, or even perceived, unless it has a value for us. It may be that this idea of an already existent value, present in the mind like a source of illumination, is what makes it possible to grasp a fact, and recognize it for what it is, without being misled by the ambiguity of appearances.

What is true of an ordinary scientific fact is equally true of the religious fact, a fact that makes for spiritual life. This is even more the case when it is a Christian fact, essentially an Idea-Fact, an insertion of the Eternal in Time, an historical existence inseparable from its meaning.

Yet these two aspects, though basically one, can be dissociated. They were distinct from the outset, from the first moment of cognizance. In the Gospel narratives, condensed as they are, we see the interval of time between the moment of *shock* and the moment of *faith*. Thus the experience of the Emmaus disciples was in the first place one of personal attraction, then came surprise, and finally faith. Later, the apostles at Jerusalem had a moment's hesitation between experience and conviction, between sight and vision. For John, as we can see from his description of the experiences of Peter and Thomas, *seeing* and *believing* are two distinct moments.

In the following pages I want to study the development of faith alone, not, as I have been doing so far, the development of the testimony. Faith was not concerned with circumstances. Absolute, from the very first experience of it, it had no need of details; these would be given later in the official narratives. It was the same with

Pascal, who was no longer interested, after his experience at Puy-de-Dôme, in any other possible experiences, but only in the meaning of that fact which was now for him the only one that counted. But faith developed, because belief in the Resurrection had to be found a place in the organic whole of other beliefs. There were various ways in which this could be effected, and there can be seen from the beginning this *polyvalence* in the views taken of an event that was wholly unique in kind.

THE STATE OF MIND OF THE FIRST CHRISTIANS

Early Christianity, it must be borne in mind, was deeply penetrated with the paschal mystery. With twentieth-century Christians this mystery is also *central*. But it no longer envelops all else. After confessing 'He rose again', Christians now pass on to other beliefs. The feast of Easter is the focus of all, but it passes. . . It is the geometrical difference between a focal point and an enveloping sphere.

One sign of the difference of viewpoint can be seen in the meaning of the Eucharist. The Resurrection, in early times, was closely linked to the liturgy of the Christian sacrifice. The apparitions had often occurred in the course of a meal. The Resurrection times were those at which Christ had eaten with his friends: repasts of joy and peace, of simplicity and mission. Certainly the repast was also connected with the Cross, it 'announced the Lord's death'. But it was the pledge of a new life, the symbol of the establishment of the Messianic kingdom, of eternity already begun in time. The *Acts* bear the memory of this indescribable impression, which had been that of the disciples.

Another reason for the difference between the Church of the *Acts* and that of the next, of *all* succeeding centuries, was that in the period of origins the Resurrection was conceived as the first moment of an imminent general resurrection. At that time, for believers, there was no unreckonable interval between Christ's resurrection and their own. They were living in a parenthesis between two parousias: that which had just faded with the Lord's presence and that which would soon reappear with his return. One might say that for them the *immanence* of Christ in their sacred repast was hardly separated from the *imminence* of his return.

For us this imminence has lost its effective religious value; all that is left is *immanence*. And it is not the experienced immanence spoken of in the *Acts*, it is an immanence of pure faith.

Moreover for them the Passion and the Resurrection were more closely connected than they are for us. The image of the Crucified, which has prevailed over that of Christ in glory, an intenser meditation on the mysteries of *Kenosis*, the fading of Christian hope owing to the vicissitudes of history and the weariness of long waiting—all these things, together with the feeling that Christianity is failing to make headway or even endure, have cast a shadow, for the perhaps too positivist Western world, on the mystery of renewal, which is the mystery of Easter. One might say that ever since the second century the Church has been living an autumnal life.

It is only in monasteries, withdrawn from the life of the world, that it is possible once again to feel its eternal spring. Or else one must seek refreshment in those movements and reawakenings reminiscent of Galilee, like that of St Francis or Don Bosco's, like every new foundation in its first beginnings: the Spirit must be seized at the very first moment, before that feeling of establishment sets in.

When 'the Way of the Cross' was instituted, with its fourteen stations, it was a reminder of Christ's three falls and made an end at the Entombment. When the 'Sacred Heart' was revealed, it was a sorrowful Heart. Time was when there was more perception of the glory, even in the Cross itself.

A. The First Phase: the Pre-Theologies of the Resurrection

Let us try to *unearth*, as archaeologists among ruins, the primitive theologies of the Resurrection.

Here we shall distinguish two initial beds: the primitive ante-Pauline theologies, gathered up and preserved by the Apostle's piety, and the Petrine theology, which Luke has preserved for us in the *Acts*.

THE ANTE-PAULINE THEOLOGY

The writings of St Paul, dating from round about the year 55, may be said to *enchase* earlier fragments, probably drawn from the earliest liturgies, and already known and recognized by the various communities in a form that was already fixed and ritual. This almost certainly takes us back to the first origins. In the East, and in any country which is totally conservative and keeps oral tradition, twenty years are no more than a day. Even the French, with their addiction to change, have preserved unaltered for a century and a half the original words of the *Marseillaise*.

MARAN ATHA
(*1 Cor.* xvi 22)

The Lord is coming. The earliest testimony is discoverable in that Aramaic invocation, a vestige of the first liturgies. Here is the echo of that first CRY, whence issued, even before the word, the chant, the call, the rite; it is a chrysalis of thought and prayer. This first cry of *Maran atha* reminds one of *Abba* (*Father*), the germ of the *Pater noster*. But it introduces faith to another dimension. It means either 'Come, Lord!' or 'The Lord is coming!' Here we have the palaeo-liturgical cell, the first atom of prayer, dogma in fission.

Jesus is called *Kurios*: absolute Lord (according to the ideas of that age) rather than 'god'. *Lord* he became visibly by his Resurrection. This Lordship extended, in primitive thought, over the three domains of heaven and earth and the world below. The Lord has come. He is going to return. *He is coming*. The Resurrection is therefore still continuing. History ever afterwards loses its value. It contains nothing more to hope for in time. Henceforward the eternal must be awaited in the eternal.

1 Timothy iii 16

No question of it, it is a great mystery we worship. Revelation made in human nature, justification won in the realm of the Spirit; a vision seen by angels, a mystery preached to the Gentiles; Christ in this world, accepted by faith, Christ, on high, taken up into glory.

In this liturgical hymn, incorporated in the first *Epistle to Timothy*, there is found what seems to be one of the first 'theologies' of the Resurrection. It may be compared with *Romans* i 3–4. It is older than this epistle, and certainly older than the preaching of Paul.

It speaks of the *sacramentum pietatis*, the 'great mystery we worship',
which has been revealed in the flesh (1),
justified by the Spirit (2),
seen by angels (3),
preached among the Gentiles (4),
believed in the world (5),
exalted in glory (6).

1, 2, and 6 describe divine events. Jesus is revealed in the flesh, or, as we should say, in time and history. He is then *justified*: sub-limated, that is, and divinized, associated with God by the power of the Spirit. He is thenceforth exalted in glory. Revelation, justifica-tion and exaltation are, as it were, three phases in the divine economy.

Corresponding to these three divine phases, there are three phases of faith: the Resurrection was seen by angels (who then, we are to suppose, in their function of messengers, announced it to men); next it was preached among the Gentiles; finally it was believed in the world.

In this hymn the whole of Gospel history is summed up in a verse; there is no mention of apparitions to men. Like the *Epistle to the Philippians*, it envisages a threefold division of the world. Heaven, at the highest level, is the dwelling-place of the angels; a mention of it is sufficient. The Gospel of the Resurrection is received by the 'Gentiles', not by Israel alone. But the history of this preaching is only a parenthesis. We are brought back to the exaltation in glory, an allusion, perhaps, to the Ascension, the last of the apparitions.

This hymn of triumph may be compared with another, a hymn of exhortation (*Eph.* v 14), which draws its liturgical and moral con-sequences. It may have been sung, in the earliest times, at baptisms. The life of the world is conceived as a sleep, a death, a night. The resounding cry that awakens it:

> Awake, thou that sleepest,
> And arise from the dead,
> And Christ shall give thee light.

The first developments, as can be seen quite clearly, are synthetic. This is the case with every germinal state. There is hardly any room for *attestation*, as we understand it today. All is absorbed by theology, the viewpoint of eternity. The events of history must be over-shadowed by 'the invisible things of God'. The divine plan stands revealed; that which is history is not eliminated, but it contracts.

THE PETRINE THEOLOGY

There are three 'discourses' of Peter in the *Acts* (ii 22–36; iii 12–26; x 34–43).

There are notable analogies of thought between the themes developed in these three passages and the first *Epistle of Peter*. This makes it possible to trace the lines of a kind of Petrine pre-theology.

God 'makes no distinction between man and man'; Jesus is 'the stone which the builders rejected'; he is the 'judge of the living and the dead'. He had visited the realm of the dead. If the first epistle was not written by Peter, this would make me think even more that the presence of these ideas was regarded by the Christian communities as tantamount to Peter's signature.

There are other points worth noticing. The first speeches in the *Acts* make a distinction, surprising to the faith of later ages, between the earthly and the risen Jesus. The first was 'a man duly accredited from God, by miracles, wonders, and signs'; he was the greatest of the prophets. Here Peter seems to be reducing his evangelic experience to the very minimum possible. But after his death Jesus is 'invested' as 'Lord and Christ'. The moment of this investiture is left vague; it may have been at the Resurrection, or it may have been at the Ascension or Pentecost. The miracles are regarded as performed on 'those who were under the devil's tyranny'. The Resurrection is also held to be deliverance from the bonds of death.

All this belongs to a very ancient theology which, even in the light of my stringent criteria, bears all the marks of authenticity; for it 'minimizes' the more developed theology of those Christian communities that saw the compiling of the *Acts*. Was it then in seed form that Peter was presenting his ideas? Did he wish to use 'economy', to 'accommodate himself' to the Jews in order not to shock them unduly? What is certain, at any rate, is that Peter translated his experience into the theology then popular: a theology that looked towards *the end* of time, gave to 'death' and its 'kingdom' an almost physical reality, and insisted on the *delegated* character of Christ's powers. Jesus is called the Servant of God, the Just, the Holy, the 'Author of Life'. The words of Peter are a good indication that this was a new theology expressed in the framework of an older, one that lent itself ill to his purpose and was far too weak to contain his own; intuition lies wrapped in envelopes that threaten to burst asunder.[1]

In the primitive state of seed, as in the first stage of an intuition, we see, alongside older elements, others as yet undeveloped, still in a state of expectancy.

In Peter's address to the centurion Cornelius, a speech more fully elaborated than the two that come earlier, he makes an important distinction between the *anastasis* and its manifestations. 'God,' he says of Jesus, 'granted the clear sight of him.'

The Resurrection is not the same as its manifestations. These are the apparitions and—what might be called the appearance of a dis-

[1] Another example of this phenomenon is to be found in the book of *Job*.

appearance—the empty tomb, warranted by the angels. Peter lets it be understood that the manifestations, whatever they were, were not in themselves necessary. God could have raised up Jesus for Jesus alone, making such a resurrection a pure act of faith. What this means is that the *divine fact* could have been announced to men by revelation, without any clear historical proofs. But in his loving-kindness God was pleased 'to manifest himself' for 'forty days', and finally to symbolize his invisible ascent to the Father's side with an ascension visible to human eyes. For forty days, a limited period (though for the Jews long enough, complete in itself), Jesus renounced the enjoyment of his glory so as to go on living among those he had chosen. He renounced, for that period of forty days, the Messianic banquet in heaven, so as to share their earthly repasts with the Eleven; such was the special tenderness of his love for them.

This *manifestation* was restricted, it is true, to the official group, to the Eleven. It hardly ever extended further. He never presented himself to 'the people at large'. But it is this separation of the favoured group from the 'whole people' that makes the testimony so necessary. The constitution of the witnesses, their organization as well as their activity—which is nothing else than the Church in the world—is the consequence of this plan of gracious manifestation. So we find, all closely bound up together, the three nuclear ideas of *historicity*, *testimony*, and *Church*.

One might go further along these lines and say that the *historifying* of events that need not have been historified was a characteristic of the economy of the Incarnation. Christ could have died a violent death, almost without witnesses. But what God willed was a Passion of exceptional historic publicity, thanks to the concourse of people for the Paschal feast, the overlapping jurisdictions of Roman and Jew, and finally the execution before everyone's eyes; all this compressed into a single evening, a night and a day, made possible a truly synoptic testimony which serves as an historical source. Similarly it was God's will that apparitions should occur, though reserved for a handful of the elect, those who were to have a mission; and these apparitions were to be both a reward for fidelity and also a source of meritorious faith for the multitudes who must believe without having seen.

The Resurrection, as I have said, was not only a human *event* but a divine *advent*. The distinction is met with again, in an ambiguous form, among those who in our day have thought they could distinguish the 'Christ of faith' from the 'Christ of history'. But the critics of this school, instead of discerning the Resurrection-in-itself and the Resurrection-for-us, lost sight of the connection between divine reality and historical reality, and ended by seeing the historical as mere legend. Peter's idea was very different. In itself the Resurrection is a *divine fact*, intervening in the *cosmos* and the *chronos* by the removal of the body and by the subsequent 'manifestations'. It was an event that might have remained in the domain of faith. God willed that it should be known just as the facts of human history are known.

B. *The Second Phase: the Pre-Theologies of the Synoptics: Moment and Duration*

I have already considered the Gospels in connection with the development of the attestation. These documents are in the nature of testimonies: the accent is on historicity.

But the three synoptics contain also a latent theology. They are catecheses, in which the facts (as in all Scripture) serve for *didaskalia*, religious instruction. Each is inspired by a special religious design; it is the work of a spiritually minded author writing after long meditation, and what is deepest in the author's mind is indicated also by the arrangement of the contents, sometimes even by his silences. This is because arrangement and the things left unsaid are often more revealing than the actual words.

The 'density' (so to speak) of the Gospel's duration is like that of human life, not the same from start to finish. At first monotonous and full of repetitions, it quickens its tempo from the going up to Jerusalem, and still more during Holy Week. In the Resurrection it attains its sublime climax. All leads up to this.[1]

MARK

The Gospel of Mark is made up of disconnected scenes. The author is little concerned with continuity. The rhythm of his narra-

---

[1] There could be a material explanation of this hurried ending of the Gospel narratives. When the writer approached the end of his scroll he would note with surprise that he had no room left; hence the necessity for abridgement. But this plausible explanation is not necessarily an argument against a profounder reason. The need for curtailment helped to indicate the speeding up of time after the Lord's Resurrection. This is just the way, in this intertwining world of ours, that the lowly and the sublime sometimes conspire.

tive is one of jolts and jerks; the night is streaked with flashes of lightning.

If (as is quite possible) the Gospel ought to end with the verse: 'They were trembling and awe-struck, and said nothing to anyone, out of fear,' one may think that Mark wanted to stress the shock to the human mind at what was about to appear, at what he had announced. His Gospel had often insisted on the *awe* inspired by the presence of Jesus. It was he who had foretold the suffering which Jesus would have to undergo, for the ransoming of many; he had also announced the new banquet, the glory of the Transfiguration (of which Peter was the principal witness), the coming of the Son in the clouds of heaven. Thus Passion and Triumph: a harsh Passion, a total Triumph.

All we find here is a summary statement of what is essential; it is a kind of *shock effect* to the human mind caused by the revelation of the 'Son of Man'. One might call it today a theology of transcendence, a theology of the instant.

MATTHEW

Here the Resurrection takes its place within the history of all that has gone before. Matthew is careful to recount it in the colours of those ancient biblical narratives in which Javé revealed his power over the whole cosmos in order to protect and save his people.

Those 'marvels' which astonish us, so little in accord with the sobriety and probability of the accounts given by Luke and John, must no doubt be understood by adopting the mental attitude of St Paul to the manna or to the rock of Horeb; before all else he sought the 'typic' significance. The earthquake and the darkening of the sky indicate primarily the confusion of the heavenly 'powers' in the cosmos; the guards 'like dead men' signify the paralysis of the powers of earth. One is reminded of the prodigies that accompanied the exodus from Egypt, itself an image of God's *raising* power, exercised in favour of his people, who were a figure of his Son.

It is in the same biblical spirit that we must understand the full meaning of the Galilean apparitions and the silence concerning those at Jerusalem. Galilee was the land of Zabulon and Naphtali, foretold by Isaias as the Galilee of the Gentiles (iv 15–16; cf. *Isaias* viii 23). Galilee, therefore, was the geographical seed of the preaching of the Gospel to the world, the figure of that human world in which it must spread. It was on a mountain in Galilee, during the Lord's first preaching, that there was promulgated that new Law of Faith, the Beatitudes. Here was an image of a new world. And Galilee, no doubt, was the scene of the Transfiguration, the first-fruits of the world to come. Jerusalem had refused to listen to Jesus, but in Galilee he had been able to proclaim his work of renewal in the presence of the assembled poor, who were full of faith and hope because they had charity.

It was the image of the kingdom of God, glimpsed by the prophets as coming to pass in the world's last age.

The risen Jesus makes a *rendezvous* in Galilee, the land of Origins, as though every new departure must depend upon refreshment at that same place where the Spirit first gushed forth for our reviving. Jesus was in his own country once more, the country whence the 'son of David' came, even though prophecy had not foretold this origin for the Messiah. He led his disciples to that last 'high place', reminiscent surely of Sinai and Garizim, of the mount of the Beatitudes and the mount of the Transfiguration, doubtless summarizing and typifying them all. Yes, it summed up all; it was the mountain of the Source, of the New Law, of the Transformation—of the Fission, one might say, that was to fill all space-time with its breath and light. What we see here is the whole earth, without any distinction of race or nation, without reference even to the privileged stock of Israel. The Resurrection appears as something without precedent, no longer linked with any announcements in Scripture. We have been lifted above Times and Origins and Conditions.

Jesus is revealed as sovereign Lord. All authority has been given him in heaven and on earth. He is truly the *Kurios* of all spiritual space and time, Lord also of eternity, King of glory, universal King. Yet at the same time he is he-who-is-with-us-every-day: truly, therefore, the 'Emmanuel', God-with-us. His transcendence is manifested by a *daily* immanence.

Jerusalem is passed over in silence: the mystical explosion has not its centre in the City. For the theologian-evangelist, the Resurrection has transferred the New Source elsewhere. Henceforth the Church has its foundation where the body of Christ is, in heaven, 'at the Father's right hand'. The highest functions on earth will be simply vicarial. The Church has for its starting-point the abstract 'mountain' of Galilee.

The evangelist would certainly have known that triad, the Resurrection, the Ascension, and Pentecost. But from his loftier vantage-point, all else seemed to have been made superfluous by the manifestation on the unnamed mountain.

If the conclusion to *Mark*, so far missing, was the principal source of *Matthew*, it may be said that these two Gospels are akin in their historical theology in that Jerusalem is so strangely absent from both. They do not deny the place it occupied, but only the significance that Judaic-Christians might tend to give it.

Here, though with more reticence (for the language of silence is the more *agapic*), these pre-theologies are in line with the explicit theologies of Paul and John. By insisting on Galilee as the land of first election and first departure, their tendency is to free the Resurrection from Jewish history and make it part of universal history. In any case, their point of view is not very 'historical', if what history ought to be is a logical and close-knit narrative. These Gospels are not concerned with the number and sequence of the apparitions. One is enough, and it achieves everything. Times also are compressed. They seem fully accomplished, as though they had reached 'the beginning of the end'. Christ reigns, and the old Time is now no more; or at any rate it is no longer a 'time of waiting'. It is the time of the history of the Church: Christ, though veiled, reigns glorified in every moment of it, repeating 'all days' his invisible and eternal presence.

LUKE

In the Gospel of Luke we have a pre-theology of a different type.

Here, unlike the others, the accent is on historical development, and on Jerusalem as centre, source, and focus. One might say that Matthew, with his idea of the eternal instant, is in the Kierkegaard tradition; Luke, revealing that slow development which gives value to all time, is rather more in Newman's.

Luke can recount only what has been already *prerecounted*, even more than *predicted*. For him, we might say, the true *figure* is not the sibylline verse, as it was in Matthew's Gospel of the Infancy, but the announcement made by an event of long ago.

The Resurrection had (as it were) been narrated already, in figure, in the Gospel of the Infancy; which is also, through Mary, the link between the Old Testament and the New. The virginal conception itself had been a figure, for it was an act of God's almighty power.

This same care of Luke's for presenting all in historical form is shown in the way he describes the Resurrection. Here history intervenes to replace presence with the sacrament of little details.

It is this that makes plausible, even though miraculous, what in the others had been sudden and abrupt, excessively condensed, or else insulated, as it were, by unfathomable silences. Instead of being an event transcending history, the Resurrection becomes a kind of second Incarnation, momentary, glorious, yet real and intimate. Jesus accepted the conditions of a human life relived; he shares meals, allows himself to be touched.

This historical life is a life of religion and worship. The Gospel itself, which opens with scenes of prayer, also ends with an act of worship. In this it could be said that for Luke all history is a parenthesis between prayers.

C. The Third Phase: The Explicit Theologies

We have seen in Luke's Gospel an explanatory design. Luke connects the Resurrection with previous history and with the history that was to follow. He sees it as a link between the two. He gathers up his pictures, his syntheses, his external themes; he arranges them, and as he does so he somehow sets them in a softer light.

Here he compresses, there he expands. The *tempo* of his work varies. Either because he wished to confine himself to history, or because he found himself overburdened with the weight of detail he had conscientiously gathered, there is no theology, properly speaking, in what he wrote.

The three evangelists I have been discussing were in the tradition of those whom Josephus describes as 'anterior Prophets'; we should call them *historians* rather than 'prophets', because their aim was to trace the divine plan where it was historically discoverable, namely *in the past*.

The case is different with those thinkers who are not so much historians as *theologians*. They, like those described by Josephus as 'posterior Prophets', were concerned with describing only the future accomplishment of the divine plans. Thus the Old Testament prophets looked primarily to the future; but Paul and John, though they certainly do not neglect the future, have their eyes on the eternal, since Christ has absorbed time and made the future a mere figure. In this new perspective the Resurrection is seen as the beginning of eternity.

THE PAULINE VIEW OF THE RESURRECTION

The Resurrection is central in the thought of Paul. At Damascus he enjoyed an apparition of Christ. He was seized thenceforward with the idea that Jesus, 'delivered up for our sins', had been raised again for our justification. Thus Passion and Resurrection are two connected acts. And since he had been privileged to have an experience of it, Paul regarded the Resurrection as the main foundation of faith.

Christ, once he had risen, acted through the Spirit. But no one stresses more than Paul the life shared in common by the risen Christ and mankind. For him, more than for others, the *anastasis* was really a communal transformation; because for antiquity there was a much closer affinity, than there is for us, between the ideas of *body* and *community*; we have dissociated society and materialized the body. The resurrection of one individual glorifies the whole of the human race. This transformation had taken place in the head, the type, the model. As for our own transformation, it is close at hand: there are those still alive who will see it. Perhaps we shall see it... The thought of Paul turns readily to the last day, jumping all intermediate history. And this last day reminds him of the first. Adam and Christ explain one another, they are two types of creation.

St Paul sees a triple division in man. It is not one we are accustomed to make. Man is not for him, as he is for us, a body and a soul; he is body, soul, and spirit. A triple division is useful in justifying a mean between two extremes. Here the extremes are Adam, 'the first', and Christ, 'the last'. Adam's body is a *psychic* body, animated by soul. Christ's is a *spiritual* body, animated by the Spirit. When man is laid in the earth, there is sown a body animated by a soul; on the day of Resurrection, what is gathered up is a body animated now by the Spirit. In other words, resurrection is a process by which bodies, which have ceased to be animated by the provisional principle we call *soul*, will be recreated and eternally spiritualized by a principle allied to the Spirit, that is to the Intimacy of God. This spiritualization of the flesh has been accomplished already in that nuclear point of the spiritual organism which is the body of Christ. It will be continued by all human beings, in different ways and at different times, in an order of succession which Paul laid down.[1] But Christ's Resurrection differs from that of men,

---

[1] St Paul's speculations on the relationship of the earthly Adam to the heavenly Christ, or on the connection of the three elements that constitute man, the *somatic*,

because his body was never subject to corruption. At the last day, no doubt, those who are then alive will avoid having to die. The Resurrection, as St Paul sees it, in a sense anticipates that final hour.

What still remains mysterious is the nature of the *intermediate state*, that of those dead already who have not yet risen. St Paul no doubt would have been greatly surprised if he had been told that this intermediate state would be so much prolonged and become the history of the Church. To meet this problem, might he perhaps have been forced to take a deeper view of 'lapse of time' and ask himself the significance, in the divine consciousness, of a temporal interval?

THE JOHANNINE GOSPEL

What one finds in John's Gospel, more than in any of the others, is a retrospective illumination. Everywhere else the premises are stated without the conclusion being drawn. Here the development is completed. And like every completed development, it is a denial of development, for it applies to the beginning what was never apparent till the end.

Thus everywhere else—in the earliest professions of faith, in the thought of St Paul, in the synoptic narratives—it is God who raises Jesus of Nazareth from the dead. The Father is the source of that work of salvation which is consummated in Jesus by the act which made the Messiah-Jesus the Lord of heaven and earth and the world below, before whom every knee must bend.

Clearly, as Christian thought (by the ways I have described) became fully aware of the divinity of Jesus and his identity with the Father, those original formulas became less and less adequate. Jesus had to be conceived as the author of his own resurrection. John, who sees the Temple as the symbol of Christ's body, makes Jesus announce, at the very outset of his ministry, his power to 'raise it up again' in three days (ii 19).

Jesus is essentially Life, having power over all flesh; he has

---

the *psychic*, and the *spiritual*, do not seem so far to have had much posterity. It may be that the promulgation of the Assumption (which has its own connection with a passage in St Paul about the order of the Resurrection) will draw attention to the *resurrection of bodies* in its relation to eternal life. The body of the Blessed Virgin, so closely connected with the body of Christ, is the second *somatic* organism of Adam's kind to enter into the state of the risen Christ, namely to become *spiritualized*, withdrawn from the cosmos and fully possessed by the Spirit.

authority, too, to take up his own life and lay it down—at *his hour*. Momentarily this power is dormant, through the effect of his dwelling in the midst of men. For John, one thinks, it was not the existence of a glorified Christ that presented any difficulty, but the existence of a Christ who was not yet glorified.

Life, eternity, and resurrection are for us too, as it were, already given. Yet nevertheless they remain objects of hope. The moment when this 'not yet' and this 'already' have an end, when there is no more expectation and no more continuance, that is the *now* of the Passion-Resurrection.

These two conjoined words, of humiliation and glory, inter-penetrate. In the Passion according to John, Christ makes use of his life-giving power. He gives birth to the Church: a new Adam, with the help of the eternal woman (for he causes his mother to share his labour) he enters into one last combat with the devil. Then, from his heart, he sheds the water-and-blood, instruments of the life-giving Spirit in Baptism and the Eucharist. Risen again, on the day after the morrow, he had nothing more to add to his work, which he was to complete, that Easter evening, by bestowing the Spirit collectively on the apostles.

John, more than the other evangelists, shows the persistence of Calvary even in glory. When Thomas touches Jesus, he touched the signs of the Cross, the wound in the side and the heart.

It is no easy matter to convey so many meanings in such little time and to associate them in such an intimate unity.

The Resurrection, for St John, is both a datable event and at the same time an event detemporalized. Jesus speaks of his 'Hour', saying it has 'not yet come'. But sometimes he lets it be understood that it has. It is not a question, here, of an eternal fact; the fact which is in John's mind is an historical fact, and in his own name he solemnly bears witness to it. But this historical fact, which recalls the passing of the Pasch, reveals an eternal reality: God's life-giving power. This *not yet* and *already* might be called the mystery of Johannine time, which is also (even more than the Platonic) an image of eternity.

For the Synoptics, the Passion-Resurrection is the simultaneous moment of summing up and sublimation. In our day it would be called the 'dialectical moment'. The times to come would merely unfold the consequences of this moment. That is why those that preceded this unique Event continue to be times of preparation.

But for John, who sees things in depth, the Resurrection is also a dialectical moment in another cycle, that of eternal history. The Incarnation may be considered as it is in the divine thought, where it subsists eternally. When the Logos became man and pitched his tent among us, he became in some sort removed from the Father: he travels, he *goes towards* the Father. The Son is as though removed from the Spirit, in the sense that not being yet glorified he has not yet the power to shed the gift of that Spirit upon the world. There is some sort of obstacle to be removed before the only-begotten Son can rejoin the Father and send forth the Spirit. What makes an end of the delay is the death-and-resurrection. Before the Event, in the 'discourse after the supper', the Johannine Jesus explains this economy, whereby eternal relationships are associated with those which subtend the history of the Incarnation on earth. Seen in this light the Resurrection is the way by which Jesus passes from this world to the Father, so that there may descend upon the world the very Spirit of the Father.

It was a grievous blow to the disciples that Jesus was to ascend to the Father without taking them with him. They had to console themselves with the thought that without his solitary ascent to the Father there would be no gift of the Spirit, which Jesus had merely anticipated by departing first, and that afterwards they in their turn would ascend to the Father.

When the Resurrection has taken place, at the very moment when Jesus ascends (has just ascended or is going to ascend) he sends the Spirit to the Eleven. It is then he stands revealed as the Re-Creator, fulfilling the prophecies by a new creation due to the Spirit, one to which the first creation was only a pedestal or prefiguration. Here was a kind of new Genesis.[1] And just as Javé spoke with Eve in the Garden, so Jesus, in another garden, speaks with the Woman. And what is this second creation by the Spirit? It is a mission of peace and purification, a pastoral mission.

When all was seen in this light, a light in the strictest sense sublime, it is understandable that the Ascension and Pentecost were not mentioned. Their historical occurrence is not denied; but John, even more than Matthew, stands in a light so nearly the light of eternity that it would spoil his design to recall the Ascension and

---

[1] At the beginning of the Johannine Gospel some think they see a division into seven days, indicating the stages of the second creation, that of pure grace. The first day concerns light, the second water; the Marriage at Cana corresponds to the seventh, a day which lasts for ever.

Pentecost as events. The event, for religious thought, is always basically the counterpart of an invisible reality. John is primarily interested in what St Augustine calls the *æternum internum*. The reality of the Ascension and Pentecost he places on Easter evening. It is on Easter Day that Jesus ascends to heaven, the few hours since his leaving the tomb being enough to represent the historical interval. Even though these mysteries, given virtually at Easter, were to be reproduced on Ascension Day and Whit Sunday (as the *Acts* testify and as the Church relives them in the liturgy), none can deny that they derive effectively from the Resurrection. On that first Sunday, though a *not yet* remained, everything was done *already*.

For John, who spoke so much of the mysterious HOUR, that hour had come.

Thenceforward the time of accomplishments gathers pace, like the Latin Mass after the moment of consecration. It can be condensed indefinitely. In this John resembles Mark, who we are told has restored us the Gospel of Peter. So by two different approaches, it would seem, we gain access to the experience of the earliest witnesses, who had less need, than their disciples had, to connect the Event with History, because they themselves had had part in it.

This does not mean that for John time is no more. There is still fishing, after the Resurrection, and Christ takes part in it. Fish are caught, meals are eaten. There is even a question of longevity, and that in connection with the most spiritual of the disciples. But after Easter Day, time, however long (that God alone knows), is a final time, it will never bring anything comparable to the *Hour*.

If, as is probable, the Apocalypse belongs to the same cycle of thought, it could be said to rise still higher above time. John's Gospel condenses and concentrates history around a truly historical, though mysterious, 'hour'. The Apocalypse transcends universal history, which it conceives as a struggle between the Woman and her male Child and the ancient Serpent; here the sacrificed Lamb in heaven considers death and resurrection in their eternal permanence.

PAUL'S SOTERIOLOGY COMPARED WITH THE THEOLOGY OF JOHN

Like the earliest professions of faith, both Paul and John see history as a parenthesis.

Christ existed before his historical manifestation, which for him had been in the nature of a limitation. Risen, he returns to the glory he had momentarily forgone; he returns to what he had been before the world began. What we are so much attached to, the 'historical', in the eyes of Paul and John is the time of Christ's abasement, who therein merits his exaltation and also shows what history should be for us: a time of conversion and return, of affirmation and decision.

Yet what Paul stresses more is the current of history, wherein Christ, though creation's head, is incorporated in creation. In Paul (as in Peter) it is God who raises up Christ, as he will raise us up. In John, Christ effects his own resurrection by the power he had received from God. He has chosen his hour. Paul prefers the popular language of the Apocalypses and of *Genesis*, the 'proto-gospel'. He refers more to the origin of Adam, to the last end, to the battle fought against sin-and-death. This is matched in many points by the Johannine idea of a battle against 'the prince of this world'; but it tends to fade out in a sublimer light. Just as for John the flesh is not evil in itself, since this is what the Logos became, so sin-death is *already* vanquished. The recapitulation is made *already*. The annihilation, the cruel and ignominious death, features that had so struck Paul (though he had not witnessed them himself), fade before the triumphant glory, visible even in the consummating sacrifice.

For John, the passing from death to life is faith. Without faith, the Resurrection, like the Eucharist, would avail nothing. And faith without physical touch is a beatitude.

In John's Gospel we see faith operative through love. It is the beloved disciple who first enters the sepulchre, who sees and believes; the discovery that the tomb is empty gives him an immediate intuition of the Resurrection. No need of prophetic texts for him, as there was for the pilgrims on the road to Emmaus. His mode of belief is almost that of believers generally: by means of signs, the meaning of which he instantly understands. In other words, unlike Mary Magdalen or Thomas, he believes in the normal manner, without having *seen*. And the lesson to draw from this is that actual experience is of no great importance: the Magdalen saw and Thomas felt, yet both had moments of uncertainty.

Faith, the bread of life, resurrection, the outpouring of the Spirit—all are bound up together. There is a tendency in *John* to think of all-important changes (and the Resurrection not excepted) as not occurring just at the instant they become manifest, but at the moment hope comes to believe in them; it is then that the seed, which is the substance, comes into being.[1] Whereas the Resurrection is seen by Paul as a process of universal sublimation, always combined with a combat against death, John's standpoint is less historical, or at any rate less turned towards the future: the *already* dominates the *not yet.*

D. Allied Developments in Dogma

In this study of developments that are explanations or consequences of the Resurrection, I now want to examine certain articles of faith which have supervened, often at very great intervals of time.

THE DESCENT INTO HELL
(*1 Peter* iii 18–20; iv 6)

The Resurrection receives its plenary meaning in the Ascension, since it was never distinct from an exaltation of Christ in glory and the apparitions were conceived as implying a termination.

If we remember that the Lordship was over three domains, *heaven, earth,* and the *world below*, it is understandable that the idea of the Ascension, that entry into the Lordship of heaven, then the earthly Lordship of the 'forty days', should lead to that of another Lordship of Christ, that exercised in 'hell'. Christ, after his death, must take possession of this third world. When? Why, during that 'dead time', from the entombment until Easter, so that freed now from all that bound him to earth, but not as yet risen, he could exercise his third authority, proclaim his victory over death in the very domain of death. This was Christ's triumph over the powers of death and over the devil, and his freeing of those whom the powers of darkness still held prisoners. The Gates of Hell could not prevail against Christ, victorious as he was, now and for ever.

For the modern mind, it must be confessed, these 'combats' and different 'domains' have rather lost their evocative power and even their religious instructiveness. But the Johannine Gospel, it seems to me, has drawn attention to another aspect of this same development of faith, one that could be called 'the evangelization outside time', the integral evangelization.

'The dead,' Jesus had said, 'will listen to the voice of the Son of

[1] Cf. *1 John* v 15: 'We are sure that he listens to all our requests, sure that the requests we make of him are granted,'

God, and those who listen to it will live' (v 25). Now between the time when the Logos ceased to animate his body and that of his possessing it again at the moment of the Resurrection, he who, like his Father, 'never ceased working' (v 17) could not, while still within the confines of this world, remain without working for human salvation.

The same idea is found in the Epiphany liturgy. It is that of the *universality* of the Gospel. Perhaps there is also the idea that, before the destiny of a soul can be determined for ever, Christ's Gospel (that of the Passion and Resurrection) must in some way or other be presented to it first. This descent into hell was affirmed very early in the Roman creed. And even if the occasion of it were merely symmetrization with the Ascension, it would contain a deep truth, in some respects now hard to appreciate, though in others it is perhaps not yet developed—like everything that has to do with spiritual activity once the time-barrier is broken.

Perhaps we should see it in conjunction with that strange phenomenon recorded only in *Matthew*, how at the moment when Jesus died the graves were opened and many bodies of holy men arose out of them; and how, after the resurrection of Jesus, they left their graves and 'were seen' by many. This passage contains the idea of a relationship, rather hard to define exactly, between the dead Jesus and the souls of the just, a relationship asserted already, by Luke alone, in the episode of the good thief, and one that could have given rise to mystical phenomena.

Hence the emergence of this first development of the faith contained in the article of the primitive creed: *descendit ad infernos*.

But for a deeper understanding of these three things, the Resurrection, the Ascension, and the Descent into Hell, faith must be carefully separated from what in the beginning had been the mental envelope. The Resurrection must be purified of the idea of a return to terrestrial life; the Ascension from the image of an ascent into the atmosphere, which is only the symbol of it; and the Descent into Hell must be purified of the image of a subterranean descent.

KINDRED DOGMAS IN MARIOLOGY

Mariology is a kind of second sphere of faith, where everything in the Christosphere may be said to have its echo. And there have in fact, as history shows, been decisions reached in this sphere of Mary's which have thrown light on characteristics of the Christosphere, as was seen at the Council of Ephesus and in the history of Nestorianism. The Nestorian distinction between two 'persons' in Jesus Christ caused no disturbance to Christian thought till it was seen to involve the divine motherhood of the Virgin. But the opposite process is more common, and there have been developments in Christ's sphere that have led minds to question how they would affect Mary.

The dogmas of the Virginal Conception and the Assumption, though promulgated at a very great interval apart, are both connected with the development of the Resurrection.

In so far as it depends on the Blessed Virgin's own testimony, the Virginal Conception is a divine fact, not an inference of faith. Luke's Gospel takes as its sources those who had been witnesses 'from the beginning', those, that is, immediately associated with the Virgin, and for essentials the Virgin herself, the only witness. But before such testimony could be sought, gathered, and (though depending on only one witness) believed, there must have existed already in the Christian mind some sort of anticipation of that virginity. And this largely derived, even before explicit belief in the Lord's divinity, from belief in the Resurrection. The way in which faith thought of the body of Christ as having escaped corruption, and left the sepulchre alive, was an invitation to reflect on the nature of that body during the earlier period. For thought like that of the Jews, referring so readily from end to origin—origin being conceived as an image of the consummation—there was a natural tendency to conceive the entry of Jesus into mortal life on the model of his manner of leaving it.

Virginity before childbirth is clearly expressed in *Matthew* and *Luke*, and doubtless too in the Gospel of John. But there is no mention in any of the Gospels of virginity *in partu*. Here can be seen a direct development of the Resurrection. Christ, so the Fathers observed, had left his mother's womb as he had left the sepulchre, virginally. Therefore Christmas, in the eyes of faith, is a unique miracle, analogous to the mystery of Easter of which it is the figure.

The Assumption is an even clearer development of belief in the Resurrection. In so far as it derives from Scripture, it can be connected with that passage in the first *Epistle to the Corinthians* where Paul, describing the resurrection, specifies the *order* (*tagma*) in which it must come about: there being varying values of worth and time according to the part played by human beings in God's work. In the same Epistle he refers to the section of *Genesis* sometimes called the 'proto-gospel', where victory over sin and death is promised to a mysterious woman. But he does not speak of that woman herself or of the *tagma* of her resurrection.

Johannine thought—in contrast to Paul's, which dwells on temporal unfolding—is not directly interested in the beginning or end of time. John is living in the 'now' of Christ and the Eternal-Now, which is the reign of the Lamb. In two contexts the woman appears: in the one she is the unnamed mother of Jesus, standing at the foot of the Cross and receiving all humanity; in the other (in the Apocalypse) she is the eternal woman persecuted by the Serpent, she who gives birth to the disciples. If we may associate the seen fact with the vision, it may be inferred that the lot of the woman, mother of the Logos, is not to be that of other members of the human race. If there is a *tagma* in resurrection, an order of value and sequence, she must be the first to rise. In our temporal language— which, temporalized as we are, we are bound to use—this privilege of order must be translated into an idea of anticipated resurrection. Finally this leads to the idea that what for us is not yet, for her is already accomplished.

The authority of the Roman See, supported by Catholic faith, has given this inference, after a long period of waiting, the authority of a divine revelation, as it had done long ago for the virginity *in partu*.